Methexiology

Methexiology

Philosophical Theology and Theological Philosophy for the Deification of Humanity

NICOLAS LAOS

Foreword by Arthur Versluis

☙PICKWICK *Publications* • Eugene, Oregon

METHEXIOLOGY
Philosophical Theology and Theological Philosophy for the Deification of Humanity

Copyright © 2016 Nicolas Laos. All rights reserved. Except for brief quotations in critical publications or reviews, no part of this book may be reproduced in any manner without prior written permission from the publisher. Write: Permissions, Wipf and Stock Publishers, 199 W. 8th Ave., Suite 3, Eugene, OR 97401.

Pickwick Publications
An imprint of Wipf and Stock Publishers
199 W. 8th Ave., Suite 3
Eugene, OR 97401

www.wipfandstock.com

ISBN 13: 978-1-4982-3385-9
HB ISBN 13: 978-1-4982-3387-3

Cataloging-in-Publication data:

Laos, Nicolas K., 1974–.

Methexeology : philosophical theology and theological philosophy for the deification of humanity / Nicolas Laos.

viii + 270 p. ; 23 cm. Includes bibliographical references.

ISBN 13: 978-1-4982-3385-9

HB ISBN 13: 978-1-4982-3387-3

1. Metaphysics. 2. Hesychasm. 3. Philosophical theology. 4. Deification (Christianity). 5. Orthodox Eastern Church—Doctrines. I. Title.

JA71 L36 2016

Manufactured in the U.S.A.

Contents

Foreword by Arthur Versluis vii

Introduction 1

Chapter 1: Being and Its Presence 75

Chapter 2: Access to Being 97

Chapter 3: The Modes of Being 124

Chapter 4: Epistemology and the Noetic Faculty of the Soul 153

Chapter 5: Mystery, Grace, and Philosophical Theology: Through Unselfishness to Deification 173

Chapter 6: Psychotherapy: The Secret Potential of the Mind 209

Chapter 7: Axiology, Ethics, and Justice 229

Bibliography 251

Glossary 261

About the Author 267

Foreword

IT IS A PLEASURE to provide some prefatory remarks and context for this book by Dr. Nicolas Laos, which represents Dr. Laos's remarkable synthesis of a wide range of sources and intellectual currents. In it, and in a previous work, *The Metaphysics of World Order*, which more or less leaves off where this book begins, he develops an unusually broad and deep analysis based in the Hellenic tradition. Here, Hellenic tradition includes the Platonic inheritance from antiquity as well as Orthodoxy and in particular Hesychastic tradition, all of which have been given not enough attention by international scholars. What distinguishes Dr. Laos's work above all, beyond its unusual scope, is his emphasis on the assertion of metaphysical truth as the touchstone for understanding political, philosophical, religious, social, cultural, and economic dimensions of modern life in a theologically informed context.

Dr. Laos's book is also unusual because it incorporates elements of what has become known as "Western esotericism," but which might better be described as those traditions in Western European tradition (including alchemy) that point us toward deeper dimensions and understanding of inner or spiritual life. After all, the word "esoteric" (bearing the meaning of "inner" as opposed to "exo-," or "outer") ultimately refers to different processes of inner transmutation and illumination, and as such has analogues in Eastern or Asian religious traditions that also reject simplistic rationalism and subject-object dualism. By emphasizing the Platonic and Orthodox traditions, Dr. Laos presents us with a philosophical and theological synthesis that in turn looks at aspects of modern political and cultural life in what for many readers will be new and surprising ways.

For the modern secular reader, some aspects of Dr. Laos's book may be daunting. He offers detailed historical accounts in order to substantiate his larger case, and the last part of the book seeks to synthesize philosophical and theological traditions in ways that unabashedly challenge rationalist and secular perspectives. But the theological dimensions of his work are integral to his argument, and must be seen in the context of the whole, not in isolation. What Dr. Laos is presenting in this book is nothing less than a challenge to most established ways of thinking about modernity and the modern world. Regardless of whether you find yourself agreeing or disagreeing with the whole or some of its parts, you will without doubt find that it presents new ways of thinking not only about the world in which we find ourselves, but also about the world as he envisions it could be. His work is original, stimulating, and provocative—without doubt, it will reward the attentive reader.

Arthur Versluis, author of *The Mystical State* and many other books
Chair of the Department of Religious Studies and Professor in the College of Arts & Letters at Michigan State University

Introduction

METHEXIOLOGY OR THE PHILOSOPHY of methexis is a system of philosophical theology and theological philosophy that is focused and founded on the concept of *mēthexis*. The Greek word *mēthexis* literally means participation and sharing. It is important to understand that *mēthexis* is something much deeper and more specific than the term "relation," because *mēthexis* emphasizes the event of an ontologically grounded union. Therefore, eros (love passion) is at the center of the methexiologists' theological method, in accordance with the New Law of Christ, namely, love,[1] and in accordance with the following biblical passages: "The kingdom of heaven is like a certain king, who prepared a marriage feast for his son,"[2] and: "I saw the holy city, New Jerusalem, coming down out of heaven from God, prepared like a bride adorned for her husband."[3]

Intimately related to methexiology is a peculiar Christocentric type of mysticism. In general, by the term "mysticism," I mean a personal experience of communion with the real truth in a way that transcends propositional language, and, instead, it involves a peculiar type of enlightened intuition. The East has been the cradle of mysticism, whose hierophants, guided by ideational and contemplative imagination, were the prophets among the Egyptians, the Chaldeans among the Assyrians, the philosophers among the Greeks, the Sramanas of the Bactrians, the Magi among the Persians—who announced beforehand the birth of the Savior, being led by a star until they arrived in the land of Judaea, and among the Indians the Gymnosophists, and other philosophers of ancient Eastern nations.

---

1. John 13:34–35.
2. Matthew 22:2.
3. Revelation 21:2.

The mystical teaching of the ancient Brahmans, who are the only interpreters of the Vedas or Holy Writings, is symbolized by an equilateral triangle circumscribed about a circle: the circle symbolizes infinity and eternity, while the equilateral triangle symbolizes Brahma, Vishnu, and Shiva, the three creative principles in the Hindu pantheon. Brahma means, when literally translated, "that which grows," and he is a symbol of evolution; Vishnu is a symbol of form, the producer of forms; Shiva is a symbol of chaos, out of which order emerges. The mystical tradition of the peoples irrigated by the Ganges and the Indus rivers was brought to the banks of the Nile by the Gymnosophists.

The mystical schools of ancient times attained their greatest prosperity in the valley of the Nile through the mysteries of Isis, Serapis, and Osiris. The Osiris mystery represents the human soul's drama. Osiris symbolizes the soul proper, namely, what in ancient Greek is called nous, the repository of the uncreated Spirit, or what the Kabbalists call neshamah. Osiris is also a Son of the Sun. However, within the profane men, Osiris is dead through the lower nature, symbolized by Set-Typhon, which means through the animal soul, particularly, through selfish thoughts and through selfish sentiments and passions. Thus, Osiris is buried in the shrine of the mummy of the material world and thrown into the Nile, which symbolizes material life. But Isis, who symbolizes the love for the divine, that is, for the real Truth, seeks, with the help of Anubis (who symbolizes divine wisdom), the parts of Osiris's fragmented corpse, to collect them and to take care of them, thus giving rise to an integrated, harmonious, and divinely illuminated higher soul, symbolized by Horus, the new divine Osiris, which subdues the demon, namely, Set.

Initiation into the Egyptian mysteries was most highly valued and was embellished with all the splendor of Eastern culture and lore. In 525 BC, the Persian King Cambyses beat the great Egyptian nation into submission, but, a thousand years before this, the Greeks had already formed their mystical schools under the influence of Egypt, and they had already instituted their famous mysteries of Samothrace and Eleusis. According to the mysteries of Eleusis, the grieving Demeter, for nine days and nights, wandered about with a torch, searching for her lost daughter, Persephone, as Isis once searched for the missing Osiris. Furthermore, gradually, the Greeks' spirit of religion assumes a philosophical color with the molding of the Orphic tradition. Rhythm and music give rise to an ecstatic existential state that takes on the meaning of a surrogate for death, and that does away with the straitjacket of the senses, so that it brings about a peculiar experience of spiritual liberation and offers entry to a world where life beyond the grave is the ultimate reality. Both Orphism and Pythagoreanism, each in its own way, made use of certain elements of this psychosocial and religious disposition and, thus, set the stage for the development of classical Greek philosophy.

Let us look at the first true history of philosophical thought, namely, the opening book of Aristotle's *Metaphysics*. Here, Aristotle sets out his two most basic results: The first result mentioned by Aristotle has to do with making the most of awareness and of its ability, firstly, to detach itself from the world of necessity, and, secondly, to relate, thereafter, to other objects independent of all endurance, objects that awake its wonder and puzzlement, and are also independent of any kind of exigency. The second result mentioned by Aristotle consists in developing the power of awareness in order to detach itself from the immediate and specific environment of the existence that it is the awareness of, and giving itself over to abstract elucidation of the problems arising from the fact of its detachment.

Ancient Greeks used the term *logos* (plural: *logoi*) in order to refer to the event of "disclosure," or truth. Disclosure proclaims and speaks about the existence of an entity in the world; additionally, it refers to a conscious being that is aware of the event of disclosure. Hence, as Martin Heidegger has pointed out, from the perspective of the Greeks' notion of truth (in Greek, *alētheia*), truth emerges from the relationship between a disclosed entity and the viewer of this disclosure. According to classical Greek philosophy, true being consists in a harmonious, meaningful, and decent order, specifically in the common logos, which is manifest in the cosmos.

The Greek word *alētheia* is a combination of the prefix "a-," signifying lack, and the Greek word *lēthe*, meaning forgetfulness. In other words, as Heidegger has pointed out, for the ancient Greeks, truth means *un-forgetfulness*, un-concealment, and disclosure.[4] Ancient Greeks managed to endow their life with a transcendent scope, namely, the scope of harmonizing the self with the cosmic logos. In this way, they managed to bridge the gap between history and eternity. According to Plato's *Timaeus* and Plotinus's *On Time and Eternity*, time is an image of eternity. This does not mean that, for Plato and Plotinus, time consists in a deterministic cycle of the world of becoming, but it means that the image—precisely,

---

4. Heidegger, *Basic Writings*.

time—points to and leads to the creative archetypal Good, the Sun mentioned by Plato in his *Republic* (514a ff.).

Plotinus argues that we must release time from the shackles of the physical world and seek the origin of time in the nature of the soul. In his book *On Time and Eternity*, Plotinus argues that "eternity" is the radiance of the substratum of the mental principle, and it is continually in a state of changeless timelessness. Moreover, in the same book, following Plato, Plotinus argues that time consists of the activity of the soul in the world, and it is an image of eternity. According to Plotinus, the term "being" refers to eternity, and "real being" in its absolute ideal state is unmanifested, whereas the term "existence" means the manifestation of being in the world of becoming. Hence, time, being guided by eternity, manifests a tendency toward perfection, and eternity manifests the participation of beings in the state of the intelligible world, precisely in a state of ontological completeness. Similarly, in the Holy Scripture, we read that, in God, the past and the future are united in eternal presence: with Whom there is no variableness, nor change of light, or darkness (Jas 1:17).

All these men formed schools, their doctrines spread throughout the world, and, thus, in Judea, schools of thought were established well before the coming of Christ, such as the Pharisees, religious conservatives, the Sadducees, political conservatives, and the Essenes, a mystical religious society influenced by Pythagoreanism and austere Stoic practices. Moreover, the Jews of the Hellenistic Egypt developed a highly Hellenized literature, on which I will say more later.

At this point, it is useful to mention that monotheism was not originally developed by the Hebrews/Israelites, and that the Hebrews were not the only monotheistic nation in the ancient world. At the zenith of ancient Egyptian civilization, Pharaoh Amenhotep IV (who reigned for approximately sixteen years; from 1352 until 1336/1334 BC), known also as Akhenaten (meaning Effective Spirit of Aten), attempted to change the polytheistic religion of Egypt into a monotheistic one by promulgating the monotheistic worship of Aten, the Sun God. Aten means bright disk, and, thus, the falcon-headed picture of Ra-Harakhti (the previous Egyptian solar deity) was replaced by the symbol of a solar disk whose rays ended in human hands some of which were holding the holy ankh, the symbol of life. In contrast to the old Egyptian solar deity, which represented the physical Sun, Aten was a symbol of the Transcosmic One, the One lifegiving source, which creates and preserves the cosmos through its light. Moses, the most important prophet in Judaism, was arguably initiated into the mysteries of the Egyptian monotheism, and, when the Egyptians decided to abandon Akhenaten's monotheistic religion and return to polytheism, it is not unreasonable to suppose that Moses preserved and expanded the monotheistic tradition among the Hebrews. Thus, Judaism became the strictest and most effective custodian of monotheism in the ancient world. Moreover, in the Hebrew Bible, the manifestations of God's glory are often described as light or fire, and one of the Hebrew names for God is Adonai, which comes from the root *ada*, which means radiant.

In ancient Greece, in the context of the Orphic Mysteries, there was a monotheistic religious dogma, and, in contrast to Homer's popular polytheistic beliefs, the Orphic hymns celebrated the One and Universal God. According to Iamblichus and Porphyry, even though Pythagoras made references to several gods, he taught that there is only one God and that the various different gods mentioned in the Greeks' Homeric popular polytheistic religion are powers or energies of the One God. In the same spirit, Plutarch, one of the most influential Platonist philosophers, believed in one, unitary, trans-temporal God, with different names for the Divinity's different aspects and energies.

Why is monotheism so important for the spiritual development of humanity? Monotheism leads to the ontological liberation of God from the cosmos, and, therefore, in the context of monotheism, the divine Logos is free from cosmic laws, that is, from cosmic necessity. In the context of pure monotheism, God's mode of existence is freedom. The essential autonomy of God from the natural cosmos implies that God relates to the natural cosmos only under terms dictated by God's own free will (in Greek, the divine *thēlema*), and, therefore, the laws that govern the natural cosmos (that is, the creation) do not govern the divine Mind (that is, the ultimate cause of creation) itself. Therefore, since God is the existential mirror in which humans see themselves, and since the qualities and the nature of the God with whom one empathizes determine one's way of thinking about oneself and about one's existential integration, the God of monotheism is the perfect archetype of humanity's historical emancipation and spiritual perfection.

However, over time, the Pharisees and the Sadducees failed to keep the fire of spiritual initiation burning. The Pharisees, in particular, became so obsessed with obeying their legal interpretations in every detail that they ignored God's mystical message of grace and mercy, and their piety was often hypocritical. The Sadducees lapsed into a formalist religious system, devoid of the inner meaning of the Bible, and they were often willing to compromise their values with the Romans and others in order to maintain their social status and extract social privileges. Jesus Christ calls the Pharisees an evil "brood of vipers" (Matt 12:34), "hypocrites" (Matt 23:23), and "blind guides" (Matt 23:16, 24), not because their ideas were evil, but because they politicized them in order to promote their own selfish purposes. Jesus charges the Pharisees with having committed blasphemy against the Spirit (Matt 12:31), because they took the law that applies to the heart (i.e., the law of the Spirit, according to Rom 8:2–11) out of its proper context and forced it upon others through political lawmaking.

Of the mystical schools of Judea, that of the Essenes was the most important. The Essenes were feeling contempt for riches, they had a communal way of life, they were praying together turning eastward, and they were meditating on divine law in a language rich in symbolism and allegory. The Essenes were submitting their candidates to three years of trials. Then, in the ceremonies of initiation, they were handing them a pick or axe and a white garment. Their fundamental maxim was: "You will love God and your neighbor, you will be virtuous."

The divine flame of spiritual initiation continued to burn and the great work was brought to completion by Jesus Christ. He appeared in an age when corruption was universal; in the midst of a people who, from time immemorial, had been subject to slavery and who eagerly expected their deliverer announced by the prophets. Jesus appeared and taught the doctrine of the potential divinity of man. Jesus Christ set a clear and eternal example of how the deified man, that is, the man who is united with the deity, approaches law, possession, and religion.

Jesus Christ's teaching about law is the following: "The Sabbath was made for man, not man for the Sabbath" (Mark 2:27). Additionally, he said: "A new commandment I give to you, that you love one another" (John 13:34). "One of the scribes came, and heard them questioning together. Knowing that he had answered them well, asked him, 'Which commandment is the greatest of all?' Jesus answered: 'The greatest is, "Hear, Israel, the Lord our God, the Lord is one: you shall love the Lord your God with all your heart, and with all your soul, and with all your mind, and with all your strength." This is the first commandment. The second is like this: You shall love your neighbor as yourself. There is no other commandment greater than these'" (Mark 12:28–31).

Jesus Christ's teaching about possession of material wealth is the following: "Most certainly I say to you, a rich man will enter into the kingdom of heaven with difficulty. Again I tell you, it is easier for a camel to go through a needle's eye, than for a rich man to enter into God's kingdom" (Matt 19:23–24). The apostle Paul observes that "the love of money is the root of all kinds of evil" (1 Tim 6:10). It is the love of money that is the obstacle to faith, not the money itself. Although Jesus never condemns material wealth as evil *per se*, he consistently addresses the danger of material possessions as a hindrance to full and sincere compliance with the New Law of Christ, which is love.

Jesus Christ's teaching about religion is the following: first of all, Jesus said to humans: "Ye are gods" (John 10:34), thus revealing that the true Christianity is a mystical path toward man's deification, and that Christ is the manifestation of every worthy religion's purpose, namely, the deified human. Whereas Jesus Christ taught the deification of the human being, the Pharisees and the Sadducees insisted on a phyletic perception of salvation, centered on the messianic destiny of the Jewish nation and founded on historical means. Jesus taught the true worship of God as follows:

> The woman said to him, "Sir, I perceive that you are a prophet. Our fathers worshiped in this mountain, and you Jews say that in Jerusalem is the place where people ought to worship." Jesus said to her, "Woman, believe me, the hour comes, when neither in this mountain, nor in Jerusalem, will you worship the Father. You worship that which you don't know. We worship that which we know; for salvation is from the Jews. But the hour comes, and now is, when the true worshipers will worship the Father in spirit and truth, for the Father seeks such to be his worshipers. God is spirit, and those who worship him must worship in spirit and truth." (John 4:19–24)

Thus, as we read in Revelation 21:22, there is no temple in the New Holy City: "And I saw no temple therein: for the Lord God the Almighty, and the Lamb, are the temple thereof."

From the perspective of methexiology, philosophical theology is possible and meaningful only under the conditions that by the term "philosophy" we mean *a way of life whose fundamental attribute is the erotic pursuit of and union with the Absolute Lover*, and that by the term "theology" we mean *the experiential knowledge of the Absolute Lover*, that is, the participation in the Absolute Lover's way of life and the experience of an ontological union with the Absolute Lover.

Symeon the New Theologian, a renowned theologian, poet, and saint of the Eastern Orthodox church, in his fifteenth Hymn, writes that Christ makes his true servants-saints his spouses, in the sense that those souls which are united with God are God's spouses. Therefore, according to methexiology, the main purpose and *finis ultimus* of philosophical theology is the study of God's beautiful mode of being and humanity's participation in God's uncreated energies, that is, in the uncreated lifeforce of God's uncreated essence.

Moreover, in the context of methexiology, theology—defined in the aforementioned "methexiological" way—brings philosophy to completion and conclusion. In other words, in the context of methexiology, philosophical theology and theological philosophy are inextricably related to each other, and, indeed, they constitute the two sides of the same coin.

Given the definitions of the terms "methexiology," "philosophy," and "theology" that I have just proposed, the philosophical constituent component of methexiology consists of the philosophical works of Plato and Aristotle, and the theological constituent component of methexiology consists of the theological works of the Hesychasts (known also as the Neptic fathers), since both these philosophical and theological traditions are centered on eros.

The Stakes Are High

Before delineating the ontological, epistemological, and ethical dimensions and the substantial arguments of the philosophical orientation that I call methexiology, I would like, in this introductory section, to briefly inform and alert my readers about the manipulation of spirituality by various power oligopolies that tend to subordinate values and principles to historical expediencies in the context of a selfish conception of "pragmatism," and they use philosophical and theological notions merely or primarily as "mental munitions" for the promotion of their selfish interests and agendas. The previous attitude, which is particularly characteristic of authoritarian and totalitarian regimes as well as of the advocates of the underlying mentality of *Realpolitik*, causes serious erosions in the moral status of humans and, implicitly but clearly, cultivates an attitude of complacent nihilism.

Given that methexiology highlights and underpins the spirit's freedom from and supremacy over history and the natural world, thus, giving primacy to spiritual goals over pragmatic ones and refusing to subdue the human mind to any necessity, I wish to compare and contrast methexiology with characteristic examples of policy-makers, organizations, scholars, and even religious leaders who adhere to the opposite view. I think that it is significant to do so, not only in order to draw a clear distinction between methexiology and politicized or, generally, manipulated spirituality, but also for three more reasons: (i) first, in order to show that, when philosophy, instead of guiding politics, becomes a servant or instrument of politics, then political power takes precedence over truth, and the human being becomes a means to the achievement of political goals; (ii) secondly, in order to show that, when political power and, in general, the achievement of historical goals are elevated to absolute principles, then the different opposing historical "camps" ultimately become spiritually similar to one another, and the creation of a world society is impossible due to a lack of transcendent, universal values sufficiently capable of cultivating and underpinning the sociality of the historical actors' souls; (iii) thirdly, in order to help my readers understand why I maintain that methexiology is an alternative existential strategy and leads to a different perception of civilization from the one that prevailed in the era of modernity, without being oblivious of the defects of other pre-modern and anti-modern social models.

Methexiology is a new philosophical orientation, and, therefore, a new existential strategy, that is, ultimately, a vision for a new civilization. In general, "civilization" means an anthropological type, and, therefore, at the most fundamental level, large-scale historical change refers to great anthropological changes: for instance, the emergence of capitalism is a historical consequence of the values of an anthropological type that gives primacy to the *exchange* value of money (that is, money trade or financial speculation) over the *use* value of money, thus transforming "money" into "capital." In particular, capitalism emerged in the fifteenth century AD, when the Papacy decided to morally legitimize and honor usury, whereas, until then, other traditional anthropological types, that is, civilizations, had never honored usury, thus precluding the development of capitalism. (Capitalism appeared on the historical scene as a peculiar form of trade organized by the Fugger family in Germany; when the Fuggers made their first loan to the Archduke Sigismund, in 1487, they took as security an interest in silver and copper mines in the Tirol.)

Furthermore, "advanced modernity" is marked by a deep crisis, which became tragically manifest in the 2000s, and which consists in a deep crisis of the nation-state, of the world-conception of *Realpolitik*, of financial capitalism, of the major Euroatlantic institutions (such as NATO and the EU),[5] of Russian nationalism, of the modern Islamic world, of Maoist China's peculiar capitalist model, and even of the model of globalization that was formed and implemented in the 1990s on the basis of the principles of advanced modernity. Therefore, at the dawn of the twenty-first century, humanity is faced with the need to extricate itself from the intellectual shackles of the previous principles and ways of life, which are in deep crisis, in order to consciously and responsibly give rise to a new major historical change.

Reflecting on my studies in the history of art and aesthetics, I realize the following: ancient agricultural civilizations worshiped nature, and, thus, their gods usually had animal characteristics; ancient nomadic civilizations worshiped the natural bond of blood, the power of the race; but, on the other hand, ancient Greek gods had human form. The human form of the ancient Greek gods was characterized by exceptional beauty, because it was expressing the ancient Greek person's quest for existential integration and perfection. According to ancient Greek mythology, the end of the human being's existence is human participation in the deity. Thus, through their mythology, Greeks gave priority to a personal approach to reality over the impersonal commands of nature and race, and, in this way, they created an anthropocentric civilization. The humanism of the classical Greek aesthetics was transformed into a theological system by Christianity, since Christians identified the Greek value of beauty with Jesus Christ, and, through Jesus Christ, Christianity stressed the personhood of God and the incarnation of the divine Logos,

---

5. During the Cold War, NATO was defending one ideology against another one, and it had important ideational attributes, but, after the collapse of the Soviet Union and the end of the Cold War, the West's military-industrial-security complex was alarmed by the end of the "communist threat" as the ready-made justifier of continued escalation of the Western nations' defense/security budgets and by the demands for "peace dividends," and, therefore, NATO, gradually, degraded into an institution that blatantly serves the interests of the West's military-industrial-security complex through military interventions for regime change and counter-terrorism operations. On November 7, 2014, RT published an interview with the prominent U.S. scholar Noam Chomsky, in which Chomsky pointedly characterized post-Cold War NATO as a "US-run intervention force." See: https://www.rt.com/shows/sophieco/202967-cold-nuclear-war-nato/

that is, the personal and, hence, free and perfect presence and disclosure of God within the sensuous world.

Spirituality, Faith, and Power Politics: A Theme in Need of a Focus

In 1887, the influential British Freemason and scholarly mystic Arthur Edward Waite pointedly wrote that "beneath the broad tide of human history there flow the stealthy undercurrents of the secret societies, which frequently determine in the depths the changes that take place upon the surface."[6] In the garb of "faith" and "spirituality," there are many hidden and secretive military Orders that manipulate targeted populations with precision around the entire world. It goes without saying that, in general, many "mystical" networks have flourished in diplomacy, defense, espionage, and business. The "Skull and Bones" fraternity at Yale University is a characteristic case in point.

Formed in 1832 by General William Russell, whose shipping firm later dominated the U.S. side of the China opium trade, this secret society became the recruiting grounds and preserve of the most important New-England-centered families, such as the Coffins, the Sloanes, the Tafts, the Bundys, the Paynes, the Whitneys, etc. In 1903, Yale Divinity School established several schools and hospitals in China that were collectively known as "Yale in China." The program "Yale in China" was an intelligence network undermining Sun Yat-sen's republican movement and supporting Mao Zedong on behalf of the Anglo-American establishment. During World War II, "Yale in China" was used by the U.S. establishment and its Office of Strategic Services (OSS) in order to install the Maoists into power.[7] "Yale in China" was run by OSS operative Reuben Holden, a member of Skull and Bones. Furthermore, "Yale in China" was closely associated with the New York-based Union Theological Seminary, which was dominated for twenty years by Henry Sloane Coffin, a U.S.

---

6. Waite, *The Real History of the Rosicrucians*, 1.

7. In other words, the "pragmatist," or rather cynical and materialist mentality, of the United States' liberal oligarchy and OSS/CIA operatives played a substantial role in China's conversion to communism. In particular, the United States Army Observation Group, commonly known as the Dixie Mission, was the first U.S. effort to establish official relations with the Communist Party of China and the People's Liberation Army, then headquartered in the mountainous city of Yan'an. This mission was launched in July 1944, during World War II, and it lasted until March 1947.

intelligence executive from the Sloane and Coffin families and a Skull and Bones member. The New-York-based Union Theological Seminary has been a major center for U.S. subversion of Asia. From the outset, the Skull and Bones fraternity has been playing a "two ends against the middle" game, whereby it aims at controlling and manipulating both the "thesis" (e.g., the USA/Euroatlantic Bloc, Liberalism, etc.) and the "antithesis" (e.g., the USSR/Russia, China, Communism, Fascism, etc.), thus keeping the peoples of the world in a state of confusion and despair, in the hope that, ultimately, people will resign themselves into accepting the "synthesis" (specifically, a particular world order model fabricated and promoted by the Skull and Bones fraternity) as the only alternative to solve the problems that the "synthesis" brokers created in the first place.[8]

In the last decade of the nineteenth century, in the context of Eurasian mysticism and geostrategic competitions, Shamzaran (Pyotr) Badmaev (a Buryat Mongol who had grown up in Siberia and converted to Russian Orthodoxy, with Tsar Alexander III acting as his godfather) articulated an occult geopolitical vision of a unified Eurasia that emphasized the unification of Russia with Mongolia and Tibet. Badmaev, known also as "the Tibetan," served for many years in the Asia department of the Russian Ministry of Foreign Affairs. He was familiar with the legend—popular in Mongolia, China, and Tibet—about the "White Tsar" who would come from the North (from "Northern Shambhala") and restore the original traditions of Buddhism. Moreover, Badmaev had a close association with a prominent Tibetan master, the lama Agvan Dordzhiyev, the tutor and confidant of the thirteenth Dalai Lama. According to Dordzhiyev, Russia represented the coming Kingdom of Shambhala anticipated in the *Kalachakra* texts of Tibetan Buddhism.[9] In a letter of December 19, 1896, Badmaev wrote to Tsar Nicolas II that his activities aimed at helping Russia to achieve "greater influence than other powers upon the Mongolian-Tibetan-Chinese East." In addition, intimately related to Russia's occult Orientalism is a neo-pagan belief in "sacred geography," which perceives the human being as a being of the earth, and not as a being of the sky, that is, as a free spirit.

In the same spirit of occult Orientalism, the Russian philosopher Nikolai Berdyaev (1874–1948) called for a "new knighthood" against

---

8. Sutton, *America's Secret Establishment*.

9. According to Tibetan Buddhism, Shambhala is a mystical kingdom of adepts in which the teachings of the *Kalachakra* (Wheel of Time) Tantric school are maintained in their purest form.

the West, and the Russian artist and archaeologist Nikolai Konstantinovitch Rerikh (1874–1947), a student of Madame Blavatsky's works,[10] promoted a Eurasian vision founded on his belief in the transcendent unity of Eurasian religions and on the argument that the doctrines of Buddhism, Islam, and Christianity are husks concealing the truth within. Thus, in the late nineteenth and the early twentieth centuries, Eurasian mysticism was inextricably linked to a cultural shift of many members of the modern Russian elite away from Orthodox Christianity and Byzantium/"Romanity," mostly to Asian cultures and "New Age" spiritualist movements. Whereas modern tsarist imperial Russia could reclaim Romanity as a descendant of the Eastern Roman Empire and thus act as a neo-Byzantine super-power in European and Eastern-Mediterranean affairs, in the late nineteenth and the early twentieth centuries, Eurasian mysticism tended to intellectually confine Russia to Orientalism and German romanticism. In fact, the late-nineteenth-century and the early-twentieth-century Russian Eurasianist scholars were not only alienated from Orthodox Christianity, but also they were alienated from and often inimically disposed toward the Greco-Roman culture.

In 1886, Jamal ad-Din al-Afghani, who had named himself "Philosopher of the East," visited Russia invited by the order of the Russian government, and he joined up with Blavatsky's publisher, Mikhail Katkoff, who wanted to implement an imperialist Russian-Orientalist ideological and geostrategic policy in Central Asia and India. Al-Afghani was descended from a Shiite Azerbaijani family from the Asadabad village of Iran, but he used the name al-Afghani to hide his Iranian and Shiite origin, because he was generally active within predominantly Sunni areas. Al-Afghani established his own Masonic organization under the auspices of the Grand Orient of France. Al-Afghani's ideology was a peculiar combination of radical, anti-Western Pan-Islamism and an attempt of utilizing Western rationality and technology in order to invigorate Islam. The nineteenth-century Russian establishment cooperated with Blavatsky, Jamal ad-Din al-Afghani, and several spiritualists in order to conduct

10. Madame Helena Petrovna Blavatsky, the founder of a mystical "school" called Theosophy, articulated a Eurasian theory of mystical imperialism. Blavatsky was a friend of Russian Tsar Nicolas II and the Oriental enthusiast Prince Esper Ukhtomsky, a close confidant of Tsar Nicolas II. In fact, Blavatsky fascinated Tsar Nicolas II and his wife, the notoriously superstitious Tsarina Alexandra Feodorovna, with her book *The Secret Doctrine*. Blavatsky's book *The Secret Doctrine* is a synthesis of several mystical traditions, but it is primarily focused on Indo/Tibetan spirituality.

its own "occult war," thus betraying its Byzantine Christian roots and departing from the spiritual legacy of the Eastern Roman Empire.

Furthermore, if we investigate the history and the identity of Sheikh Hassan al-Banna, the founder of the Muslim Brotherhood, the relationship between the Muslim terrorist network ISIS/Daesh and the Baathist regime that was dictatorially established in Iraq in 1968, the hidden connections and operations of Hezbollah's Secretary-General, Sayyed Hassan Nasrallah, as well as the relationship between the Norwegian terrorist, Freemason, and neo-Templar Anders Behring Breivik and the ethos of several neo-Templar Orders, we can easily realize that there is a deep, substantial, and clandestine relationship among spiritual masters, terrorism, and imperialism.

In the nineteenth century, the Ottoman Empire was in a period of decay, and the Western Great Powers decided to integrate the Islamic world into the global capitalist system. Great Britain was right to pursue the dissolution of the corrupt and obscurantist Ottoman Empire,[11] but the British foreign policy was guided by *Realpolitik* and not by any noble ideas. Thus, following the traditional divide-and-conquer strategy, Great Britain concentrated its diplomacy in World War I on wresting the *Hejaz* (i.e., the Islamic holy cities of Mecca and Medina) from the control of the Ottoman Empire and on spreading the ideology of nationalism throughout the Arabo-Islamic world. This goal of the British diplomacy was achieved when "Sharif" Husain, the Ottoman-appointed "Sharif" (ruler) of Mecca, was induced by the British Empire to rebel against the Ottoman caliph and to establish an autonomous authority over the *Hejaz* under British protection. By 1916, the Ottoman caliph had lost control over Mecca and Jeddah, and, in 1919, he lost control over Medina, too, since Ottoman troops within the city of Medina were induced to rebel against Fakhri Pasha.

Finally, on March 3, 1924, the Ottoman Caliphate was abolished, and, on March 7, 1924, Sharif Husain, who had been exercising *de facto* local control over the *Hejaz* since 1916, claimed the Caliphate for himself. But the British Empire's policy was different from Sharif Husain's plans. Thus, Great Britain assisted Abd al-Aziz Ibn Saud to move against Sharif Husain and to wrest control of the *Hejaz* from him. Ibn Saud was a "puppet" of the British diplomacy. In particular, during Sharif Husain's rebellion against the Ottoman caliph and during the imposition of Sharif

---

11. Byron, *The Byzantine Achievement*; Portal, *The Slavs*.

Husain's rule over the *Hejaz*, Ibn Saud was receiving a monthly sum of 5,000 pounds sterling from the British Treasury in return for his policy of neutrality, which was then serving the interests of the British Empire. But when Sharif Husain claimed the Caliphate for himself, Great Britain urged Ibn Saud to move his forces against Sharif Husain.

In 1902, the Saudis captured Riyadh as a result of an alliance between a tribal chief and the religious leader of the Wahhabi religious sect. The alliance ensured that the *Najdi* Saudis would be under the control of the Wahhabis and would seek to enforce Wahhabism in the "heartland" of Islam, that is, in the *Hejaz*. Wahhabism is founded on a modern Sunni reformer called Ibn Abd al-Wahhab (d. 1792); it is a puritanical, formalist, and fanatical perception of the *Sharia*, and its mentality resembles that of Oliver Cromwell's English Puritanism.

According to the researcher Dr. John Coleman, the Muslim Brotherhood was created by the great names of the British Intelligence.[12] In its dealings with Gamal Abdel Nasser (Egyptian Prime Minister, 1952–70), the British government used espionage, diplomacy, bribery, and even direct military might to retain control over Egypt and the Suez Canal. The newly founded CIA was also concerned about Nasser's policy, because Nasser showed signs of tilting to the Soviet Union. The Muslim Brotherhood was an obvious ally against Nasser, because he had banned it in Egypt after it was involved in a failed assassination attempt on his life in 1954. In general, the Muslim Brotherhood rejected Nasser's policy. In June 1955, the British intelligence agency MI6 was already cooperating with the Muslim Brotherhood in Syria to undermine and destabilize the new government that showed strong left-wing tendencies and a desire to forge an alliance with Egypt. The Muslim Brotherhood became an even more important Anglo-American intelligence asset after Nasser announced the Egyptian takeover of the Suez Canal. According to the researcher Stephen Dorril and the investigative journalist Mark Curtis, the Muslim Brotherhood was linked to British intelligence through the British explorer and travel writer Dame Freya Stark prior to World War II, and the Shah's regime in Iran considered it to be closely associated with British Freemasonry;[13] "the CIA also approved Saudi Arabia's funding of

---

12. Coleman, "What Really Happened in Iran."
13. Curtis, *Secret Affairs*, 62.

the Muslim Brotherhood to act against Nasser, according to former CIA officer, Robert Baer."[14]

During the 1950s and the 1960s, Nasser persistently implemented a strict policy against the Muslim Brotherhood, and, during the same period, Saudi Arabia hosted Arab Muslim Brotherhood exiles. The strong presence of Muslim Brotherhood exiles in Saudi Arabia spawned a new Salafist movement, which is a hybrid of Wahhabism and other post-1960s Islamic movements, and it has been associated with literalist and puritanical approaches to Islam. When the then Syrian President Hafez al-Assad launched his own harsh crackdown against the Syrian branch of the Muslim Brotherhood in the early 1980s, a new wave of Muslim Brotherhood exiles moved to Saudi Arabia. In the 1980s, the Muslim Brotherhood evolved, spread, and spawned a virulent network of radical jihadists, including Al-Qaeda.

With regard to the Assad regime in Syria, it is worth pointing out that the Assad family, which started ruling Syria in 1970, has deep connections with the French establishment and the French Freemasonry, particularly, the Grand Orient of France. The Assads are Alawites, who are a Shiite sect, which the French entrusted with the ruling of Syria in the 1970s. In 1936, Ali Sulayman al-Assad, the father of Hafez al-Assad, was one of eighty Alawite notables who signed a letter addressed to the French Prime Minister saying that "[the] Alawi people rejected attachment to Syria and wished to stay under French protection." However, in 1946, Hafez al-Assad joined the Arab Baath Party, which espoused a pan-Arabist socialist ideology, and, in 1970, after dictatorially displacing the corrupt and unpopular Jadid's government, he established his own autocratic Baathist regime in Syria. Like many other members of the Syrian establishment, Hafez al-Assad was a Freemason.[15] Even though the Assad regime is secular and has traditional ties with the West, particularly, with France, the U.S. and its allies, including Turkey, Saudi Arabia, and Qatar, in 2011, initiated a series of subversive operations against the government of Bashar al-Assad, who was elected President of Syria on July 10, 2000, succeeding Hafez al-Assad, his father, who had led Syria for thirty years and died in office a month prior. The reasons for the United States' and its allies' decision to overthrow the Assad regime in Syria include their decision to stop cooperating with Baathist governments and substi-

---

14. Ibid, 63.
15. Sfeir, "Les francs-maçons en terres d'Islam."

tute them with weaker and, thus, more easily manipulated ones as well. Thus, in 2011, the U.S. and its allies started using jihadists, including the Al-Nusra Front (i.e., Al-Qaeda in Syria), in order to fight against Bashar al-Assad's government.

In order to understand the history of jihadism, it is also important to bear in mind that, in 1978, U.S. President Jimmy Carter's National Security Advisor, Zbigniew Brzezinski (a Polish-born nobleman whose family hailed from the most anti-Russian part of Poland, and who acquired significant political power through the Trilateral Commission), advised Carter to transfer pro-Saudi fighters, called "mujahedeen" (later called "Taliban"), into the then-Soviet-allied Afghanistan, in order to create there a wave of terrorism that would render the Soviets unable to preserve their Afghan ally, and, thus, help to bring down the Soviet Union.[16] Moreover, when, in February 1979, after Mohammad Reza Shah's overthrow, Ayatollah Khomeini, a radical Iranian Shiite religious leader, took over the leadership of Iran, Brzezinski argued that, because Khomeini's Shiite fundamentalism was coupled with an anti-Soviet policy, Khomeini's government could become part of a U.S.-controlled anti-Soviet alliance.[17]

As regards the relationship between the Muslim terrorist network ISIS/Daesh and the Baathist regime that was dictatorially established in Iraq in 1968, Kyle W. Orton wrote in *The New York Times*, on December 23, 2015, that in the 1980s the then U.S.-backed Baathist Iraqi dictator Saddam Hussein "allied with Islamists, notably the Muslim Brotherhood, to destabilize his regional rival in Syria," and, in 1986, "the Pan-Arab Command, the Baath Party's top ideological institution, formally reoriented Iraq's foreign policy toward an alliance with Islamists";[18] "the campaign of Islamization intensified further after Iraq's devastating defeat in Kuwait in 1991 and the subsequent Shiite revolt, culminating in 1993."[19] Thus, during the 1990s, Salafist and other radical Sunni elements were integrated into Iraq's Baathist regime, giving rise to the capture of great parts of Northern Iraq by ISIS/Daesh militants in the post-Saddam Hussein era.

In the case of Hezbollah's Secretary-General, Sayyed Hassan Nasrallah, too, it is difficult to distinguish between the identity of a religious

16. Brzezinski, "Interview."
17. Engdahl, *A Century of War*, 171.
18. Orton, "How Saddam Hussein Gave Us ISIS."
19. Ibid.

18   Methexiology

leader and that of a military Order's leader. Through Hezbollah's international network, the Beirut-based Shiite cleric Sayyed Hassan Nasrallah promotes a radical Shia ideology. During NATO's wars against the former Yugoslavia (1991–2001), the Euroatlantic alliance backed Hezbollah to fight in Kosovo against the Serbs and to assist in the creation of the Sunni nation of Bosnia.[20] In 2002, "Geostrategy-Direct," an online newsletter edited by veteran journalist Robert Morton, wrote that the Dutch government released a report that detailed the alliance between the United States and militant Islamic organizations to help Bosnian Muslims; in particular, according to that report, the United States provided a green light to groups on the State Department list of terrorist organizations, such as Hezbollah, to operate in Bosnia.[21] This explains why Nasrallah often gets a good image and a good press in the West, compared to other terrorist outfit leaders and is not demonized like them.

However, Nasrallah controls a big international network of diamond mining and diamond cutting experts as well as diamond mining equipment suppliers.[22] This network, whose members compete ambitiously in the international gemstone market, has given rise to a challenging Shiite actor in the diamond industry, since, in the 2000s, Hezbollah teamed up with Iran and formed a nexus with Venezuela and Cuba against the U.S. and the State of Israel. During the 1990s, the 2000s, and the 2010s, the diamond dispute led to several attacks on Lebanon by the Israeli Armed Forces. Hezbollah has transferred diamond-mining technology to South East Asian nations, particularly, to Myanmar, Cambodia, Vietnam, Thailand, Philippines, and Indonesia, thus making it imperative for the U.S. to set up a naval base in Bangladesh. Additionally, Hezbollah is believed to have raised significant funds by dealing in so-called "conflict diamonds" in Sierra Leone, Liberia, and Congo, a practice that has reportedly been copied by al-Qaeda.[23] In the 2010s, the United States and the State of Israel teamed up with Saudi Arabia to counter their Shiite competitors in the diamond market, and they have bargained with Saudi Arabia's regime for the creation of a Salafist/Wahhabi satellite state in the diamond-rich Pattani area (one of Thailand's Southern provinces) and in the Philippines on the lines of Kosovo in Bosnia.

20. Geostrategy-Direct Intelligence Brief, "U.S. Gave Green Light to Terrorists in Bosnia."
21. Ibid.
22. Levitt, "Hezbollah Finances."
23. Ibid.

It is worth pointing out that Shia Islam has a deep mystical tradition, and, according to Angel Millar, it "has developed a complex theory of transmission of initiatory knowledge (*'ilm*, i.e., the esoteric interpretation of the Qur'an) to the elite believers (*khasa*)."[24] Shia Islam emphasizes more the mystical, prophetic, and messianic aspects of the Islamic religion, whereas Sunni Islam focuses more on the legalist, moral, and political aspects of the Islamic religion. Furthermore, several Sunni teachers have articulated a stunningly brutal Islamic hedonistic calculus. For instance, Al-Suyuti (known also as Jalaluddin), a fifteenth-century AD Egyptian religious scholar, juristic expert, and teacher, and one of the most prolific Sunni Arab writers of the Middle Ages, has described the Muslims' conception of Paradise as a state in which, each time a Muslim sleeps with a Houri (erotic companion), he finds her a virgin, and, additionally, as a state in which "the penis of the Elected never softens," and "the erection is eternal," each "chosen one" being married to seventy Houris.[25] Thus, at first hearing, the mystical teachings of Shia Islam create the impression that they cultivate a spiritually deeper, more mature, and freer consciousness than Sunni Islam. However, this is not the case, because Shia Islam's relationship with history is as problematic as Sunni Islam's. In particular, Sunni Islam seeks to totally formalize historical becoming through a suffocating, religious legal system (occasionally coupled with an Islamic hedonistic calculus), while Shia Islam seeks to give an end to historical becoming.

Whereas Christian mysticism, especially Hesychasm (which I shall elucidate and defend in the present book), understands mysticism as a way of spiritualizing history, and, therefore, as a way of endowing history with a transcendent meaning, which underpins the spiritual freedom and creativity of the historical actor, the Shiites' perception of mysticism gives rise to a negation of history altogether and, thus, to a peculiar type of nihilism (since it refuses to accept the real value of history). Any belief system that denies the real value of history for the sake of an eschatological vision renders its adherents unable to undertake their historical responsibilities in a creative and efficient way. Moreover, when a person who negates the value of history forms the impression that his eschatological vision clashes with his actual historical conditions, he is prone to violent sentimental explosions, since not only is he unable to reconcile

24. Millar, *The Crescent and the Compass*, 19.

25. Quoted in Papanicolaou, *Islam vs. the United States*; see also: http://www.movieguide.org/news-articles/bookguide-islam-vs-the-united-states.html

his eschatological expectations with history, but he also persistently experiences a psychologically traumatic contradiction between eschatology and history, and, thus, he tries to annihilate historical reality (including human beings) as a source of discontent.

However, after the terrorist attacks of September 11, 2001, the U.S. launched a "Global War on Terrorism" (GWOT), which has the essential ingredients of the twelfth-century AD French and Spanish inquisitions, and it underpins several U.S. imperialist military interventions in geo-economically crucial areas of the Middle East.

On July 26, 2011, the Reuters journalist Michael Holden wrote that, "at a secret location in London in April 2002, nine far-right extremists gathered together to form 'The Knights Templar Europe,' a small pan-European group," and, nine years later, on July 22, 2011, one of those at this meeting, Anders Behring Breivik, "caused the sort of carnage the group had discussed as being an essential part of their campaign, the bombing and shooting rampage that killed at least 76 people in Norway."[26] The Breivik manifesto and video enhance the suspicion that Breivik was associated with a larger movement of neo-Templar Crusaders in defense of "Judeo-Christian" Europe.

A video attributed to Breivik shows some remarkable similarities to a video that has been released by the leader of a self-professed Knights Templar group called Order 777. The leader of the Order 777 is a former anti-Muslim terrorist and bomber from East Germany, by the name of Nick Greger ("Commander Mad Nick" or "madnick77").[27] The videos that have been released by the Order 777 and Breivik use a Zionist-Christian and neo-fascist rhetoric in order to urge "Judeo-Christian" Europe to unite against Islam and globalist multi-culturalism as enforced by the UN and the United States. A fact not highlighted in these videos is that, of the nine men celebrated at its outset, all but two (Eugene Terreblanche of South Africa and Laurent Nkunda of the Democratic Republic of the Congo) were notorious criminals (mainly, drug traffickers), namely: Charles Taylor, self-installed president of Liberia, Samir Geagea, militia leader in Lebanon, Milorad Ulemek, a Serbian gangster and Breivik's mentor, Johnny Adair, former Protestant militia leader in Northern Ireland, and Irish militia hitmen Gary Smith and (allegedly) Billy Wright.[28]

26. Holden, "The Knights Templar Europe."
27. Gardham, "Violent Videos of Oslo Killer's 'Mentor.'"
28. Scott, "Norway's Terror as Systemic Destabilization."

The profiles of the Order 777 and of Breivik match with the structure of the "deep events" that have been studied by Peter Dale Scott, a former Canadian diplomat and English Professor at the University of California, Berkeley.[29] By the term "deep event," one should understand an event that is obscured and/or misrepresented in mainstream media, and whose origins are mysterious and often attributed to marginal outsiders, but, in reality, they intersect with powerful and covert forces intending to influence history. Russian sources have linked Ulemek, Breivik's mentor, with Vladimir Filin, the Russian leader of Far West LLC, a group of former Soviet military intelligence officers that has developed into a multinational linchpin between organized crime and the global intelligence and corporate establishment, and it enjoys connections to the intelligence networks of Israel, Turkey, Saudi Arabia, Russia, Great Britain, and the United States.[30] Moreover, Far West LLC "is said to have CIA-approved contractual dealings with Halliburton for geopolitical purposes in the Caucasus, as well as dealings in Iraq with Diligence LLC."[31]

It goes without saying that militant Islam *predates* the Western Crusades, and, therefore, it is a lie that the Crusaders were the first aggressors. For instance, Egypt was conquered by the forces of Islam in 647 AD, Cyprus and Armenia were conquered by Muslims in 653 AD (Cyprus was liberated in 965 AD by the Byzantine Army), Constantinople was first attacked by the armies of Islam in 678 AD, Andalusia and Granada, in Spain, were conquered by the forces of Islam in 711 AD (liberated in 1492 by Ferdinand and Isabella), Avignon, in France, was conquered by the forces of Islam in 719 AD, Paris was attacked by Muslims in 732 AD, Sicily was conquered by Islamic forces in 828 AD, Malta was conquered by the armies of Islam in 870 AD (liberated in 1090 by the Normans), etc. However, the First Crusade started in 1095 AD. Arguing that the militant Islam predates the Western Crusades is one thing, but trying to justify the Crusaders' ethos is another. In the Middle Ages, not only did the Crusaders fail to contain the Islamic world, which by the eleventh century AD had almost transformed the Mediterranean Sea into a Muslim lake, but they also undermined and looted the Eastern Roman Empire. Moreover, since the Crusaders were very poorly educated, several of them, during their stay in the Middle East, were influenced by

29. Scott, "Korea (1950), the Tonkin Gulf Incident, and 9/11."
30. Scott, *American War Machine*, 188.
31. Scott, "The Global Drug Meta-Group."

Islamic and other Oriental schools of mystical belief, and, therefore, far from defending Christian theology, they became agents of non-Christian belief systems in the West.

It is also important to mention that, after the East-West Schism (1053) and the Fall of Constantinople to the Ottomans (1453), several Western Sovereigns, following policies dictated by narrow-minded selfish calculations, and underestimating the significance of great cultural and identity issues, allied with the Ottoman Empire. In 1536, the Franco-Ottoman alliance was established between King Francis I of France and the Turkish sultan of the Ottoman Empire Suleiman the Magnificent. Even though the Franco-Ottoman alliance was designated as "the impious alliance," or "the sacrilegious union of the Lily and the Crescent," it endured because it served economic interests of both parties.[32] King Charles IX of France (1560–74) was another significant Western ally of the Ottomans; he even gave free use of France's main naval base at Toulon to the Ottomans and converted the Cathedral of Toulon into a mosque to accommodate the Muslim fleets.

The policy of Queen Elizabeth I of England (1533–1603) was beneficial to the Ottomans, too, and her pirate flotillas, captained by Sir Francis Drake, plundered the Spanish galleys that were coming back to Spain from America loaded with gold. By stealing a large portion of Spain's gold, Queen Elizabeth I of England rendered Spain unable to build a navy powerful enough to fight Islam.

Judaizing Christians, the Qur'an, and neo-Templarism

In the context of church history, one of the earliest Christian heresies was that of the Judaizing Christians. In the fourth century AD, in the city of Antioch (which was founded in 300 BC by Seleucus I Nicator, one of Alexander the Great's generals), there were two big Jewish synagogues that exerted significant spiritual influence on the local Christian community. In particular, in the fourth century AD, the Judaizers, or Judaizing Christians, were promoting a syncretistic attitude toward Christianity and Judaism, they were getting blessings and amulets from Jewish rabbis, and many of them were even celebrating Easter together with Jews on the fourteenth of Nisan, in violation of the relevant canons of the First Ecumenical Council. On the other hand, from the perspective of Orthodox

---

32. Merriman, *Suleiman the Magnificent*, 133.

Christianity, Jesus Christ's gospel is the disclosure of the *telos* (i.e., the ultimate, transcend purpose) and the perfect fulfillment of biblical Judaism (i.e., of the Old Testament). Hence, in the Christian era, the true Israel[33] is the New Israel of Jesus Christ's church.

Between 386–87 AD, John Chrysostom, who was then a Presbyter, and later he became Archbishop of Constantinople, wrote of the Jews and of Judaizers in eight homilies *Adversus Judaeos*. Chrysostom argues that the heresy of the Judaizing Christians is a "very serious illness," and he describes it as follows: "there are many in our ranks who say they think as we do," but "some of these are going to watch the festivals and others will join the Jews in keeping their feasts and observing their fasts," adding that he intends to "drive this perverse custom from the church right now."[34] John Chrysostom emphasizes that, because of the Jews' decision to deny Jesus Christ, the Jewish synagogues lack communion with the Incarnate Logos of God, who is the ultimate source of the significance and the end of the Old Testament. Thus, according to Chrysostom, even though the holy books of the Old Testament are kept in every Jewish synagogue, Christians should not worship God in Jewish synagogues; in John Chrysostom's own words, "let no man venerate the synagogue because of the holy books."[35]

One of the most influential movements of the Judaizing Christians was that of the Ebionites. The Ebionites taught that Jesus of Nazareth was God's Messiah (messenger), but they rejected his ontological divinity, and they insisted on the necessity of following Jewish law and rites (for which reason they strongly opposed the apostle Paul, who taught that, through Jesus Christ, the law of the life-giving Spirit has liberated humanity from "the law of sin and death"[36]). Hippolytus of Rome, the most important third-century theologian in the Christian church in Rome, wrote in his *Refutation of All Heresies*, 7.22: the Ebionites "live conformably to the customs of the Jews, alleging that they are justified according to the law, and saying that Jesus was justified by fulfilling the law." Moreover, Epiphanius of Salamis (who was Bishop of Salamis, Cyprus, at the end of the fourth century), in his *Panarion* 30, argues that "Ebionites

---

33. In Hebrew, "Israel" literally means "triumphant with God," and "who prevails with God" (Genesis 32:28, 35:10), that is, it means the people of God.
34. *Adversus Judaeos* (Patrologia Graeca, Vol. 48), 844.
35. Ibid., 851.
36. Romans 8:2.

are very like the Cerinthians and Nazoraeans; the sect of the Sampsaeans and Elkasaites was associated with them to a degree."

Judaizing Christians also had an influence on early Islam. In 595 AD, Mohammed married Khadijah, who is commonly regarded by Muslims as "the Mother of the Believers." Khadijah had a cousin who was called Waraqah ibn Nawfal. Waraqah ibn Nawfal was an Ebionite priest, and he exerted significant influence on Mohammed's religious thought. In 1978, a Lebanese Maronite priest using the pen name Abu Musa al-Hariri authored a book in Arabic entitled *Qiss wa Nabi* (Nabi means Prophet, and Qiss means Priest), which was the culmination of his long research in ancient Islamic and Christian texts.[37] In this book, Abu Musa al-Hariri, whose real name is Father Joseph al-Qazi, elucidates Waraqah ibn Nawfal's spiritual influence on Mohammed: Waraqah ibn Nawfal recognized Mohammed's religious tendencies and leadership capabilities, and he hoped that Mohammed would succeed him as the Ebionite leader of Mecca. Thus, Mohammed's perception of the Bible (Old and New Testaments) and the biblical stories that are included in the Qur'an are molded by the teachings of the Ebionites. In fact, the Qur'an itself mentions that, when Mohammed first began to preach among the poor of Mecca, he called them not to any particular religion called "Islam," but to the monotheism of Abraham. Mohammed's perception of Abraham's faith reflects the heresy of the Ebionites. Thus, in the Qur'an, specifically in Sura 5:73, Mohammed writes that those who equate Jesus, "the Messiah, son of Mary," with God, and, in general, those who believe in the Christian doctrine of the Holy Trinity are "disbelievers." After Waraqah ibn Nawfal and Khadijah died, Mohammed decided to follow some of his converts to the city of Medina, where his message and lifestyle became more radical: his message became one of conquest and imperialism, and his lifestyle became peculiarly hedonistic. Thus, in the Qur'an, specifically, in Sura 9:5 (Medina, 113th), Mohammed writes that, "when the sacred months are over slay the idolaters wherever you find them."

In the Middle Ages, especially after the East-West Schism, Western Christianity rejected the Eastern Orthodox Church's teachings about the deification of humanity through Jesus Christ, and it endorsed a moralistic and largely legalistic theology. Thus, ignoring the mystical theology of

---

37. See: http://www.muhammadanism.org/Arabic/book/hariri/priest_prophet_book.pdf. In 2010, Abu Musa al-Hariri was interviewed on the Arabic TV show "Daring Question," and during that interview, he identified himself as Father Joseph al-Qazi; see: http://islamexplained.com/.

the Eastern Orthodox Church, several medieval Western mystics started looking for consciousness-expanding experiences in Oriental schools of mystical belief, primarily in Arabo-Islamic and Jewish mystical texts. Moreover, nineteenth-century romanticism signaled a revival of occultism and chivalry. In the context of nineteenth-century romanticism, several Western mystics developed and propagated neo-Templar legends according to which the medieval Knights Templar acquired secret knowledge by interacting with Muslim and Jewish mystics during their stay in the Middle East. In particular, the nineteenth-century neo-Templar legends cultivated a syncretistic theology that reflected the teachings of the Ebionites, Gnosticism, and non-canonical gospels.[38] Thus, in the nineteenth century, several Freemasonic organizations were significantly influenced by various types of Judaizing Christianity, and they compromised or even abandoned the original Christian and European identity of the first Masonic Lodges.[39]

38. In classical Antiquity, the term "canon" acquired the meaning of a rod or measuring stick, and it was metaphorically used to describe the essential teachings of a school of philosophy. The early church used the term "canon" to denote which texts were to be included in the Holy Bible, as opposed to those that were to be excluded. There were two basic criteria for determining the canonicity of Gospels. The first criterion was apostolic authorship; for instance, the Gospels of Mark and Luke bore the stamp of Peter and Paul's authority, respectively. The second criterion was more complex: the Gospel's content had to deal with salvation, and, of course, the Gospels that would ultimately be included in the Holy Bible should be theologically consistent with one another. For instance, the "infancy gospels" of Thomas and James, though of great antiquity, were discarded, because they were found to be misleading in teaching the salvation of humanity, and they were filled with extravagant accounts of Jesus Christ's childhood and adolescence. The church began to separate the canonical Scriptural texts from the non-canonical ones in the early centuries; specifically, one can refer to the following ecclesiastical texts: Apostolic Canon 85; Council of Laodicea (364 AD), canon 60; Council of Carthage (418 AD), canon 32; Athanasius of Alexandria, 39 Festal Epistle (367 AD). All these attempts were finally assessed, combined, and confirmed by the Sixth Ecumenical Council (691 AD), canon 2, and further ratified by the Seventh Ecumenical Council (783 AD).

39. In 1846, the English cleric, schoolmaster, topographer, and writer Reverend Dr George Oliver—who was elected Deputy Provincial Grand Master of Masons for Lincolnshire in 1832, and who was appointed an honorary member of the Grand Lodge of Massachusetts, with the rank of Deputy Grand Master, in 1840—published his *Apology for the Freemasons*, in which he emphasized that the traditional medieval Masonic organizations were explicitly serving both the church and the state, and many Masonic degrees are Christian, and only Christian Masons espousing the Christian Trinitarian doctrine can be admitted to them. Moreover, according to Reverend Dr George Oliver (ibid), on several occasions, in England, the Grand Masters of Masonry were selected from the highest dignitaries of the church, such as the following: Austin the Monk

Spiritualism, Ideological Wars, and World Order

When we study the history of spirituality, in general, it is useful to bear in mind that spiritualism has been used by various elites in order to promote religious syncretism, and, through religious syncretism, to establish an empire. For instance, Arthur Balfour, 1st Earl of Balfour—who was the Prime Minister of the United Kingdom from July 1902 to December 1905, and later Foreign Secretary—was a member of a mystical society called Hort's Apostles and President of the Society for Psychic Research (S.P.R.). Moreover, Balfour not only headed the S.P.R., holding séances at his home, but also he initiated a group called the "Synthetic Society," whose goal was to create a one-world religion, which, in turn, would spiritually underpin a new world order that was being promoted by the League of Nations, in which Balfour was instrumental. Balfour invited a certain Frederic Myers of the S.P.R. to join the Synthetic Society, and together they created the "preamble of all religions," according to which "our . . . material world is interpenetrated and to an extent acted upon, by another order of things, an unseen spiritual world," and "the metetherial realm (is) a World Soul," and "linked to all . . . is a Universal Spirit."[40]

The Charter of the United Nations—whose name was coined by United States President Franklin D. Roosevelt and was first used in the Declaration by United Nations of January 1, 1942, when representatives of twenty-six nations pledged their governments to continue fighting together against the Axis Powers—was signed on June 26, 1945. The United Nations (UN) officially came into existence on October 24, 1945, when the Charter had been ratified by China, France, the Soviet Union, the United Kingdom, the United States, and by a majority of other signatories. After the establishment of the UN, Alger Hiss became its acting Secretary-General. Alger Hiss was a U.S. State Department official, and he was accused of being a Soviet spy in 1948 and convicted of perjury in connection with this charge in 1950. However, before he was tried and convicted, Hiss cooperated with Joseph E. Johnson (who later became Secretary of the Bilderberg Group) in writing much of the UN Charter

---

(597 AD), Bennet, Abbot of Wirral (680 AD), St. Swithin (856 AD), St. Dunstan, Archbishop of Canterbury (957 AD), Gondulph, Bishop of Rochester (1066), Peter de Rupibus, Bishop of Winchester (1216), Walter Giffard, Archbishop of York (1272), William of Wykeham, Bishop of Winchester (1357 AD), Henry Chichely, Archbishop of Canterbury (1413), William Waynfleet, Bishop of Winchester (1443), John Poynet, Bishop of Winchester (1552), etc.

40. Gauld, *The Founders of Psychical Research*, 305–10.

in a way that, to a significant extent, reflected principles of the Soviet Union's constitution and of Karl Marx's *Communist Manifesto*.

The first official UN Secretary-General was Trygve Lie, who was a high-ranking member of Norway's Social Democratic Labor Party, which was an offshoot of the Third Communist International. The second UN Secretary-General, Dag Hammarskjold, was a Swedish socialist, who openly supported communist policies, and the third UN Secretary-General, U Thant, was an acknowledged Marxist and an advocate of world federalism. The study of the early history of the UN and of the mentality of the first UN Secretary-Generals helps one to understand the philosophy on which this international institution has been founded.

It goes without saying that, throughout the twentieth century, the UN was never a communist, anti-capitalist institution. However, the UN has used the secular, materialist cosmopolitanism that characterizes Marxism in order to promote and implement its own globalist agenda by deconstructing traditional metaphysics and identities and by manipulating international ideological, geopolitical, and economic conflicts. Moreover, in 1982, Norman Dodd was interviewed by the U.S. film-maker and journalist G. Edward Griffin regarding the time that he spent as the head researcher for the Reece Committee, and, in that interview, Dodd stated that, in 1954—when he was the newly appointed chief investigator of what was called the Congressional Committee to Investigate Tax-Exempt Foundations—he realized that major tax-exempt foundations of the USA, including the Ford Foundation and the Carnegie Endowment for International Peace, immediately after the end of World War II, became involved in a clandestine operation whose objective was the creation of a world-wide collectivist state, including the Soviet Union, which would be ruled from behind the scenes by those same interests which then controlled those U.S. tax-exempt foundations.[41]

In fact, communism/socialism (i.e., the ideology underpinning "left wing" political parties) and fascism/Nazism (i.e., the ideology underpinning extreme "right-wing" political parties) are merely variants of a common underlying collectivist ideology that justifies the sacrifice of the individual human being for the sake of a historical objective that a collectivist elite propagandizes as something historically necessary, noble, or even sacred, yet, in reality, it is determined and dictated by the

---

41. The transcript of the ground-breaking 1982 interview of Norman Dodd by G. Edward Griffin can be found in the following link: http://realityzone.stores.yahoo.net/hiddenagenda2.html.

selfish interests of the corresponding collectivist elite. In general, the mainstream left-versus-right political paradigm is mainly a propaganda ploy by which the propagandist can promote a liberal, a fascist, a communist, or a socialist variant of collectivism, depending on one's mission.

The liberal variant of collectivism consists in the liberal collectivists' thesis that the individual has to conform to impersonal, objective, necessary economic laws, which supposedly are similar to the natural laws, yet, in reality, they are ideological underpinnings of a system of liberal oligarchy and technocratic capitalism, in the context of which individualism becomes a shadow of itself. For instance, the liberal variant of collectivism is the founding ideology of the European Union (EU), the European Central Bank (ECB), the Federal Reserve System (Fed), and the International Monetary Fund (IMF). The EU, the ECB, the Fed, and the IMF traditionally support financial oligopolies, economic regimes of imperfect competition, and state-sponsored austerity programs, which contradict the theory of free market system, according to which no firm or consumer should be able to significantly affect the market price, and all (or almost all) currently available information should be already incorporated into the market price. For instance, in the 1990s, in the 2000s, and in the 2010s, it became clear that, through currency swaps and other economic agreements, a banking cartel composed of the Federal Reserve System, the European Central Bank, the Bank of England, the Bank of Switzerland, the Bank of Japan, and the Bank of Canada aims at establishing a global oligarchical financial/monetary regime, whose foundations were laid by the 1985 Plaza Agreement, and which was significantly invigorated by the establishment of a USD/Euro swap line between the Federal Reserve System and the European Central Bank in December 2007, as well as by the fact that, in 2011, the Federal Reserve System, the European Central Bank, the Bank of England, the Bank of Switzerland, the Bank of Japan, and the Bank of Canada agreed to coordinate their actions concerning the management of global liquidity. This financial oligarchy, which creates money out of thin air and operates as an overlord of the real economy, can only corrupt and destroy a free and fair market.[42]

---

42. For more details, see Rickards, *The Death of Money*. From 2008 until 2014, the Fed was printing more and more money, but the velocity of money was plunging, that is, people were neither borrowing nor spending extra money. In fact, in 2014, in the U.S., the velocity of money was worse than in 1929 (the first year of the Great Depression). Moreover, in 2014, in the U.S., the Misery Index (which is defined as the sum of the real unemployment rate and the inflation rate) increased to 32.89, that is, it was worse than in the Great Depression (the Misery Index in the Great Depression

Moreover, in the same spirit of liberal collectivism, in 1997, George Soros, a notorious financial speculator, wrote an essay entitled "The Capitalist Threat," in which he argued that the main contemporary threat to what he calls an "open society" is a fully free economic market.[43] Inherent in Soros's concept of "the open society" is his ideology of liberal collectivism, because he maintains that "people must be free to think and act, *subject only to limits imposed by the common interests*";[44] it is exactly this perception of "the common interests" that, in the context of liberal collectivism, underpins and justifies the expansion of state authority, which, in turn, is ultimately manipulated by the most powerful members of the social establishment, namely, by the liberal oligarchs, such as George Soros himself. In fact, the super-rich are aware that the only economic institution that is more powerful than themselves and can really eliminate their oligarchical privileges is the free economic market itself, and that the state is the most effective instrument by which they can manipulate the market, since the state has tremendous power to mobilize and control the masses and acquire popular legitimacy. Thus, many members of the super-rich class are advocates of the liberal variant of collectivism, which they usually call a "mixed economy."

The fascist variant of collectivism consists in the fascist collectivists' thesis that the individual is real only to the degree that one conforms to particular conceptions of national interest and national destiny that are always defined by a ruling "national" elite whose rule stems exactly from its exclusive privilege and absolute power to define the corresponding nation's interest and destiny. Thus, for instance, within the context of the Bilderberg Group—which is NATO's elitist private exclusive membership club—the elite of the liberal variant of collectivism cooperates with the elite of the fascist variant of collectivism in an effective way in order to establish a shared vision of world order. In fact, the Bilderberg Group has had Nazi connections from the very beginning. The first conference of the Bilderberg Group was held at the Hotel de Bilderberg in Oosterbeek,

---

was 27). During the "economic boom" years of the 1950s and the 1960s, in the U.S., every dollar of debt that was created corresponded to $2.41 worth of economic growth (Gross Domestic Product growth); during the stagflation years of the late 1970s and the early 1980s, in the U.S., every dollar of debt that was created corresponded to only $0.41 worth of economic growth; in 2014, in the U.S., every dollar of debt that was created corresponded to only $0.03 worth of economic growth.

43. Soros, "The Capitalist Threat."
44. Ibid.

Netherlands, from 29 to 31 May 1954. From 1954 until 1975, the chairman of the Bilderberg Group's steering committee was Prince Bernhard of Lippe-Biesterfeld, later Prince Bernhard of the Netherlands (after he married Princess Juliana, the future Queen of the Netherlands), who was a member of the "Reiter-SS" of the Nazi party, and of the National Socialist Motor Corps. Moreover, John Foster Dulles—who served as U.S. Secretary of State under Republican President Dwight D. Eisenhower from 1953 to 1959—was instrumental in setting up the Bilderberg Group. In 1954, John Foster Dulles testified in favor of a bill designed to return vested German enemy assets, such as those of the General Aniline and Film Company (GAF), to their previous owners, and his brother, Allen Welsh Dulles, the first civilian Director of the CIA, was responsible for Operation Paperclip, which enabled many Nazi scientists (among others) to settle in the United States and start working for the U.S. government in various capacities.

It is also worth pointing out that, in the context of the Cold War, CIA chief Allen Dulles created a series of secret armies of fascist terrorists, including former Nazis, across Western Europe and Turkey with the coordination of NATO, known as stay-behind organizations. The most infamous stay-behind organizations were the Italian "Operation Gladio," and the Turkish "Counter-Guerrillas."[45] The chief ideological inspiration of the fascist stay-behind networks was Julius Evola (1898–1974), who articulated a radical anti-egalitarian, anti-liberal, authoritarian political theory founded on Saint-Yves's and Papus's occult authoritarianism, known as "synarchism,"[46] on René Guénon's traditionalism, and on occult Nazism.

45. Ganser, *NATO's Secret Armies*.

46. In 1888, Papus (whose real name was Gérard Anaclet Vincent Encausse) and Joseph Alexandre Saint-Yves d'Alveydre founded the Kabbalistic Order of the Rose-Cross (OKR+C), which came to be regarded as the "inner circle" of the Martinist Order. Through the OKR+C, they were promulgating "synarchism." Synarchism is an occult system of religious syncretism and authoritarian rule by secret societies, which the advocates of synarchism perceive as a "trans-religious" priestly class in direct communication with the "Ascended Masters" of Agartha, a legendary city that is said to reside in the hollow earth. Agartha is intimately related to the myth of Shambhala, popularized by Madame Blavatsky as the legendary home of the Aryan race. Like Shambhala, Agartha was situated in Central Asia, and, thus, it is also related to Eurasian occultism and the Turkish Counter-Guerrillas, who developed the "Ergenekon," a clandestine, Kemalist, ultra-nationalist organization. The name "Ergenekon" is derived from a Turkish legend according to which Ergenekon is a mythical place located in the valleys of the Altai Mountains, in Eurasia, serving as a model for the synarchist

The fascist variant of collectivism is used by the ruling oligarchy in order to manipulate the radicalization of the petty bourgeoisie (the lower middle social class), since, historically, fascism is the main political expression of the radicalization of the petty bourgeoisie. Additionally, during the twentieth century, as I already pointed out, the Western ruling oligarchy used fascists on several occasions as the established system's "mastiffs." On the other hand, historically, the main political expression of the radicalization of the proletariat is communism, and, therefore, the ruling oligarchy plays fascism and communism against each other in order to keep people intellectually imprisoned in collectivist ideologies. Thus, for instance, Jacob Schiff, head of the New York investment firm Kuhn, Loeb and Co., was one of the principal financial supporters of the Bolshevik revolution, and he personally financed Leo Trotsky's trip from New York to Russia. In the February 3, 1949 issue of the *New York Journal-American*, Jacob Schiff's grandson, John Schiff, was quoted by columnist Cholly Knickerbocker as saying that his grandfather had given about $20 million for the triumph of Communism in Russia. Because Jacob Schiff was a key member of New York's financial cartel, an advocate for passage of the Federal Reserve Act, and a Zionist activist, he used Marxism in order to bring about regime change in Russia, where Tsar Nicolas II was following a policy that was opposite to the interests that Jacob Schiff represented.

The communist and the socialist variants of collectivism consist in the communists' and, generally, the socialists' thesis that the individual is real only to the degree that he or she conforms to particular conceptions of class interest and class struggle that are always defined by a ruling communist/socialist party elite whose rule stems exactly from its exclusive privilege and absolute power to define the working class's interest and destiny.

The possibility of a dialectical synthesis between the liberal variant of collectivism and the communist one became strikingly manifest in the 1971 meetings between the then U.S. National Security Advisor Henry A. Kissinger and the then Chinese Premier Zhou Enlai, which paved the way to the following groundbreaking events: the 1972 summit between the U.S. President Richard Nixon and the Communist Party of China Chairman Mao Zedong, the formalization of relations between the two

---

idea of the mythical realm of Agartha. These mythical motifs, combining occultism, authoritarianism, and geopolitical determinism, are the main spiritual underpinnings and garbs of several fascist movements.

countries, irrespectively of their declared ideological opposition to each other, and the development of a peculiar type of Chinese capitalism, in the context of which capitalist economic relations are coupled with an absolutist government exclusively controlled by China's Communist Party. Moreover, prominent Western socialists, such as António Guterres, former President of the Socialist International and former Prime Minister of Portugal (1995–2002), Lionel Jospin, former leader of the French Socialist Party and former Prime Minister of France (1997–2002), as well as John Smith (1938–94), former leader of the UK's Labor Party, have been actively involved in the Bilderberg Group. In fact, John Smith had also been a member of the Steering Committee of the Bilderberg Group.

Whenever ideological "warlords" of the aforementioned collectivist "camps" go to war with one another, as it happened in World War II, for instance, they do not fight over ideology, since, in essence, they are all collectivists, but they fight over dominance, that is, over who is going to rule. However, Jesus Christ has explicitly warned Christians against these events, saying: "You know that the rulers of the nations lord it over them, and their great ones exercise authority over them. It shall not be so among you."[47]

As Tatiana Goricheva, a prominent dissident scholar in Russia, pointedly argued, "talking about God is dangerous."[48] The creation of a world-wide collectivist state presupposes a corresponding convenient mythology and necessitates subversion of genuine Christianity, because genuine Christianity teaches the deification of the human being through the incarnation of the divine Logos, thus, endowing the individual human being with infinite, ontologically grounded (precisely, God-given) value. Jesus Christ's ministry in the world is clear: "having stripped the principalities and the powers, he made a show of them openly,"[49] and he taught that each individual human being is a potential god,[50] through and due to one's personal relationship with God, who, for this reason (that is, for the deification of humanity), was self-disclosed within history.

On the other hand, Robert Muller, a Belgian-French civil servant who served as Assistant Secretary-General of the United Nations for four decades, has argued as follows: "We must move as quickly as possible

---

47. Matthew 20:25–26.
48. Goricheva, *Talking About God Is Dangerous*.
49. Colossians 2:15.
50. John 10:34.

to a one-world government; a one-world religion; under a one-world leader."⁵¹ Muller's arguments about world government and spirituality underpin the increased representation of religions in the UN, especially of so-called New Age organizations. It is worth pointing out that one of Muller's major philosophical mentors was the Jesuit priest and philosopher Pierre Teilhard de Chardin, who has argued that, "although the form is not yet discernible, mankind tomorrow will awaken to a 'pan-organized' world."⁵² According to Robert Muller, "Teilhard [de Chardin] had always viewed the United Nations as the progressive institutional embodiment of his philosophy."⁵³

Robert Muller, who won the UNESCO Prize for Peace Education in 1989 for his World Core Curriculum, is associated with two different branches of the Theosophical movement: one is the Share International, a group that believes that "Maitreya," the "World Teacher," is about to return soon,⁵⁴ and the other is Alice A. Bailey's Arcane School and Lucis Trust. In fact, Muller has openly admitted that The Robert Muller School is philosophically founded on the occult teachings set forth in the books of Alice A. Bailey, the founder of the Arcane School and the Lucis Trust, according to Bailey's Tibetan teacher, Djwhal Khul.⁵⁵ Between 1979 and 1984, Robert Muller published seven articles in *The Beacon*, which Alice A. Bailey's Lucis Trust describes as "a magazine of esoteric philosophy presenting the principles of Ageless Wisdom as a contemporary way of

51. Kinman, *The World's Last Dictator*, 81.

52. Chardin, *The Future of Man*, 170.

53. Muller, and Zonneveld, eds, *The Desire to Be a Human*, 304.

54. In March 1982, the Share International printed an article written by Robert Muller under the title "The Future of the United Nations."

55. Robert Muller's manual for the World Core Curriculum says: "the underlying philosophy upon which The Robert Muller School is based will be found in the Teachings set forth in the books of Alice A. Bailey by the Tibetan Teacher, Djwhal Khul . . . and the Teachings of Morya as given in the Agni Yoga series books"; see: Robert Muller School, *World Core Curriculum: Foundation*, 1. Alice A. Bailey (1880–1949)—born Alice LaTrobe Bateman—was a writer of more than twenty-four books on theosophical subjects, and she was one of the first writers to use the term "New Age." Her writings are based on the teachings of Madame Blavatsky (the founder of the Theosophical Society), Singh gurus, and Muslim mystics ("Sufis"). In the 1910s, Alice Bailey became a member of the Theosophical Society, and, in 1921, she married Foster Bailey, who was a senior official of the Theosophical Society. In 1922, Alice and Foster Bailey founded the Lucis Trust, whose activities include the Arcane School, World Goodwill, Triangles, a quarterly magazine called *The Beacon*, and a publishing company primarily intended to publish Bailey's books.

life."[56] In 1995, the UN asked the Temple of Understanding, founded by Bailey's Lucis Trust, to host the fiftieth anniversary of its founding and to organize two inter-faith services.

Promoting religious freedom is one thing, but promoting religious syncretism—that is, fusing different religions into one globalist religion, whose purpose is to be a mythological underpinning of globalization—is a totally different thing. Globalist decision-makers, such as Robert Muller, and New Age "schools," such as the Theosophical Society and the Arcane School/Lucis Trust, argue that one of the major factors provoking international turmoil and even conflicts is the sheer fact that there are different religions, and they assume that any expression of a genuine theological faith, that is, any statement of the belief that a religious person is speaking the real truth, is politically threatening and unacceptable. The aforementioned globalist decision-makers and New Age "schools" believe that, if people stop speaking about the real truth and state that their religious convictions are merely subjective cultural paths and conditional loyalties, humanity would be spared the risk of cultural or, more specifically, faith-based conflicts and, generally, violence. Thus, the aforementioned globalist decision-makers and New Age "schools" promote a romantic approach to religion, they attempt to build alliances among different romanticized religious communities, and they detest classical ontology, since the latter is focused on the issue of truth.

The aforementioned globalist and New Age fantasy is founded on an implicit assumption that talking about truth is necessarily less important than talking about political order and harmony. Moreover, given that, in the context of secular modern political thought, "political order" has no ontologically grounded and universal definition, and, thus, it is bound to be defined by the most powerful historical actors in any particular segment of space-time, it logically follows that, in the context of the aforementioned globalist and New Age perceptions, political *power* is more important than *truth*. Being concerned about truth implies that one recognizes that there are things about humanity and the world that transcend historical necessity and are absolute values. On the other hand, ceasing to be concerned about truth means that one admits that political power has the last word. As the British Christian anarchist scholar Gilbert K. Chesterton has wisely argued, the individual's relationship with the deity endows one with intrinsic, absolute value and with the

---

56. See: https://www.lucistrust.org/el/books/the_beacon_magazine

authority to criticize the government, whereas, by abolishing the relationship between the individual human being and the deity, the government becomes the God.[57]

Thus, neither the fact that there are different religions nor doctrinal theology itself is necessarily a cause of global turmoil, but, on the contrary, the communities that are primarily and sincerely concerned about truth are crucially important for the spiritual health of humanity. Since doctrinal theologians, philosophers focused on ontology, and, generally, religious persons will not readily give up their claims to truth in response to the appeal from ephemeral political authorities to be at one for the sake of a political order, they give witness to the spiritual freedom of humanity. However, the following question emerges: what is the cost of religious diversity to social cohesion? My answer is that *religious diversity and even religion itself undermine social cohesion only if and to the extent that a religion is politicized, that is, it compromises with the logic of historical necessity.*

From the perspective of my theory of methexiology, the ultimate purpose of any worthy religion is to expand humanity's soul in order to make the human being capable of receiving the Absolute into one's soul. Thus, a truly religious person is in communion with God and in a eucharistic, that is, metaphysically fraternal, relationship with his or her fellow humans. The belief in an absolute religious truth is the ultimate underpinning of the sociality of the human soul, and it implies that one is spiritually independent from history. Religion becomes a cause of antisocial behavior and even of violence *only* if and to the extent that it has betrayed its metaphysical essence and has submitted to the spirit of history. For instance, jihadist terrorists are not violent because they are very religious, but, on the contrary, they are violent because their metaphysical thought is so poor and disordered, and their relationship with the deity is so agitated that they believe that their historical failures are failures or defeats for God, and, therefore, they resort to crime to save their god's (in reality, their idol's) face in front of other historical actors. In other words, religious violence suggests a deep crisis in one's relationship with the deity and an essentially antireligious shift from a life founded on metaphysical principles to a life founded on the logic of historical necessity.

The more sincerely one is concerned about truth, and the more solid one's belief in the truth of his convictions is, the more noble one's attitude

---

57. Chesterton, *The Man Who Was Thursday*.

toward history will be. The less developed one's metaphysical thought is, and the more insecure one feels about one's relationship with God, the more plebeian one's attitude toward history will be. Thus, Jesus Christ said to Pilate that his kingdom "is not of this world,"[58] and he taught his disciples that it is the knowledge of truth that will make them free.[59] Moreover, Jesus Christ told his disciples to globalize Christianity, making disciples of all nations,[60] and he disclosed to them that he is "the way and the truth and the life,"[61] and that the perfect communion between humanity and God the Father is possible only through Jesus Christ,[62] but he stressed that his disciples should never use coercion, violence, or deceit in order to expand the Christian faith: "Whoever wants to come after me, let him deny himself, and take up his cross, and follow me."[63] However, in John the Evangelist's Revelation 1:5, we read that no authority of this world is really sovereign, and that God has the last word in history, since the Incarnate Logos of God, namely, Jesus Christ, is "the ruler of the kings of the earth."

Noopolitics and Mental Wars: Secret Aspects of Spirituality

Intimately related to philosophy and mysticism is noopolitics (derived from the Greek compound *nous* + politics = mind-centered politics). Whereas "geopolitics" is the conduct of politics in the geographical space, "noopolitics" is the conduct of politics in the network (or system of networks) that is created by the communication among conscious entities. Thus, noopolitics is concerned with people's fundamental significations (or values), culture, institutions, and technologies. At the center of noopolitics is the concept of "myth," that is, the spiritual core, or ultimate meaning, of beings and things. By the term "myth," one should

---

58. John 18:36. Moreover, with regard to the ethos of the historical Jesus Christ and the early Christians, one may refer to the following ancient non-Christian sources: Tacitus, *Annals*, 15:44; Pliny, *Epistles*, 10:96; Josephus, *Antiquities*, 18:63–64.

59. John 8:32.

60. Matthew 28:19.

61. John 14:6.

62. John 14:6.

63. Mark 8:34.

understand the capacity of an idea to inspire, to direct, and to motivate people according to the myth's central idea.

The term "noopolitics" (*Noöpolitik*) was coined by the defense experts John Arquilla and David Ronfeldt in a seminal RAND Corporation study of 1999.[64] Arquilla and Ronfeldt defined noopolitics as the network-based geopolitics of knowledge. Thus, in the context of noopolitics, the members of the international system are studied as conscious organisms and as phenomena molded by conscious communication. The key conclusion of noopolitics can be summarized as follows: by ruling a population's fundamental significations (or values) and myth, one commands that population's system of institutions and technologies; by ruling a population's system of institutions and technologies, one commands that population geopolitically, too.

In the context of noopolitics, power and technology are primarily directed toward man's psychic life, particularly, his memories, attention, and fundamental values. Thus, by being directly and inextricably concerned with mythology and symbology, Freemasonry has tremendous noopolitical significance. In particular, by "chiseling" the consciousness of its members and by organizing its members into a particular spiritual "edifice," each Freemasonic Order is essentially and *de facto* a great noopolitical operation.

Consciousness is that state of being which enables us to develop the functions that are necessary in order to know our environment as well as the events that happen around us and within ourselves. The significance of the riddle of consciousness and of techniques of consciousness change can be fully understood if we bear in mind that consciousness cannot make meaningful statements about one reality, but it can refer to, describe, and evaluate comparative realities as perceived by different instruments, including the central nervous system, which is the instrument that "reads" all the instruments of the human organism. The central nervous system interlocks with the immunological system, the endocrine system, the neuro-muscular system, etc., and, hence, every judgment that a human being makes is a synergetic process of the human system as a whole. Moreover, biochemical events can even cause religious and mystical experiences.[65]

---

64. Arquilla, and Ronfeldt, "The Promise of Noöpolitik."
65. See, for instance, Ropp, *Drugs and the Mind*.

In the context of the study of the interplay between mysticism and consciousness research, several researchers analyze findings from brain imaging and electroencephalographic (EEG) research. On November 6, 2014, Sage Lazzaro wrote in the *Observer* that "researchers achieved brain-to-brain communication where one person was able to control the movements of another person's hand by simply thinking about it";[66] the study was published on November 5, 2014 by The University of Washington, and "it involved three pairs of participants working together to play a computer game" that "involved firing a cannon and intercepting rockets to protect a city."[67] Each pair was comprised of a "sender" and a corresponding "receiver": each of the senders who were placed in front of the computer game could not physically interact with it, but he could only think about moving one's hands to fire the cannons and intercept the rockets; each of the corresponding recipients sat in a distant, dark room without being able to see the game, and their right hands were positioned over touchpads that controlled the game. The senders were connected to EEG machines, and their partners wore caps equipped with technology that stimulates the part of the brain that controls hand movements. Thus, when a sender thought about moving his hands to shoot the cannon, his partner's brain received the message to do so via signals sent from his partner's brain to his over the Internet.

The aforementioned psychological, biological, and technological discoveries, which lead to the conclusion that the American psychologist Timothy Leary was right when he argued that the term "reality" should be replaced by the term "reality tunnel,"[68] stem from the more fundamental argument that "reality" is a system of abstractions.

As I shall explain in this book, in the context of Western philosophy, the origins of the argument that "reality" is a system of abstractions can be traced back to Augustine of Hippo's theology and the medieval scholastics. Moreover, in chapters 2, 3, and 4, I maintain that reality can be perceived as a system of abstractions only if and to the extent that one identifies the terms "consciousness" and "mind" with each other, and I defend arguments that have been put forward by Plato, Aristotle, and the Orthodox Christian mystics known as the Hesychasts according to which the term "mind" (in Greek, *nous*) should *not* be identified with the

---

66. Lazzaro, "It's Now Possible for One Person's Brain to Control Another Person's Movements."

67. Ibid.

68. Leary, et al, *Neuropolitique*.

term "consciousness," thus restoring traditional ontology without negating the significance of abstraction.

Each person's "reality tunnel"—being a consequence of one's genetic program, one's early imprints, one's subsequent conditioning, one's learning experiences, and of whatever experiments one has done in reprograming one's nervous system—can be altered through psychotherapy, yoga, general semantics, neurolinguistic programing (NLP), psychedelic drugs, and brain tuning machines. In fact, the most extreme and most effective ways in which the world super-structure and secret services control members of the elites are the manipulation of the instinct of reproduction (especially through paraphilias) and the manipulation of the central nervous system (especially through psychedelic drugs, which are particularly useful in order to suspend the targeted persons' inhibitions); several mystical fraternities and private exclusive membership clubs are used for such purposes. Inasmuch as one exists in one's own "reality tunnel"—which is a state similar to the one that Plato describes in his myth of the cave[69]—one's existence and identity can be manipulated by the forces that handle one's reality tunnel through psychotherapy, yoga, general semantics, neuro-linguistic programming (NLP), psychedelic drugs, and brain tuning machines, and, thus, one finds oneself in a hypergame situation in which different reality tunnels compete with one another. The previous situation changes dramatically when one exits one's reality tunnel in order to seek the *real truth;* this radical spiritual quest, namely, the pursuit of the real truth, is the essence of traditional metaphysics and, more specifically, the object of my theory of methexiology, which I elucidate in the present book.

In 1980, two Psychological Operations (PSYOP) officers of the United States Army, namely, Colonel Paul E. Valley and Major Michael A. Aquino, authored a treatise entitled *From PSYOP to MindWar: The Psychology of Victory*, which was published by the 7th Psychological Operations Group of the United States Army (Presidio of San Francisco, California, 1980). In that treatise, they discussed the use of psychotronic and electromagnetic weapons for brain manipulation. In particular, the biggest part of humanity's thinking process consists in "pattern thinking," that is, it is subconscious, and many of the ways in which these patterns come into existence are mechanical, in the sense that they are consequences of senses and sensory perceptions that people are not aware of.

69. Plato, *Republic*, Book 7, section 7.

The various brain frequencies are a characteristic case in point: Alpha waves (i.e., neural oscillations in the frequency range of 8–12 Hz) put one in a pleasant mood; Beta waves (i.e., neural oscillations in the frequency range of 12–27 Hz) put one in a somewhat nervous and confrontational mood; Theta waves (i.e., neural oscillations in the frequency range of 3–8 Hz) put one in a creative mood (Theta is also a very receptive mental state, and, thus, it is useful for hypnotherapy and self-hypnosis using recorded affirmations and suggestions); Delta waves (i.e., neural oscillations in the frequency range of 0.2–3 Hz) are the slowest brainwaves, and Delta is the mental state when one is in deep sleep (according to a Hindu mystical tradition that is known as "Advaita Vedanta," if one can stay aware or conscious while in deepest dreamless sleep, a deep meditative state that is called "jagrat sushupti" is said to be achievable; this paradoxical type of consciousness is linked to high cortical activity, which happens during the delta-sleep); Gamma waves (i.e., neural oscillations whose frequencies are 27 Hz and above) are associated with the formation of concepts, high levels of concentration, language and memory processing, as well as various types of learning.

It is important to mention that Michael A. Aquino is not only a prominent Psychological Operations officer of the United States Army, but he is also a highly influential black magician. During the summer solstice of 1975, Michael A. Aquino consecrated the "Temple of Set," a left-hand path initiatory order, in Santa Barbara, California, by practicing a "greater black magic" ritual that resulted in what Aquino regards as a supernaturally revealed text entitled *The Book of Coming Forth by Night*. In 1969, Michael A. Aquino joined Anton Szandor LaVey's "Church of Satan," but, in 1975, he left the church of Satan, and, followed by other former members of the church of Satan, he founded the Temple of Set, arguing that LaVey had lost the mandate, which, according to Aquino and his advocates, the "Prince of Darkness" then transferred to Aquino and his Temple of Set. During 1969–70, Aquino was assigned to the 6th PSYOP Battalion, 4th Group, Vietnam. As an HA Command & Control Team Leader, he was responsible for both tactical (HB) teams in combat operations and audio-visual (HE) teams in the Civil Operations & Revolutionary Development Support (CORDS) program, and he flew numerous PSYOP air support missions throughout III Corps Tactical Zone with both the U.S. Air Force and the U.S. Army aviation. In 1990, as one of the U.S. Army's first officers to be certified in Joint Space Intelligence by the U.S. Air Force, Aquino was assigned to J2 HQ U.S. Space Command, where in Section X, out of the Cheyenne Mountain NORAD complex, he was involved with those files until he retired from the Active USAR in 1994.

Furthermore, especially from the 1940s onward, several mystical groups have been investigating the issue of UFOs from the perspective of the concept of "extra-dimensional beings" and in the context of studies and experiments in the field of "altered state of consciousness"[70] (ASC). Such studies have been methodically developed and promoted by the Borderland Sciences Research Foundation (formerly Associates), which is a non-profit organization based in California, informally organized in 1946 and legally incorporated in 1951 as the "Borderland Sciences Research Associates Foundation" by founder Meade Layne,[71] later renamed "Borderland Sciences Research Foundation" in 1968 under Riley Crabb.[72] Relevant information is contained in the so-called *The Vault*, which is the new Freedom of Information Act (FOIA) library set up by the FBI.[73] Lynn E. Catoe, who was the senior bibliographer of a government publication researched by the Library of Congress for the United States Air Force Office of Scientific Research entitled *UFOs and Related Subjects*, argues that "a large part of the available UFO literature is closely linked with mysticism and the metaphysical," and that "many of the UFO reports now being published in the popular press recount alleged incidents that are strikingly similar to demonic possession and psychic phenomena."[74]

The twentieth-century neo-mythology about humanity's contacts with physical aliens and physical UFOs gives one a cosmic theory that, supposedly, explains everything and, also, gives one a place in the universe. In fact, back in the 1950s, the psychoanalyst Carl G. Jung studied the issue of "flying saucers," and he authored a relevant book in which

---

70. The expression "altered state of consciousness" was brought into common usage from 1969 by the prominent psychologist and parapsychologist Charles T. Tart, who received his doctoral degree in psychology from the University of North Carolina at Chapel Hill in 1963, and then he received postdoctoral training in hypnosis research with Professor Ernest R. Hilgard at Stanford University.

71. Meade Layne was an early researcher of ufology and parapsychology, and, prior to his public work studying UFOs, he was professor at the University of Southern California and English department head at Illinois Wesleyan University and Florida Southern College. He coined the term "interdimensional hypostasis" in order explain flying saucer sightings.

72. Greenfield, *Secret Cipher of the UFOnauts*.

73. http://vault.fbi.gov/

74. Catoe, *UFOs and Related Subjects*.

he argued that UFOlogy is a new, emerging mythology and even a new religious phenomenon in the context of which extraterrestrials tend to replace traditional angels and demons.[75] Thus, UFOlogy is a powerful noopolitical instrument, and several secret intelligence organizations are involved in research projects and experiments related to UFOlogy and altered state of consciousness.

For instance, the U.S. branch of the fringe-Masonic Ordo Templi Orientis (O.T.O.) that was founded in 1969 by a U.S. military officer named Grady Louis McMurty (whose "retired" rank was Lieutenant Colonel) is tied to the U.S. military intelligence and the CIA. In 1943, McMurty was stationed in England, where he became a student of the occultist and British spy Aleister Crowley,[76] who was the leader of the British branch of the O.T.O. Crowley elevated McMurty to the eleventh degree of the O.T.O., giving him the name "Hymenaeus Beta" in November 1943. The German occultist Karl Johannes Germer,[77] also known as "Frater Saturnus," was the successor of Aleister Crowley as the Outer Head of the Order (O.H.O.) of the O.T.O. from 1947 until his death in 1962. In October 1962, Germer died from complications following a prostate operation at the age of seventy-seven, without naming a successor as head of the O.T.O. Thus, Kenneth Grant of Britain, Hermann Metzger of Switzerland, and Marcelo Ramos Motta of Brazil claimed succession to Germer. But, in 1969, in California, McMurtry decided to restore the O.T.O. by invoking his emergency orders from Crowley that gave him authority (subject to Karl Germer's approval) to "take charge of the whole work of the Order in California to reform the Organization," and he assumed the title "Caliph of O.T.O.," as specified in Crowley's letters to McMurtry

---

75. Jung, *Flying Saucers*.

76. Churton, *Aleister Crowley*.

77. Germer worked as a military intelligence officer in World War I and received first-class and second-class Iron Crosses for his services to Germany. In 1923, he sold his Vienna property and founded the publishing house and magazine "Pansophia Verlag" in Munich. During January and February 1926, Germer and his wife, Marie, stayed at the "Abbey of Thelema," which was Aleister Crowley's occult center in Cefalù, Sicily, in Italy. In 1926, Germer moved to the USA with his wife, and, in 1927, he founded the publishing house "Thelema-Verlags-Gesellschaft," which published German versions of Crowley's works. In 1941, Crowley appointed Germer as X° for the free German-speaking peoples and legate in the USA. Germer's ideology was a peculiar version of occult Nazism, and, thus, since 1942, Germer and his wife, Sascha, believed that they were being monitored by the FBI. After Crowley's death, Germer, as the new O.H.O. of the O.T.O., transferred the headquarters of the O.T.O. to California, since he was living in Barstow, California.

from the 1940s. His witnesses were the prominent occultists Israel Regardie and Gerald Yorke ("a veteran British intelligence agent"[78]), who both supported him, even though other O.T.O. Obediences refused to accept McMurty's leadership.

The O.T.O. Lodges that were placed under McMurty's control and administration became experimental laboratories for the CIA's psychological programs. In particular, Alex Constantine argues that "Germer died during the period the CIA had chosen to move mind control experimentation from academic and military labs into the community," and "a number of intelligence agents with occult interests already had their hooks into the O.T.O."[79]

In 1919, Aleister Crowley, in his "Dead Souls exhibition" held in Greenwich Village, New York, included what he called the portrait of Lam; "Lam" is the Tibetan word for way or path, and "Lama" is he who goes. According to Crowley, the portrait of Lam was a drawing he made of an entity he had invoked repeatedly in 1918. Crowley's Lam is the original motif of what Americans call the "grey aliens." In 1987, Kenneth Grant, one of Crowley's successors in the O.T.O., formalized the "Lam Workings" into what came to be known as the cult of Lam. Since Crowley's time, several occultists, such as Michael Bertiaux in the 1960s and a group of O.T.O initiates in the 1970s, following Crowley's path, have claimed to have intentionally and successfully contacted Lam through magical evocations, and they consider Lam to be a trans-mundane, extraterrestrial entity. The cult of Lam is a characteristic case of UFOlogy. Moreover, Monsignor Corrado Balducci (1923–2008), who was a Roman Catholic theologian of the Vatican Curia and the Vatican's chief demonologist and UFOlogist, has cultivated and exploited UFOlogy, specifically, people's belief in extraterrestrials, in order to adjust UFOlogy to the Vatican's noopolitical strategy.

Apart from using UFOlogy for the conduct of psychological operations, several governments use the neo-mythology of UFOs as a means of disinformation in order to conceal particular technological achievements for reasons of national security. For instance, from 1891 to 1893, Nikola Tesla, the famous Serbian American physicist, inventor, electrical engineer, mechanical engineer, and futurist, gave a series of lectures in which he presented his invention of flying "saucers," and, around 1937, Werner

78. Constantine, *Virtual Government*, 103.
79. Ibid, 103.

von Braun was in Los Alamos, New Mexico, testing Tesla's "saucer" technology which then developed into a high-technology weapon program of Nazi Germany.[80] Amidst the first wave of so-called UFO sightings in 1950, Professor Giuseppe Belluzzo, a prominent engineer and former Italian cabinet minister, who personally worked in a German-Italian "flying saucer" project in the 1940s, was quoted in the Italian daily newspaper *Il Giornale d'Italia*, on March 24–25, 1950, saying that, at least as regards the cases of UFO sightings of which he was aware, flying saucers are not alien space ships, but they are man-made, rational constructions, and that Great Powers launch such "discs" to study them; the day after, several newspapers published Belluzzo's claims, such as *Il Corriere della Sera, Il Messaggero, La Nazione, La Stampa, La Gazzetta del Popolo*, etc.[81]

The Creation of the Ecumene

The Greek civilizations of the Aegean Sea constitute the cradle of Europe's prehistoric architecture and technology as well as the cradle of Europe's philosophy.[82] By the fourteenth century BC, trade relations between Mycenae and the Celts were already flourishing, and, in the sixth century BC, Greeks from Phocaea founded Marseille, which soon became a major cultural center for the dissemination of the Greek civilization among the Celts. In his *Geographica*, IV, 181, Strabo writes that Marseille was schooling the Celts to be fond enough of the Greeks to write even their contracts in Greek, and that was one of the most important educational centers in the Roman Empire. In his *De bello gallico*, I, 29:1, Gaius Julius Caesar writes that, "in the camp of the Helvetii, lists were found, drawn up in Greek characters." Moreover, in *De bello gallico*, VI, 14:4, Gaius Julius Caesar writes about the Druids (namely, the priests of the Celts): "in their public and private transactions, they use Greek characters."

Furthermore, the civilization of ancient Rome was a Greek creation. First of all, according to Roman mythology, the city of Rome was founded by Romulus, son of the Greek god Ares. The first ruler of Rome was Janus, grandson of Erechtheus, an archaic king of Athens. The Roman (Latin) alphabet was derived from the Greek one, and the first known Roman author is the Greek dramatist and epic poet Livius Andronicus

---

80. Lyne, *Pentagon Aliens*.
81. For more details, see also Lafayette, *The German UFOs*.
82. Hawkes, *The Prehistoric Foundations of Europe to the Mycenaean Age*.

(third century BC). The ancient Greek religion was adopted by the Romans during the classical era, that is, long before the Hellenistic era. For instance, the Temple of Demeter in Rome was built by Greek artificers in 493 BC. Ancient Roman art was derived from Greek art, and many Roman artists came from Greek colonies and provinces. For instance, some of the Greek antecedents of Roman art were the following: Polygnotos (noted for his wall murals), Apollodoros (the originator of chiaroscuro), Zeuxius, Parrhasius, Phidias, Lysippos, Praxiteles, Agasias, Cleomenes, Aristeas, Demophilos, Gorgasos, etc. Many of the art forms and methods used by the Romans (such as high and low relief, free-standing sculpture, bronze casting, vase art, mosaic, cameo, coin art, fine jewelry and metalwork, funerary sculpture, perspective drawing, caricature, genre and portrait painting, landscape painting, architectural sculpture, and trompe l'oeil painting) were developed or refined by ancient Greek artists.[83] Moreover, the intellectual roots of Roman law can be traced back to the book *Dodecadeltos* (in Latin, *Duodecim tabularum*), which was written by the Greek philosopher and jurist Hermodorus, who was born in Ephesus, in the fifth century BC, and he was a student of the famous Greek philosopher Heraclitus.

In 334 BC, Alexander the Great had already liberated the Greek inhabitants of Ionia from the Persian yoke, and he went to Gordium, the Phrygian capital, to spend the winter. By that time, he had already conceived the "ecumene," that is, the creation of a spiritually grounded world order and, indeed, a world *society*. In the last year of his life, he had a deep understanding of the notion of ecumene, and, in fact, he had created the ecumene. According to Arrian's *Anabasis* (Book VII, 11), Alexander the Great "prayed for other blessings, and especially that harmony and community of rule might exist between the Macedonians and Persians." Alexander the Great did not simply found an empire; he founded the "ecumene," that is, the first type of globalization in the history of mankind. Thus, Hermann Bengtson argues that neither the Roman Empire, nor the triumph of Christianity's march, nor the Byzantine Empire, nor the Arab civilization could have been achieved without Alexander the Great's work.[84]

In his book *On the Fortune or the Virtue of Alexander*, I, 329a–d, Plutarch points out that Alexander the Great gave effect to Zeno's

---

83. Piper, *The Illustrated Library of Art*.
84. Bengtson, *History of Greece*.

cosmopolitan political ideal. Zeno, the founder of Stoicism, wrote in his *Republic* that we should consider all men to be of one community and one polity and that we should all have a common life and common order. Furthermore, Plutarch points out that Alexander the Great did not follow Aristotle's advice to treat the Greeks as if he were their leader, and other peoples as if he were their master. Instead, according to Plutarch, Alexander the Great believed that he came as a heaven-sent ruler to all and as a mediator for the whole world, and, therefore, those whom he could not persuade to unite with him, he conquered by force of arms, but he bade all his subjects consider as their fatherland the whole inhabited earth, as their polity his camp, as akin to them all virtuous men, and as foreigners only the wicked. Thus, Alexander the Great created a multicultural polity. With respect to his attitude toward Asia, Plutarch (Ibid., I, 330c–e) emphasizes that Alexander did not overrun Asia like a robber, but Alexander's goal was to render all upon earth subject to one law of reason and one form of government.

Instead of building up an empire merely by establishing regimes based on physical-spatial unity, Alexander the Great was founding new cities that were centers of the Greek *paideia*,[85] and, at the apex of his imperial career, he declared the brotherhood of all men, thus uniting the existential dimensions of space and time. If one conquers space, but he fails to conquer the human factor, that is, if the superiority of his cultural proposal is not acknowledged by others, then his spatial conquests will be lost within a relatively short time interval. Geopolitical calculations can yield power, indeed; but, if they are not combined with a sufficiently attractive cultural proposal, even the most ingenious geopolitical calculations will end in failure, because they will be defeated by time. Culture leads to a dynamic understanding of space and unites it with time, like an artifact, whose truth is being continually formed and reformed over time. Alexander the Great was the first world leader who transcended national differences, and he anticipated the apostle Paul's universalism by forging a spiritual unity between the Greeks and the barbarians.[86]

---

85. In his book entitled *Paideia: The Ideals of Greek Culture*, W. W. Jaeger explains that *paideia* is a word that we translate as education, but, according to ancient Greeks, *paideia* means not only the rearing and education of children (*pais* is the simple Greek for child), but also culture and civilization, and, generally, the spiritual accomplishments of an age or people; it was rendered in Latin as *humanitas*.

86. Tarn, "Alexander: The Conquest of the Far East."

The Punic Wars played a decisive role in the fate of the ecumene. They were a series of three wars fought between Rome and Carthage from 264 BC to 146 BC. They started in 264 BC, when the Roman Republic decided to ally itself with the Mamertines (which means "sons of Mars"), a group of thugs and pirates, who were living in Messina, which was besieged by King Hieron II of Syracuse and the Carthaginians. In his *Histories*, I, 12:5, Polybius explains the historical significance of the First Punic War: it was "the first warlike expedition of the Romans beyond the shores of Italy."

When, after their victory in the Second Punic War against Carthage, the Romans decided to march out toward Pherae, an ancient Greek town in southeastern Thessaly, against the Greek kingdom of Macedonia, many Greek city-states allied with the Romans, and, for this reason, at the Battle of Cynoscephalae (in Thessaly), in 197 BC, the Roman army, led by Titus Quinctius Flamininus, managed to defeat King Philip V of Macedon. Philip V of Macedon was an ally of Antiochus III the Great, a Seleucid Greek king and the sixth ruler of the Seleucid Empire (ruling over the region of Syria and large parts of the rest of the Middle East). When Antiochus III the Great learned that his ally, Philip V of Macedon, had been defeated by the Romans, he decided to attack the Romans and drive them out of Greece. But, by the time Antiochus III the Great and his huge army arrived in Thessaly, Philip V of Macedon had become the leader of the Roman army, and, therefore, he turned against Antiochus III the Great. At the Battle of Thermopylae, in 191 BC, the allied forces of the Romans, Philip V of Macedon, and several Greek city-states defeated Antiochus III the Great.

After, Philip V's death, Perseus, son of Philip V, became the new king of Macedon. Perseus decided to attack the Romans, since the Roman army was small, and the primary cause of the Romans' power was their alliance with Greek city-states. However, at the Battle of Pydna, in 168 BC, Perseus was defeated by the Romans, because the Roman general Lucius Aemilius Paullus had bribed several officers of Perseus's army.[97] It is worth pointing out that Perseus refused to employ Gallic mercenaries, because he wanted to liberate and unite the Greeks without any foreign assistance. Finally, in 146 BC, the Roman statesman and general Lucius Mummius, exploiting the Greek civil wars, and primarily a conflict between Corinth and Sparta, conquered the Achaean League and brought

---

87. Polybius, *Histories*, 29.

all of Greece under Roman control. However, because the Romans were unable to maintain direct political authority over Greece, they offered autonomy to all Greek city-states, and, during the so-called Roman occupation period (i.e., from the first century BC until the third century AD), most of the Roman emperors, who admired Greek culture, acted as benefactors to the Greek cities, and especially Athens. Thus, Jacques Pirenne argues that the Roman Empire was a "Hellenistic state,"[88] and Francis E. Peters uses the terms "Latin Hellenism" and "Greek Hellenism" in order to describe the extent of Greece's cultural influence on Rome.[89]

The Christianization of the Ecumene

Given that the dominant civilization of the ancient ecumene was the Greek one, the study of the issue of the Christianization of the ecumene is reduced to the study of the issue of the Christianization of the Greeks.

From the perspective of classical Greek philosophy, the human soul is relatively capable of introducing harmony into its movements and of acting in such a way that human life has some order, because and to the extent that it has achieved to gaze at that which is timeless, that is, the deity, the absolute good.[90] The absolute good is the ultimate purpose, the end (*telos*), of being, because it is simultaneously the order of the constitution of each work and of reality as well as their completion. This is the kind of goodness that each positive work tries to actualize, whether it is the work of the divine constructor mentioned in Plato's *Timaeus* 29a–d, or the work of the painters, the builders, the shipwrights, the trainers, and the physicians mentioned in Plato's *Gorgias* 503–4, or the work of those who practice the art of weaving, which can be used as a model for the study of statesmanship, as mentioned in Plato's *Statesman* 279a–b. Hence, everything that takes place in the world exists due to its end (ultimate purpose). The deity is the end that gives meaning to the whole cosmic becoming, because of the erotic attraction that the deity exerts: seeking the order that they have to actualize and the perfection that they have to achieve, all beings respond positively to the universal eros, whose ultimate object is the perfection of the deity.

---

88. Pirenne, *The Tides of History*.
89. Peters, *The Harvest of Hellenism*.
90. Plato, *Phaedrus* 247c–d.

According to Plato and Aristotle, *theoria* (spiritual gaze) brings the philosopher's life to completion and conclusion, and *theoria* should not be identified with scientific theorizing. From the perspective of the classical Greek philosophers, *theoria* means direct knowledge of the eternal being and identification with it. For this reason, "the life of *theoria*" is the philosopher's mode of life, that is, it consists in love of wisdom. Wisdom is the beginning and the result of philosophy, which gazes at and accesses the totality of the being of the cosmos and, together with the gods, it enjoys the pleasures of the mind. Thus, *theoria* consists in the event of man's participation in the deity and echoes religious experiences. According to Plato, man's access to the deity is a transcendental experience, and, apart from the development of human reason, it necessarily presupposes psychic cleansing or cure,[91] and, similarly, according to Aristotle, humanity's access to the deity presupposes the perfection of the human mind.[92] In particular, according to Aristotle, *theoria* is an energy of the mind, which comes from the outside; the mind, Aristotle maintains, is "the divinest part of us,"[93] and it is "the true self of each, inasmuch as it is the dominant and better part."[94]

Furthermore, in order to understand the history of the Greek metaphysical thought, in general, and the underpinnings of Hesychasm, in particular, one should bear in mind the interaction and synthesis of the Greek philosophical tradition with the Jewish scriptural tradition in the context of the Ptolemies' Greek kingdom of Egypt. First of all, in the context of the Ptolemies' Greek kingdom of Egypt, a significant part of the Jewish community of Egypt was Hellenized. In particular, many Jews of Egypt used to take Greek names (such as: Apollonius, Artemidoros, Diodotus, Demetrius, Dionysus, Diophantus, Heracleia, Heracledes, Hermeias, Theodotus, Theodorus, Dositheus, Jason, etc.), and they were proud of their Greek culture and manners. The Jews of the Hellenistic Egypt developed a highly Hellenized literature: the historiographer Demetrius, a Jewish courtier of Ptolemy IV, wrote an exposition of the Jewish religion following a philosophical style, which indicates the Greek spiritual influence on the Jews of the Hellenistic Egypt; Artapanus of Alexandria, another famous Hellenized Jew, wrote an allegorical novel in which

---

91. Plato, *Symposium* 212a; *Republic* 443d–e, 509b6–10
92. Aristotle, *Metaphysics* 1072b18–24; *Nicomachean Ethics* 1177a20–21.
93. Aristotle, *Nicomachean Ethics* 1177a16.
94. Ibid., 1178a2–3.

Moses is presented as the founder of the Orphic Mysteries (i.e., of the pagan Greeks' monotheistic mysteries); a Jew named Ezekiel composed a Greek tragedy on the theme of the book of Exodus; Philo the Elder wrote an epic poem *On Jerusalem* in Homeric hexameters; Theodotus wrote an epic poem *On Shechem* (an Israelite city of the tribe of Manasseh), in which he connects the name of Shechem with Sikimios, son of the Greek god Hermes; and the Jewish philosopher Aristobulus of Paneas put forward the theory that Pythagoras and Plato had knowledge of the Bible. Under Greek philosophical influences, the Jewish worship practices were enriched with teachings about the interpretation of the Jewish religious texts, that is, with a philosophical activity, and the expressions "God the Most High" and "I am that I am" are indications of Platonic influences on the interpretation of the Bible. In the context of their cultural interaction with the Jewish scriptural tradition, many Greeks, on their side, turned their mind toward the Jewish monotheistic and prophetic theology, since it is focused on direct and personal communion with God. Titus Flavius Josephus (37–ca. 100 AD), also called Joseph ben Matityahu, an ethnic Jew and priest of Jerusalem, studied the relations between the Greeks and the Hebrews in his historical book *Antiquities of the Jews*, in his polemical work *Against Apion* (I, 12:60–68), and in his book *Jewish War*, in which he introduces himself with the Hellenized version of his name: Iosepos.

The Orientalization of the Greek philosophical tradition, that is, the synthesis of Greek philosophy with Oriental mystical religious traditions, was further enhanced and enriched by the Hermetic cult, which prevailed in Hellenistic Alexandria, in Egypt. Tobias Churton writes about the history of the Hermetic cult that, a century after Alexander the Great conquered Egypt and founded his city, Alexandria, in 331 BC, Greek settlers in Alexandria had begun to apply the epithet *megistos kai megistos theos megas* (greatest and greatest the great god) to the god Hermes, and that this dignity derives from the epithet "two times great," which Egyptians had applied to Hermes's Egyptian equivalent, the god Thoth. In Hermopolis, Thoth was believed to have hatched the World Egg. The Graeco-Egyptian Thoth-Hermes was the spirit of inventiveness. Sometime between the first century BC and the end of the first century AD, a new figure appeared: "Hermes Trismegistus" (Thrice Greatest Hermes), a name with which Greek settlers in Egypt unified the Greek god Hermes and the Egyptian god Thoth, since both were associated with magical knowledge, the dead, and healing. According to the Hermeticists' legends, the *Hermetica* was a collection of forty-two books of

Hellenistic Egyptian magical wisdom that were written by Hermes Trismegistus, who was believed to be an ancient patriarch of civilization and the founder of a philosophical religion focused on man's purification and union with the deity.

At this point, it is important to mention that the aforementioned process of the Orientalization of Greece, far from contradicting the humanist core of the Greek philosophy, was a process through which the spiritual core of the Greek aesthetics was perfected. If we study history of art, we see that ancient agricultural civilizations worshiped nature, and, thus, their gods usually had animal characteristics, and ancient nomadic civilizations worshiped the natural bond of blood, the power of the race. On the other hand, ancient Greek gods had human form. The human form of the ancient Greek gods was characterized by exceptional beauty, because it was expressing the human quest for perfection, and, according to ancient Greek mythology, the end of the human being's existence is man's participation in the deity. Thus, through their mythology, ancient Greeks gave priority to a personal approach to reality over the impersonal commands of nature and race, and, in this way, they created an anthropocentric civilization.

The humanism of the classical Greek aesthetics was transformed into a theological system by Christianity, since Christians identified the Greek value of beauty with Jesus Christ, and, through Jesus Christ, Christianity stressed the personhood of God. According to Irenaeus of Lyons' book *Against Heresies*, 3, 19:1, the central dogma of Christianity is that "the Logos became man, and the Son of God became the Son of man: so that man, by entering into communion with the Logos and thus receiving divine 'sonship,' might become a son of God."[95] Furthermore, Gregory of Nazianzus (known also as Gregory the Theologian) has stressed that the Christ Mystery signifies not only the Incarnation of the divine Logos but also the deification of the human flesh.[96] Thus, ultimately, the Greeks adopted the Orthodox Christian doctrine of the Incarnation of the divine Logos, because they understood it as a metaphysical thesis that completed and perfected the classical Greek humanist philosophy.

Greek philosophy needs mystical religious experiences in order to arrive at its completion and perfection. Hesychasm is the Christocentric perfection of the Greek concept of *theoria*. What defines a Hesychast is

---

95. *Patrologia Graeca*, Vol. 7:1, 939.
96. Ibid., Vol. 36, 353B.

that he or she poses and answers the "how" question in a very specific way: "how can a human attain *theoria*?" Or, in other words, "how can a human attain direct communion with the absolute good, or the deity, just as Moses and Hermes Trismegistus did?" Or, more specifically, "how can a human experience the uncreated light of God's glory, which was manifested during Christ's Transfiguration?"

Aristotle argues as follows: "We ought not to obey those who enjoin that a man should have man's thoughts and a mortal the thoughts of mortality, but we ought, so far as possible, to achieve immortality."[97] In particular, according to Aristotle, God's activity is the activity of *theoria*, and "the whole of the life of the gods is blessed," whereas human life is blessed "only in so far as it contains some likeness to the divine activity."[98] But the classical Greek conception of *theoria* was imperfect because of the following reason: the Greek mind discovered *theoria*, that is, the perfect mode of life, but, as Aristotle has pointed out, man, faced with physical reality, realizes that his own will and powers cannot overcome natural necessity.[99] In particular, as Aristotle has pointed out, man, being composed of mind and body, cannot unceasingly be in the state of pure *theoria*, but only during rare, pleasant moments of his life.[100] From the previous perspective, therefore, the life of the Greek philosopher is tragic.

The awareness of the tragedy of human life by the Greek philosophers, that is, the Greek philosophers' awareness of the contradiction between the spiritual freedom that characterizes the life of *theoria*, on the one hand, and human subservience to natural necessity, on the other, is the ultimate source of inspiration for the classical Greek tragic poets. Thus, for instance, Sophocles, in *Oedipus Tyrannus*, a tragedy devoted to the issue of punishment, writes: "Alas, generations of mortals! How mere non-being I count your life!"[101] Similarly, Euripides, in *Hippolytus*, describes the tragedy of the human being as follows: "the life of mortals is wholly trouble. . . . Anything we might love more than life is hid in a surrounding cloud of darkness. Thus, everything that shines on earth

---

97. stotle, *Nicomachean Ethics*, 1177b31–33.
98. Ibid., 1178b26–27.
99. Ibid., 1112a21–26.
100. Ibid., 1177b11.
101. Sophocles, *Oedipus Tyrannus*, 1186.

disappoints us, because we have neither knowledge of another life nor proof of an afterlife. We are governed by mere tales."[102]

Hesychasm addresses exactly the aforementioned Greek philosophical problem, precisely, the relationship between the created and the uncreated, and the possibility of the created human being participating in the uncreated God. According to Hesychasm, the only uncreated essence is God's essence, and, therefore, God's essence is *totally inaccessible* and *totally unknowable*. However, the Hesychasts emphasize that God exists hypostatically, precisely, as a communion of three hypostases (i.e., the divine Nous [Mind], called the "Father," the divine Logos/Word, called the "Son," and the Holy Spirit), and, therefore, God is not constrained by His essence, and His mode of being is totally free. Thus, the divine Logos can be incarnated without diminishing his divinity. In addition to His uncreated essence and His uncreated hypostases, God has uncreated *energies*, too. God's uncreated energies, known as His omnipresence, omniscience, omnipotence, providence, etc., are the life-force of His essence, that is, His capacity to perform work. *With regard to His uncreated essence, God is totally alien to creation, but, with regard to His uncreated energies, God is present in creation, in accordance with His hypostatic mode of being, precisely, in accordance with His personal will.*

Since the essence of the human being is created, a human cannot be united with God at the level of God's essence. The union between humanity and God at the level of God's hypostases (i.e., the "hypostatic union" between the divine and the human natures) took place only once, that is, in the case of Jesus Christ, the Incarnate Logos of God. Therefore, apart from Jesus Christ, human beings cannot be united with God at the level of God's hypostases, either. *However, each human being can participate in God's uncreated energies,* since, according to Hesychasm, the human mind is the repository or closet of God's uncreated energies, and the Incarnation of the divine Logos restored the human nature's ability to bear the uncreated grace of the Holy Spirit, sent by the Father in the name of the Son (John 14:26). In fact, for the Hesychasts, human participation in God's uncreated energies, that is, the union between humanity and God at the level of God's energies, is the essence of pure theology and the kind of *theoria* that the Greek philosophers had been seeking before Christ. Without the Incarnation of the Logos of God, pure theology and the kind of *theoria* that the Greek philosophers had been seeking before

---

102. Euripides, *Hippolytus*, 189–97.

Christ would have remained "hid in a surrounding cloud of darkness," and humanity would have continued to be "governed by mere tales," as Euripides writes in *Hippolytus*. Thus, from the perspective of Hesychasm, love is a disposition of the soul by which one prefers no being to the participation in God's uncreated energies.

In addition to the essence/energies distinction, the Hesychasts emphasize the distinction of the human mind, being construed as the repository or closet of God's uncreated energies, and, therefore, as a source of uncreated, divine knowledge, from the human intellect, being construed as the seat of human reason, and, therefore, as a source of created knowledge. Jesus Christ himself referred to the mind as a spiritual closet; in particular, in Matthew 6:5–6, we read that Jesus Christ taught the following about praying: "When you pray, you shall not be as the hypocrites, for they love to stand and pray in the synagogues and in the corners of the streets, that they may be seen by men. . . . But you, when you pray, enter into your closet, and having shut your door, pray to your Father who is in secret, and your Father who sees in secret will reward you openly."

Moreover, there are significant similarities between the Hesychast notion of the mind as the repository or closet of God's uncreated energies and the Kabbalistic doctrine of the "neshamah," as it is presented in the *Sefer Ha-Zohar* (Book of Splendor), an important text of Jewish mysticism filled with arcane symbolism and erotic language. The *Zohar* first appeared in Spain in the thirteenth century AD and was published by a Jewish writer and rabbi named Moses de León. According to the *Zohar*, the neshamah stands above all the parts of the soul, it is the supernal power by which a human knows the Holy One, it obeys His precepts, and it can be conceived as our spiritual umbilical cord that connects us to God and to each other. The biblical term *neshamah* literally means breath, and it can be broadly understood as the "soul proper" and the ability to become partakers of God. In the Old Testament, there are several references to the *neshamah*, such as the following: Isaiah 30:33: breath of God as hot wind kindling a flame; 2 Samuel 22:16 and Job 4:9: as destroying wind; Job 32:8 and 33:4: as cold wind producing ice; 1 Kings 17:17, Isaiah 42:5, Job 27:3, and Daniel 10:7: breath of man; Genesis 2:7 and Job 34:14 and 36:4: breath of life and God's breath in man; Isaiah 2:22: man in whose nostrils is but a breath.

The Division of the Ecumene

In 330 AD, the first Christian ruler of the Roman Empire, Constantine the Great, transferred the imperial capital from Rome to Byzantium. In the seventh century BC, Byzas, son of the king of Megara (a city-state near Athens), created a Megarian colony in a location where the Golden Horn, an important natural harbor, meets the Bosporus and flows into the Sea of Marmara; Byzas named that city Byzantium after himself. The location of Byzantium attracted Roman Emperor Constantine the Great, who, in 330 AD, refounded it as an imperial residence and the capital of the Roman Empire; after his death, the city was called Constantinople (literally, the "city of Constantine"). Between 330 AD and 1453 AD, Constantinople (known also as the "New Rome") was the capital of the Roman Empire. However, when Emperor Theodosius the Great (fourth century AD) divided the Roman Empire between his two sons, Arcadius in the East and Honorius in the West, the Adriatic Sea became the new border between East and West.

In the first centuries of the Christian era, many Christians felt uncomfortable with Greek philosophy, because many gnostic "schools" challenged Christianity by putting forward philosophical arguments, and because philosophy, in general, poses questions that the early Christian church was not ready to tackle in a systematic way. Thus, an early Latin church father, Tertullian (active in the second and the third centuries AD), in his *De Praescriptione Haereticorum* 7, posed the question: "What has Athens to do with Jerusalem?" Tertullian answered the previous question in the negative, thus fomenting a cultural clash between philosophy and Christianity, whereas, as I have already argued, early Greek church fathers, such as Justin Philosopher and Martyr and Clement of Alexandria, were pursuing a synthesis between philosophy and Christian theology.

Justin Philosopher and Martyr, one of the early Greek church fathers, argues, in his *Dialogue with Trypho* II, 1, that "philosophy is, in fact, the greatest possession, and most honorable before God, to whom it leads us and alone commends us; and these are truly holy men who have bestowed attention on philosophy." In the same spirit, another prominent early Greek church father, Clement of Alexandria, argues, in his *Stromata* VI, 7:55, that "philosophy yearns for the wisdom which consists in rightness of soul and speech and in purity of life." In addition, in his *Stromata* I, 20:100, Clement of Alexandria argues that the primary task of Greek philosophy is the defense of the Christian faith: "in rendering the attack of sophistry impotent and in disarming those who betray truth and wage war upon it, Greek philosophy is rightly called the hedge and the protective wall around the vineyard."

On the other hand, Tertullian was the first Christian apologist who wrote in Latin, not because he didn't know Greek, but because he wanted to deter Christendom from the use of the Greek philosophical language. In his theological essays, Tertullian uses legal terms, instead of philosophical ones, and he articulates a legalist exposition of the Christian faith. Moreover, the first Latin translation of the Bible, known as the *Vulgata*, accomplished by the Dalmatian scholar Jerome, who was commissioned by Pope Damasus I (d. 384 AD), is replete with Latin legal terms and concepts, thus underpinning and promoting a legalist approach to Christ's gospel.

The transfer of the Roman Empire's capital from Rome to Constantinople by Constantine the Great had important spiritual consequences, because it was favorable to the Greek culture. In particular, as a result of the transfer of the imperial capital from Rome to Constantinople, the Greek church could develop under the direct protection of the Roman emperor and control the education of the imperial capital, whereas Rome had to develop without having any powerful imperial institution by its side and to deal with several barbarian invasions. Thus, the See of Rome decided to fill the power vacuum and to give primacy to secular goals, precisely, to inducing barbarian hordes to adhere to the Christian church and to the Roman Empire's institutional system. In other words, for both cultural and geopolitical reasons, the See of Rome arguably succumbed to the lure of historical power at the expense of the metaphysical essence of Christianity.

As a consequence of the aforementioned cultural and geopolitical reasons, the See of Rome and the See of Constantinople (the "New Rome") have followed different paths. The central and guiding vision of the Greek East is the deification of humanity, whereas the central and guiding vision of the Latin West is the historical fulfillment and self-affirmation of humanity. The spiritual divergence between East and West increased when the Western Roman Empire and the See of Rome were conquered by German tribes in the ninth century AD.

In 476 AD, Odoaker, a German soldier, deposed Romulus Augustulus and proclaimed himself King of Italy, signaling the end of the Western Roman Empire. In 751 AD, Childeric III, the last Merovingian King of

Frankia, was deposed by Pope Zachary at the instigation of Pepin the Short, a son of the German Frank Charles Martel, mayor of the palace of Austrasia (the eastern part of the Frankish Kingdom). In 754 AD, in Paris, at the Basilica of St. Denis, Pope Stephen II—who had left Rome to beg the Frankish King for assistance against the Lombards—anointed Pepin the Short King of the Franks a second time, and he bestowed upon him the additional title of "Patricius Romanorum" (Patrician of the Romans); this is the first recorded crowning of a civil ruler by a Pope. In 768 AD, Carloman I and Charlemagne, the two sons of Pepin the Short, each inherited a half of the Kingdom of the Franks upon their father's death. Carloman I, who had the personality of a bureaucrat, as opposed to Charlemagne, who was an ambitious warlord, died in 771 AD. Thus, Charlemagne annexed Carloman's territory, and, in 774 AD, he became King of Italy, too. While still consolidating their grip on Gaul, the Franks had already conquered northern and central Italy by the middle of the eighth century, pretending that they were liberators of the See of Rome from Lombard oppression. At this time, the Papacy was preoccupied with the iconoclastic controversy, opposing both the Roman emperors and the patriarchs of Constantinople, who supported the iconoclastic movement. The Franks applied the policy of "divide and rule," playing one Roman party against the other, and, finally, they condemned both the iconoclasts and the Seventh Ecumenical Council (786–87 AD) at their own Council of Frankfurt in 794 AD, even though Pope Hadrian I was a staunch supporter of the Orthodox practice, which was also supported by the Seventh Ecumenical Council.

In the early Middle Ages, the German tribes adopted Christianity, mainly as a means to better social status in the Roman Empire, and they used Christianity in order to conquer the Western part of the Roman Empire and the See of Rome from the inside. Boniface, the first Archbishop of Mainz, described the situation of the Frankish church in the eighth century as follows: "The Episcopal Sees . . . have been given, for the most part, into the possession of avaricious laymen or exploited by adulterous and unworthy clerics for worldly uses. . . . Among them are bishops who . . . are shiftless drunkards, . . . who march armed into battle and shed with their own hands the blood of Christians and heathens alike."[103]

In 800 AD, Charlemagne was crowned Emperor of the Holy Roman Empire of the German nation by Pope Leo III on Christmas day at Old

---

103. "Boniface to Pope Zachary on His Accession to the Papacy" (742 AD); *Patrologia Latina*, Vol. 89, 744.

Saint Peter's Basilica. In 799 AD, Charlemagne and his army protected Pope Leo III from his enemies, who had accused Pope Leo III of adultery and perjury, and they had attempted to kill him, and, on December 1, 800 AD, Charlemagne held a council in Rome, thus solidifying the pontificate of Pope Leo III, who, in return, strengthened Charlemagne's position by crowning him "Augustus of the Romans." The coronation of Charlemagne—an illiterate, megalomaniac German warlord—in 800 AD, as emperor of the "Holy Roman Empire" (which was essentially a German empire) signals an important spiritual change in the West: a significant part of the West was essentially cut off from its Greco-Roman cultural heritage, and it was subjugated to the crude power of the German tribes, which, gradually, together with the subjugated See of Rome, formed a new historical entity, precisely, a Western European geopolitical and geocultural entity that was politically dominated by the Carolingian Europe and spiritually founded on scholasticism and legalism. By the term "Carolingian Europe," I refer to a geographical area that includes the Western part of Germany, a great part of France, the Benelux countries, and the Alpine region. Historically, the Carolingian Europe corresponds to the medieval Frankish Kingdom that was founded by Charlemagne in 800 AD.

On the other hand, the mystical spirituality, precisely, Hesychasm, of the Greek East expanded throughout the Slavic world in the fourteenth century AD; thus, as the distinguished scholar Dimitri Obolensky has pointed out, "Byzantium, Bulgaria, Serbia, Romania, and Russia were all affected by this new cosmopolitan movement [Hesychasm]," and, "through this "Hesychast International," whose influence extended far beyond the ecclesiastical sphere, the different parts of the Byzantine Commonwealth were, during the last hundred years of its existence, linked to each other and to its center and perhaps more closely than ever before."[104] By the ninth century AD, in the region that, in the modern era, corresponds to the states of Bulgaria, Serbia, and Romania, the foundation of the culture of the Slavs who lived there was Byzantine. In the region that, in the modern era, corresponds to the states of Russia and Ukraine, the dominant culture had three components: an inherited pre-Christian pagan component and two acquired components derived from Christianity and Byzantium.

---

104. Obolensky, *The Byzantine Commonwealth*, 390.

After the fall of Constantinople to the Ottomans, in 1453, Russia became, geopolitically, the most important representative of and heir to the Eastern Roman Empire (Byzantine civilization) and, geopolitically, the most important Christian Orthodox nation. In the fifteenth century AD, Ivan III Vasilyevich, known also as Ivan the Great, who was a Grand Prince of Moscow and Grand Prince of all Rus, tripled the territory of his state, ended the dominance of the Golden Horde[105] over the Rus, renovated the Moscow Kremlin, and laid the foundations of the Russian state. Ivan III married Zoē Sophia Paleologina, a Byzantine princess and niece of the last Byzantine Emperor, Constantine XI Palaiologos.

It should be mentioned that, from its dawn, the Russian civilization has been a multicultural one, and Russia had significant political and commercial ties with Central Asian and Middle Eastern states as early as the ninth century AD. Thus, the Christocentric ecumenism and the multicultural character of the Eastern Roman Empire (Byzantium) were particularly appealing to the Russians. In the late ninth century AD, Scandinavian warrior-traders, the Varangians, gradually took control of the major waterways from the Baltic to the Black Sea. This process began in about 860 AD, when the people of Novgorod invited the Varangian Prince Rurik to become their ruler. In 882, Rurik's successor, Oleg, captured Kiev, where he was succeeded in about 912 by Rurik's son, Prince Igor. The Rurik dynasty survived as rulers of Russia until 1598.

By the tenth century AD, the Russian city-states of Novgorod, Pskov, Smolensk, Suzdal, Kiev, and Vladimir had been established on the basis of an elaborate pagan culture and a prosperous trading system. The main trading partners of the Rus, as these people came to be known, were Byzantium and the Greeks who had lived for several centuries on the northern shores of the Black Sea. Moreover, during this period, the Rus were frequently attacked by nomadic Asian tribes, such as the Khazars, the Pechenegs, and the Polovtsians.

From the beginning of the ninth century, the Russian world was increasingly exposed to Christianity. Patriarch Photius of Constantinople, in his "Encyclical to the Eastern Patriarchs" (866 AD), writes that Greek Orthodox missionaries were active in Russian society in the middle of the ninth century. Additionally, as early as 846 AD, the Persian geographer Ibn Khordadbeh wrote in his *Book of Roads and Countries*

---

105. The Golden Horde was a Mongol and later Turkicized khanate established in the thirteenth century AD and originating as the northwestern sector of the Mongol Empire.

about Rus-Christians who traded with Byzantium and the Middle East. It should be mentioned that Novgorod and other Russian merchant cities prospered without joining the initial capitalist movement, which was primarily a Western phenomenon, and this is another element that indicates the cultural and political affinity between Russia and Byzantium.

In the second half of the tenth century AD, a large part of southern and central Rus was united under Prince Vladimir of Kiev's rule. He then adopted Orthodox Christianity as the official religion of the Rus. The Russian Orthodox Church adhered to the Byzantine Orthodox pattern completely, and it creatively assimilated pre-Christian Russian folk traditions. The adoption of Byzantine Christianity by the Rus played a key role in the development of Russian literature and marked the beginning of literacy after the adoption of the new alphabet. Two brothers from Thessaloniki, Cyril (826–69 AD) and Methodius (815–85 AD), created the alphabet for the Russian liturgical language, which was influenced by Greek linguistic models and was the common literary language of all the Christian Orthodox Slavs. Moreover, Byzantine art was another important cultural bridge between Byzantium and Russia throughout the Middle Ages.

In the thirteenth century AD, Alexander Nevsky (1219–63), Prince of Novgorod, Grand Prince of Kiev and Grand Prince of Vladimir, played a key role in preventing the submission of Russia to the Roman Catholic Pope and the Germans. In 1193, Pope Celestine III declared the Northern Crusades, encouraging the Holy Roman Empire (i.e., the Germans) and the Kingdom of Sweden to advance eastward, into Latvia, Estonia, and Lithuania. Within a decade, much of the region was under Teutonic control. Alexander Nevsky stood on the shores of Lake Peipus determined to halt the German knights' encroachment on April 5, 1242. Marching his army out onto the frozen water, Alexander Nevsky scored a major victory at the Battle of the Ice. Thus, he prevented the Teutonic Knights from entering Russia, and he hardened the dividing line between the Papacy and the Orthodox Church. He was canonized by the Russian Orthodox Church in 1547, and his principal feast day is 23 November.

With regard to religion, the Slavic world and, generally, the Russians are spiritual descendants of the Eastern Roman Empire (Byzantium), since they have adopted Byzantine Orthodoxy. However, the genuine Byzantine Orthodoxy, especially its mystical tradition, namely, Hesychasm, is founded on a Christocentric synthesis of classical Greek philosophy (i.e., Plato's, Aristotle's, and Plotinus's ontological theories), Jewish scriptural tradition, and Christ's gospel, whereas, in the Middle Ages, the Slavs and the Russians adopted Byzantine Orthodoxy without having previously assimilated the Greek philosophical tradition, which is embedded in and underpins Byzantine Orthodox theology. Thus, Russia and the Slavs are characterized by a spiritual dichotomy between their "myth," which is inextricably linked to Byzantine Orthodoxy, and their "logos," which has been strongly influenced by Western modern philosophy and political thought. In other words, the Slavs' and the Russians' myth and religion have been molded by Byzantine Orthodoxy, whereas their mainstream philosophical thought has been molded by Western modernity.

For instance, Tsar Peter the Great (1672–1725) was a sympathizer of German Protestantism, and Empress Catherine the Great (1729–96) was an adherent of the Enlightenment. In the same spirit of apostasy from their Byzantine Orthodox roots, often masked behind a pietist and moralist rhetoric, Tsar Alexander I was one of the founders and masterminds of the "Holy Alliance," an authoritarian system of international governance which was formed in Paris in 1815 by the Sovereigns of Russia, Austria, and Prussia, who thus attempted to "export" and universalize their authoritarian, absolutist, and essentially inhuman political regimes. Moreover, Georges Florovsky has written that, in the seventeenth century, Metropolitan Peter of Kiev (Petro Mohyla) founded a Roman Catholic school within the Russian Orthodox Church, and, thus, "for generations the Orthodox clergy was raised in a Roman Catholic spirit and taught theology in Latin."[106] As a result of the predominance of Western intellectual "schools" in the modern Russian elites, a desk reference book for Russian Orthodox clergy, authored by Sergei Vasilevich Bulgakov and "officially sanctioned" and published by the Russian Orthodox church in 1913 addresses the teachings of Hesychasm under a section devoted to "Schisms, Heresies, Sects, etc.," and its treatment of Hesychasm echoes the accusations of Gregory Palamas's scholastic critics and chief antagonist, the Calabrian Uniate monk Barlaam.[107] Additionally, for several centuries, while many Russian tsars were nominally Orthodox Christians, in reality they maintained a brutal, essentially anti-Christian, regime, and they treated most of their own people as slaves.

During the Soviet regime, the Russian Orthodox church was unable to give witness to Hesychasm, and, due to the KGB's suffocating

---

106. Florovsky, *Collected Works, Volume 5: Ways of Russian Theology: Part One*, 72.
107. Nedelsky, *Palamas in Exile*, 18.

control over the Orthodox Patriarchate of Moscow, the Russian Orthodox church was compelled to adjust ecclesiology to the state policy. Given that Marxism-Leninism is a purely modern Western and materialist ideology, the Soviet regime rendered the Patriarchate of Moscow incapable of giving witness to Hesychasm. In particular, the intrinsic anti-Christian ethos and legacy of Marxism has been thoroughly analyzed by Richard Wurmbrand in his book *Marx and Satan*.[108]

The aforementioned cultural adventures and contradictions of the Slavic world and, especially, of Russia have been aptly addressed by the Russian novelist Fyodor M. Dostoyevsky and by the Russian theologian Georges Florovsky. In the modern era, Russian philosophical thought has been dominated by Enlightenment scholars, existentialists, Marxists, New Age mystics, and a few sympathizers of Fascism, who are all representatives of modern Western intellectual currents. For this reason, in the modern world, Russia has great geopolitical power, but it is has little "soft power,"[109] since it cannot articulate a coherent alternative existential proposal of potentially global relevance.

The Political Significance of Methexiology

Those who have a plebeian ethos, such as the bourgeois plutocracy and the Marxist leaders, are hungry for power due to their spiritual poverty and psychological perversion, and, therefore, they are unable and too poor to give. On the other hand, methexiology underpins and gives rise to an aristocratic ethos, and a true aristocrat is one who manifests his aristocracy by *giving*. Therefore, methexiology underpins and gives rise to an ethical transition from a plebeian, that is, brutal quest for selfish power to a noble ideal of giving and even of giving one's own self for the sake of the idea of the Good.

---

108. We might also note that Vladimir I. Lenin had been trained on the Isle of Capri in the cult beliefs of the Emperor Tiberius, who murdered Christ.

109. In his book *The Future of Power* (New York: Public Affairs, 2011), Joseph Nye, Jr. has discerned "hard power," which is the ability to get what you want through coercion and/or payment (i.e., through "sticks and carrots"), and "soft power," which is the ability to get what you want through attraction, which arises from the attractiveness of a country's culture, institutions, and political behavior. In other words, according to Nye's typology of power, hard power consists in commanding others to "change their behavior against their initial preferences" and/or in the ability to control agendas, whereas soft power consists in "the ability to affect others' preferences so that they want what you want"; see Nye, Jr., *The Future of Power*, 11.

The necessary underpinning of the survival of a superior humanity is neither the state nor the race, but humanity's transparency to the transcendent, namely, the ultimate source of the meaning of existence. Everything that takes place in the world exists due to its end, or purpose, or logos. Thus, the pursuit of the source of the significance of beings and things gives rise to a specific epistemology: by the term "knowledge," one should not merely refer to one's intellectual penetration into the essence of a being. By the term "knowledge," one should primarily refer to the knowledge of a being's end, or logos. In other words, my theory of methexiology implies a teleological epistemology, in the context of which beings are not merely substances, but every being's substance is continuously united with its meaning. Therefore, when one refers to a union or a society of beings, he should not necessarily mean a natural, or substantial, type of unity, that is, he should not necessarily mean the absorption and elimination of the particular into the general, nor should he mean that a being is constrained by the coercive logic of its nature. By contrast, from the perspective of my teleological theory of knowledge, unity or society means the participation of a set of beings in the same meaning, that is, in the same ultimate existential purpose, or in the same ultimate will.

As a conclusion, human society should not be regarded as a consequence of the common nature of human beings. Human society does not stem from the general conception of "humanity." If human society is regarded as a consequence of the common nature of human beings, then its unity is founded on the logic of nature, which seeks the affirmation of instincts, and, thus, the society of human beings does not differ from that of bees or ants, and it necessarily counters freedom of consciousness. On the other hand, from the perspective of methexiology, which I propose in this book, the foundation of human society is not nature, but a transcendent logos, namely, the source of the significance of beings and things, which transcends individual consciousness and yet can be participated by the human being. Therefore, from the perspective of my theory of methexiology, the society of human beings is founded on humanity's spiritual freedom, since it is a consequence of a decision of human beings to agree on the meaning of certain things that characterize their lives.

My theory of methexiology gives rise to a theocentric political system that endows human freedom and value with ontological underpinnings in complete agreement with the Bible. First of all, in the Old Testament, in 1 Samuel 8:1–21, we read that Samuel was displeased when Israelis said to him, "Give us a king to judge us," and, after he prayed to

God, Samuel passed on God's warning to the people who asked him for a king: sovereignty belongs only to God, and, if people choose a man to be their sovereign king, then, someday, their human king will exploit and oppress them. However, since "the people refused to listen to the voice of Samuel," the latter, after praying to God, decided to listen to people's voice and make them a king. Thus, according to this passage, not only does sovereignty belong only to God, but also a temporal king's authority stems from people's approval and God's concession. In the same spirit, in the New Testament, we read that the ultimate authority is not any historical institution or ruler, but God himself (Acts 4:19 and 1 Cor 6:1–6). Additionally, in Colossians 2:15, the apostle Paul writes about the impact of Jesus Christ's ministry on worldly rulers and principalities: "Having stripped the principalities and the powers, he made a show of them openly, triumphing over them in it [i.e., the cross]."

Far from negating the quest for freedom that underpins the theory of human rights, methexiology leads to a theocentric type of philosophical conservatism in order to assert a vision of human freedom that, by being metaphysically founded, is essentially more radical than the most radical requests and visions of modern liberals, since methexiology is aimed at the *deification* of humanity.

What do I mean by the term "philosophical conservatism," as opposed to other tenets of conservatism? I mean an attitude according to which one should examine every aspect of a being or thing and preserve every element of that being or thing that has a value. In other words, my conception of philosophical conservatism consists in respecting, protecting, and retaining everything that has a value. In fact, my conception of philosophical conservatism is, to a large extent, inherent in the etymology of the English word "conservatism," which is derived from the Latin prefix *con-* (meaning "together," "with," and "from every aspect") and the Latin verb *servare* (meaning "to watch over" and "to guard"). Similarly, the Greek term *syntereticōs* (meaning conservative) is derived from the Greek prefix *syn-* (which is equivalent to the Latin prefix *con-*) and the Greek verb *terō* (meaning "to retain," "to keep," and "to examine"). On the other hand, the dominant tenet of modern Anglo-American conservatism stems from its advocates' limited imagination and from their attempt to control and restrain people's imagination. Moreover, in contrast to my conception of philosophical conservatism, revolutionary conservatism, which was a German national conservative movement prominent in the years following the First World War, is a reaction against the principles of the French Revolution and the Jacobins, it is a politicized expression of old German nobility's aesthetics, and it aims at preserving the political privileges of the elites *vis-à-vis* the "mob"; as Armin Mohler has pointedly observed, the advocates of the Conservative Revolutionary movement can be regarded as the "Trotskyists" of National Socialism.[110]

Both the dominant tenet of modern Anglo-American conservatism (which is intimately related to the intellectual passivity of British empiricism) and the Conservative Revolutionary movement (which is intimately related to the German national character's propensity for extreme voluntarism) tend to use humanity as a means to historical ends; the first uses people as a means to the preservation of the established regime, while the latter uses people as a means to the historical manifestation of the national spirit's power. In contrast to both modern Anglo-American conservatism and the Conservative Revolutionary movement, my conception of philosophical conservatism gives primacy to metaphysics over history, it endows humanity with a metaphysical, that is, *a priori*, value, and, therefore, it precludes the use of humanity merely as a means to any historical end.

Without metaphysics, human beings are determined by the powers of nesting, digesting, and congesting, like monkeys for instance. Additionally, without metaphysics, the political system reduces to a tragic and funny process according to which monkeys rule other monkeys.[111] If politics does not have any metaphysical underpinnings, then the question of whether a monkey A or a monkey B is the ruler is funny and, ultimately, insignificant. Methexiology teaches self-mastery through personal communion between oneself and the Good-in-itself, also called the deity. Furthermore, methexiology is "pro-life," not only in quantitative terms, but also in qualitative terms, precisely, methexiology is "pro" the best of what humans can make of themselves.

The theocratic element that is inherent into methexiology aims at limiting and guiding government "from above," that is, metaphysically, and not merely through secular libertarian arguments or through social contract theory. Only an ontologically solid truth with which humans can establish a personal relationship can *really*, that is, ontologically, endow the human individual with an *a priori* value and with sacredness and, thus, *really* limit government's powers. Within the context of

---

110. Mohler, *Die Konservative Revolution*.
111. See also Deloire and Dubois, *Circus Politicus*.

methexiology, "freedom from" is inextricably linked to "freedom to," in the sense that human freedom from arbitrary and oppressive authorities is inextricably linked to and dependent upon humanity's existential potential and *telos*, specifically, the deification of humanity. Thus, at the political level, my theory of methexiology underpins a system of theocratic anarchy.

A theocratic anarch is a person who contests that the human individual has an ontologically grounded, intrinsic nobility stemming from the essential ability of the human being to participate in God's uncreated energy and, thus, to be deified. Furthermore, from the perspective of theocratic anarchy, "anarchy" does not signify democracy carried to its logical conclusion, but it signifies the universalization of nobility through metaphysics. The "anarch" is not an ideologically driven "anarchist," but a spiritually free person. Thus, whereas liberals silence the difference between "civil *rights*" and "civil *liberties*," emphasizing the first while ignoring or even suppressing the latter, theocratic anarchy safeguards civil liberties by endowing them with metaphysical authority. Civil rights refer to government policies that protect individuals from discrimination by the government or other individuals, whereas civil liberties refer to the constitutional protections of citizen's freedoms from government abuse. By emphasizing civil rights, while simultaneously silencing and suppressing civil liberties, liberal regimes degrade into liberal oligarchies, since they justify the expansion of government power and manipulate people's consciousness by claiming that, in these ways, they act as protectors of people's civil rights, which, thus, become a synonym for a government-controlled conception of "political correctness."

Judges 9:8–15 is one of the most eloquent libertarian pieces of the Bible:

> The trees set out to anoint a king over themselves. They said to the olive tree, "Reign over us." But the olive tree said to them, "Should I stop producing my oil, with which they honor God and man by me, and go to wave back and forth over the trees?" The trees said to the fig tree, "Come and reign over us." But the fig tree said to them, "Should I leave my sweetness, and my good fruit, and go to wave back and forth over the trees?" The trees said to the vine, "Come and reign over us." The vine said to them, "Should I leave my new wine, which cheers God and man, and go to wave back and forth over the trees?" Then all the trees said to the bramble, "Come and reign over us." The bramble said to the trees, "If in truth you anoint me king over you, then come

and take refuge in my shade; and if not, let fire come out of the bramble, and devour the cedars of Lebanon."

In the aforementioned symbolical biblical passage, authoritarian power attracts a tyrannical, corrupt, and culturally poor personage, symbolized by the bramble, whereas it is passed over by the virtuous personages, symbolized by the olive tree, the fig tree, and the vine, all of whom chose a life of service to humanity and of devotion to God over the might of the shrub state. Thus, as we read in Acts 5:29, "Peter and the apostles answered, 'We must obey God rather than men.'"

Intimately related to my conception of Christian libertarianism, or theocratic anarchy, is a system of political economy that is founded on the following three libertarian principles:

1. The foundation and the core of the economic system must consist in a system of personal property rights and voluntary exchanges of goods and services, and taxation should be minimal.

2. The economic system must preclude any symbiotic relationship between business and government; in other words, every type of state capitalism should be eliminated. In this sense, the U.S. military-industrial complex, the Western financial oligopolies, the International Monetary Fund, the Eurozone, and the big welfare state institutions (which are extremely socially expensive in terms of taxation) are characteristic examples of capitalist institutions that contradict and actively impede the operation of the free market. International trade should be as free as possible, "corporate welfare" (that is, government handouts to business) should be minimized, and the distribution of economic information should be as efficient as possible.

3. Economic decision-making, even with regard to issues that are assumed to belong to the sphere of the so-called "welfare state" (e.g., social security, education, administration of justice, etc.), should be as much decentralized, free, and privatized as possible, thus leading to the substitution of the welfare state by a society founded on mutualism and voluntarism. In this context, government welfare should be replaced with private charity and with a negative income tax system,[112] and the social security system should be privatized.

---

112. Assume that X is a family of n members, and that a minimum income of $k is desirable for this type of families. If X's earned income is less than $k, then X can be

Additionally, custodial sentence (serving a prison term) and capital punishment (death) should be abolished and replaced with alternative sentences, such as psychotherapy programs, community service, fines, probation, and restitution.

There is an absolute antinomy between Marxism and Christianity, and, therefore, there is an absolute antinomy between Marxism and methexiology, too, because, in 1859, in his Preface to *A Contribution to the Critique of Political Economy*, Karl Marx argued that "it is not the consciousness of men that determines their being, but, on the contrary, their social being that determines their consciousness."[113] Marxism is a populist and eschatological (hence, quasi-religious) imaginary creation and social movement that excites desperate people by proposing a vision of earthly justice.

As it has been pointed out by the prominent British philosopher Bertrand Russell, the secular eschatology and the quasi-religious nature of Marxism are modeled on a materialist interpretation (precisely, distortion) of the Bible in accordance with the following correspondences:

Bible	Marxism
Yahweh	Dialectical Materialism
Messiah	Marx
The Chosen People	The Proletariat
The Church	The Communist Party
The Second Coming of Christ	The Proletariat Revolution
Hell	Punishment of the bourgeoisie/capitalists
The thousand year reign of peace	Communism

Whereas Marx's secular utopia is founded on a vision of earthly justice, in the name of which any crime can be justified (as it happened in the Soviet coalition and in Maoist China in the twentieth century), genuine Christianity believes in the justice of the heavens. The Christians' belief

---

assisted by applying a negative income tax. That is, the national income tax might be structured so that, while X pays taxes to the government for income earned in excess of $k, the government will make negative tax (subsidy) payments to X on the amount by which X's earned income falls short of $k.

113. Avineri, *The Social and Political Thought of Karl Marx*.

in the justice of the heavens does not mean that Christians seek to find justice only in the afterlife, but it means that a genuine Christian's perception of justice never submits to any historical necessity, or to any coercive legal order. A genuine Christian would never redistribute wealth, unless he had previously changed people's conscience in such a way that people's own perception of justice would motivate them to voluntarily redistribute their wealth. In particular, a genuine Christian's perception of justice does not dictate that one who has no shirt should take another person's shirt, but it dictates that one who has two shirts should voluntarily share with the one who has none.[114]

Methexiology and World Order

Any international order is caused radically (in the ontological sense) by something else, namely, by the intentionality of the consciousness of the international actors. Any international order is not a "given" to be reckoned with by the particular members of the world system, but it is a creation of consciousness. Therefore, a humane and viable world order is a world order of particularity, that is, a "multipolar system," a term that has been highlighted by the Russian geopolitician Alexander Dugin of the State University of Moscow. However, even though multipolarity gives rise to the ontology of freedom in the field of international relations, it entails important risks, too, and, therefore, multipolarity must be interpreted in a way that combines existential otherness (individuality) and sociality.

The first risk that is inherent in the theory of multipolarity is that, by over-emphasizing the actors' existential otherness and by isolating the actors' existential otherness from their socialization in the world system, multipolarity can cultivate aggressive individualism (in this case, by the term "individual," I mean an international-political actor, e.g., a state, a civilization zone, etc.), instead of promoting the idea of personhood. A "person," or hypostasis, is a socialized individual, or an-individual-in-a-relationship. Therefore, international-political actors (e.g., states and civilization zones) can become "persons" only if they are partakers of a truth that transcends them. As a result of its participation in the transcendent, an international-political actor acquires an individual value (exactly due to its relationship with the transcendent), and the different

---

114. Luke 3:11.

international-political actors that are aware of their participation in the transcendent constitute an international-political society, that is, they recognize each other as members of a truth that can be participated by each one of them but transcends every one of them. In other words, international-political actors can become persons only if they have a common, universal, existential mirror in which they can look at themselves and evaluate themselves.

The second risk that is inherent in the theory of multipolarity is that it may cultivate the mentality that people are necessarily—that is, ontologically—constrained by geopolitical categories or that people are necessarily prisoners of geopolitical divisions. On the contrary, due to the freedom of spirit, humanity is not a being of the earth (in Greek, *gaia*), but is a being of a "place beyond heaven," according to the terminology that is used by Plato in *Phaedrus*. Humanity is determined by geopolitical necessities only if and to the extent that it compromises its spiritual freedom, and, therefore, it decides to be ontologically self-degraded. Thus, according to John 4:24, Jesus Christ said to a Samaritan woman that there would no longer be limitations of geography in worshiping God, for "God is spirit." In other words, humanity's relationship with its existential purpose transcends geopolitics and "sacred geography." Furthermore, science and technology, which are creations of the human mind, in the image of God's creative activity, enable humanity to overcome geographical necessities by providing humans with potentially unlimited economic resources.

The ontology of particularity is a condition *sine qua non* for the creation of a world order worthy of human beings. However, we must answer the following question: how can one socialize the actors of the international system, and, furthermore, how can one prevent particularity from degenerating into aggressive and destructive individuality (e.g., aggressive nationalism/communitarianism)?

The relations among international-political actors are unthinkable without the event of communication. Hence, the event of communication in the international sphere manifests each world order not simply as something instituted, that is, historically given, but as something constituted, that is, constantly realized (structured and restructured) as an event of intentional communication. Each actor of the world system (nations, transnational organizations, civilization zones, etc.) is ontologically founded on communication, which means that there is no such thing as a pure international-political subject, conceivable in itself, and simultaneously communication is founded on a concrete and free international-political hypostasis.

In world politics, as in the context of societal relations, in general, a person cannot exist without communication, and, therefore, the globalists are right to the extent that they recognize and declare the ontological significance of communication. Simultaneously, communication should never deny or suppress the person, and, therefore, the anti-globalists are right when they recognize and declare the ontological significance of otherness. The previous arguments lead us to what the Greek church fathers, in general, and the Hesychasts, in particular, mean by the term "hypostatic mode of being," or personhood. Thus, methexiology, being founded on Hesychasm, urges us to think about international relations in terms of communion.

Methexiology can operate as a very important spiritual underpinning of the United Nations by promoting the idea of an "international-political hypostasis," or "great political hypostasis." In principle, the United Nations belongs to no particular international-political actor, since it is intrinsically international, and, therefore, in principle, it can serve every international-political actor. From this perspective, the United Nations has an unrivalled moral status in the international-political system.

Methexiology can further empower the United Nations by highlighting the United Nations as a global society of international-political hypostases. In the context of such a model of global society, each and every international-political actor could freely experience its existential otherness, but, simultaneously, it would be socialized through its participation in a universal truth, that is, in a truth that transcends history and individual interests. In particular, the universal truth that can transform the United Nations into a global society of international-political hypostases is the freedom of the human being from historical necessity and the acknowledgement of the human being as the universal mediator who unifies the world with its existential purpose. This image of a universe that reveals its vocation through humanity has been stressed by Maximus the Confessor and is particularly significant for an ontologically grounded humanism, which should be the spiritual foundation of every institution of global governance.

The aforementioned approach to international relations, which emphasizes the transformation of the international-political actors into international-political hypostases ("individuals-in-relationships") and the transformation of the United Nations into a global society of international-political hypostases, posits that the deeply Christian values of conciliarity and discretion should be the norm in a prescriptive way, thus constraining the use of coercive power and threats. Without the concept of "international-political hypostasis," society reduces to a fragile association of individual interests or to a coercive rationalist order, in which individuals are aggregated like objects. In other words, without the concept of "international-political hypostasis," the attempt to create a viable world society is chimerical.

As a conclusion, in the sphere of international politics, methexiology can be understood as a meta-political "custodian" of humanity's sociality and as the most solid metaphysical foundation of humanism. By looking at politics from a meta-political standpoint, that is, from outside the political sphere itself, methexiology can grasp the reason and the purpose of the entire political stage, since a methexiologist transcends mere individuality and is aware that his identity is located in his communion with the universal Logos and with his fellow humans, who are also partakers of the universal Logos. The kind of humanism that stems from methexiology is based neither on the Cartesian "cogito" (I know) principle nor on the Heideggerian "sum" (am) principle, but it is based on the awareness that our humanity is grounded on and stems from our divinity, in accordance with Jesus Christ's proclamation "You are gods" (John 10:34).

According to methexiology, the human being is ontologically and morally prior and hence superior to any historical entity (state, nation, economic system, etc.), since "God created humankind in his image" (Gen 1:27). Even though human beings are shaped by the historical communities to which they belong, their value and their existential purpose transcend every historical community. This is the essence of methexiology's cosmopolitanism. Thus, even though each community may have its own ethics (that is, its own concrete morality stemming from a rational social order where rational institutions and laws provide the content of conscientious conviction), the value of the human being as a potential god overrides every system of social ethics. From the previous perspective, methexiology provides a metaphysical underpinning for human rights and for a world order centered on the divinity of man, and it urges us to evaluate civilizations according to the degree to which they recognize the divinity of man and help man to become aware of and actualize his potential divinity.

The Structure of this Book

I have organized the present book along seven chapters as follows:

Chapter 1: Being and Its Presence: In this chapter, I study the concept of being and the different aspects of being throughout the history of philosophy, and I expound methexiology as an ontological orientation.

Chapter 2: Access to Being: Seeking the being, the philosophizing mind can choose among several paths to the conception of being. These "paths" are the methods according to which the philosophical activity may take place. In this chapter, I study and evaluate the different philosophical methods, and I expound the methexiological method.

Chapter 3: The Modes of Being: Being is not a simple reality, but it is receptive of attributes that correspond to its constitutive elements and powers. Each of these elements and powers is a parameter of the ontic function. This chapter is concerned with the different ways in which the modes of being have been studied throughout the history of philosophy and with the Hesychasts' theory of God's essence and energies. I elucidate the importance of methexiology for the study of the modes of being.

Chapter 4: Epistemology and the Noetic Faculty of the Soul: From the perspective of my theory of methexiology, "soul" is the totality of the faculties and the attributes of the human being that transcend pure biology. Moreover, the term "soul" refers to the personal manner in which each human being manifests life. The purpose of this chapter is to study the problems of knowledge and truth and the Hesychasts' theory of the mind and to elucidate methexiology's contribution to epistemology.

Chapter 5: Mystery, Grace, and Philosophical Theology: Through Unselfishness to Deification: In this chapter, I elucidate the nature of methexiology as a philosophical theology and as a theological philosophy, and I compare and contrast it with other attempts that have been made in the field of philosophical theology, such as John Milbank's "Radical Orthodoxy" and Oliver Davies's "Transformation Theology."

Chapter 6: Psychotherapy. The Secret Potential of the Mind: This chapter is given over to an examination of different theories of psychotherapy (paying particular attention to Freud's and Jung's thoughts) and to the study of the nature, the structure, the powers, and the problems of the human soul from the standpoint of methexiology.

Chapter 7: Axiology, Ethics, and Justice: In Plato's *Apology* 38a, Socrates argues that "the unexamined life is not worth living." This chapter is devoted to the study of the nature of moral consciousness (conscience), to the examination of different theories of the moral criterion (e.g., Bentham and Mill's utilitarianism, Adam Smith's principle of sympathy, Kant's moral rationalism, etc.) and to methexiology's contribution to axiology, ethics, and the theory of justice.

1

Being and Its Presence

THE CONCEPT OF BEING is the most central concept of philosophy. The primary problem of every philosophical enquiry consists in the ascertainment of the reality of its object and, more particularly, of that reality that is presumed to be the reality *par excellence*, namely, the reality of being. Throughout the history of philosophy, the most general definition of being is the following: being is a structurally united, unique, and autonomous reality that lasts either by being "closed" (i.e., isolated) in itself or by tending to transcend its nature, expanding itself beyond its substantial constraints. In the first case, one conceives of being in a static way, whereas, in the latter, one conceives of being in a dynamic way. The basic perception of being that is formed by philosophizing consciousness originally stems from the real presence of man himself, but, at a later stage, this perception undergoes conscious processing in the context of which it is abstracted from its particularities, and, in this way, it facilitates the conception of the corresponding idea and the identification of its difference from and its functional connection with the world into whose functional presence the corresponding idea is integrated.

Every philosophical enquiry is concerned with the issue of being. Even when philosophical enquiry seems, *prima facie*, to be astounded at the cosmic order and to aim at investigating and interpreting the miracle of the world itself, it refers to the human being in an indirect way (i.e., from distance), and it aims at explaining the peculiar presence of the human being. On the one hand, humanity is related to the world, everything may seem to be an outgrowth of the world, and man persistently tries to be integrated into the world according to the terms of a new equilibrium established by him. On the other hand, man imposes himself as the most magnificent manifestation of being, irrespective of whether one understands the human being in a static way (i.e., in isolation) or in a dynamic way (i.e., extended in the world). The idea of the human being as an independent and, to a large extent, free "whole" and, furthermore, as an indivisible actualization of a structural program underpins both materialist types of philosophical realism, such as the philosophies of Democritus (460–370 BC) and Epicurus (341–270 BC), and spiritualist types of philosophical realism, such as Plato's theory of ideas and Gottfried Wilhelm von Leibniz's monadology.[115]

The first cosmologizing Ionian philosophers (sixth and fifth centuries BC) sought the primary, mainly material, essence from which, according to their arguments, both the cosmic reality that surrounds the human presence and man himself as the "crown" of the cosmic reality had originated.[116] In particular, according to Thales of Miletus, that primary essence was water; according to Anaximenes, it was air; according to Heraclitus, it was fire and the continuous changing of reality; according to Anaximander, it was infinity (in Greek, *ápeiron*), an endless, unlimited mass subject to neither old age nor decay, which perpetually yields fresh materials from which everything we can perceive is derived; according to Empedocles, it was a system of attractive and repulsive functions of the elements of matter. However, it was Parmenides, a Presocratic Greek philosopher from Elea in Magna Graecia, active in the earlier part of the fifth century BC, who first articulated a conception of being according to its wholeness, its uniqueness, and its dynamism, and he founded ontology as the focus of the philosophical investigation of reality.

From Parmenides's perspective, being is a whole (in Greek, *houlon*), specifically, a unique set that imposes itself by being, and it opposes everything that is not. In the context of Parmenides's ontology, being and non-being are not reducible to each other: "For this shall never be proved, that the things that are not are."[117] The previous dualist argument is the starting point of the classical Platonic perception of ideas as "real beings"[118] (in Greek, *ōntos ōnta*). However, in his dialogue *Sophist*, Plato

115. Laos, *The Metaphysics of World Order*, chapters 1 and 3.

116. Graham, *Explaining the Cosmos*.

117. Parmenides, *Poem of Parmenides*, VII.

118. Proclus, *Initia philosophiae ac theologiae ex Platonicis fontibus ducta*, 152. Additionally, see Laos, *The Metaphysics of World Order*, chapter 1.

reconsidered the issue of being, and he argued that being and non-being are the extreme terms of an ontological series whose intermediate terms are the non-being of being and the being of non-being. According to Plato, the previous intermediate ontological terms (i.e., the non-being of being and the being of non-being) explain the presence of the world. In Plato's *Sophist*, the Stranger argues that, contrary to Parmenides, non-being is an essential condition of the existence of any object, because every object, except only being itself, participates in otherness in relation to being, and, therefore, in the extent to which they are "other than being," they must be described as "non-being." According to the Stranger, movement and rest and all other "forms," with the sole exception of being itself, are "non-beings," because, even though they participate in being, they participate also in otherness in relation to being, and, therefore, they are not identical to being.

Moreover, in the third century AD, the aforementioned Platonic argument was endorsed and developed further by Neoplatonism. In his *Enneads*, Plotinus identified four hypostases (or underlying states or substances). In particular, Plotinus's ontology is based on an ontological series of four hypostases: the totally transcendent "One" (which is beyond all categories of being and non-being, containing no division, multiplicity or distinction); the first emanation from the "One" is the "Nous" (which can be construed as "the divine mind" or "order"), which Plotinus identified (at least metaphorically) with the Demiurge (who can be construed as the "divine Architect") of Plato's *Timaeus* (unlike the "One," the "Nous" is not a self-sufficient entity, but it is capable of contemplating both the "One," as its prior, as well as its own thoughts and the ideas that are in its spiritual nature and they correspond to Plato's ideas); from the "Nous" emanates the "Soul" (in Greek, *Psychē*), the dynamic, creative temporal power, which itself is subdivided into the upper aspect, or "World Soul" (precisely, the contemplative part that governs the world and remains in contact with the "Nous," ensuring that the individual embodied souls eventually return to their true divine state within the "Nous"), and the lower aspect, which, according to Plotinus, is identified with "Nature," and it allows itself to be multiply divided into individual human souls. Finally, Plotinus, using the terminology of Plato's *Sophist*, describes matter as non-being.

In his own ontological works, Dionysius the Areopagite[119] proposes a hierarchical ordering of beings according to their natural placements

---

119. The works of Dionysius the Areopagite are commonly referred to as the *Corpus*

and their freedoms and, also, according to the simultaneous immediacy of the unknown God's presence. In the context of Dionysius the Areopagite's ontological hierarchy, matter is not merely described as non-being, since, according to Dionysius the Areopagite, there is an epistemological, yet non-ontological, continuity between the Absolute and matter. During the era of modern philosophy, the perception of continuity between the Absolute and matter was reformulated by Baruch Spinoza's monistic philosophy, in the context of which there is an ontological continuity between the Absolute and matter (in contrast to Dionysius the Areopagite, Spinoza espoused pantheism).[120]

Aristotle, mainly in his *Metaphysics*, articulated an ontology that provides a solid philosophical foundation for the interpretation of reality. In his ontology, Aristotle emphasized the distinction between being potentially (potentiality) and being actually (actuality). The previous distinction depends on a process of change ("becoming") according to which being is increasingly actualized and imposed, following its "entelechy," a model that is intrinsic to being and constitutes the program of actualization of being; the previous program (i.e., entelechy) remains unchanged, independently of the particular changes that being may undergo. According to Aristotle, being is the simplest possible presence that can be perceived by the human mind, but it is not totally simple; being can be thought of as a resultant of categories.[121] In his *Categories*, Aristotle argued that the categories of being are ten, namely: substance, quantity, quality, relatives (relation), somewhere (location), sometime (time), being in a position (position), having (possession), acting, and being acted upon (undergoing). In addition, in Aristotle's philosophy, substances are further divided into first and second: first substances are individual objects; second substances are the species in which first substances (i.e., individuals) inhere.

Aristotle's successors, including Plotinus, classified the categories of being as follows: substance, form, relation (between substance and form), time, and space. The previous categories are characteristics associated with being. Aristotle, like Plato, transcended the Parmenidean antithesis between being and non-being; Aristotle's method of transcending it was based on the distinction between being potentially and being actually. The entirety of medieval ontological thought was preoccupied with

---

Areopagiticum or *Corpus Dionysiacum*.

120. Laos, *The Metaphysics of World Order*, 60–61.

121. The word "category" is derived from the Greek *kategorein*, meaning to predicate.

Plato's and Aristotle's solutions to the problem of the antithesis between being and non-being, a problem that was originally posed by Parmenides in the fifth century BC and continues to exist as an object of philosophical debate and enquiry in the context of modern philosophy.[122]

In his *Topica*, the Roman philosopher and statesman Cicero (106–43 BC) mentions that Aristotle "was not known to the rhetorician, inasmuch as he is not much known even to philosophers, except to a very few," because "the obscurity of the subject" discouraged them from reading Aristotle's books (I.1). Thus, in ancient Western Europe, a few philosophers wrote introductory textbooks on Aristotle's philosophy. One such textbook was Cicero's aforementioned *Topica* (Cicero wrote *Topica* for the benefit of his friend Gaius Trebatius Testa). Another such textbook was Porphyry's *Introduction to the Logical Categories of Aristotle* (known simply as the *Introduction*).

Porphyry was a Syrian student of Plotinus's. In 268 AD, Porphyry experienced a serious depressive episode, and he wanted to commit suicide. His teacher convinced him not to. In his book *On the Life of Plotinus*, Porphyry writes that Plotinus told him that the tendency to commit suicide does not spring "from reason but from mere melancholy," and he advised him "to leave Rome" (11). Following Plotinus's advice, Porphyry left for Sicily. In Sicily, in 270 AD, Porphyry learned about Plotinus's death. A few years after Plotinus's death, Porphyry returned to Rome and became the head of Plotinus's school there. During his stay in Sicily, Porphyry wrote his seminal book *Introduction*. In the sixth century AD, the Roman philosopher Boethius translated Porphyry's *Introduction* in Latin, and, in the same century, the Syrian theologian Sergius of Resaina translated it in the Syrian language. Moreover, in the eighth century AD, Porphyry's *Introduction* was translated in the Armenian language, and, in the tenth century AD, it was translated in Arabic. In the cultural history of both Western Europe and the Arabs, Porphyry's *Introduction* was the first systematic educational textbook on logic.

In his *Introduction*, Porphyry studies Aristotle's arguments about "what genus, difference, species, property, and accident are." In the first chapter, Porphyry poses the following problem: whether genera and species "subsist (in the nature of things) or in mere conceptions only; whether also if subsistent, they are bodies or incorporeal, and whether they are separate from, or in, sensibles, and subsist about these." However, Porphyry does not provide an explicit solution to the previous problem,

---

122. Scruton, *Modern Philosophy*.

which he himself posed, and he argues that a solution to the previous problem "requires another more extensive investigation."

Why does Porphyry's *Introduction* not provide an explicit solution to the aforementioned ontological problem? The answer lies in the Neoplatonic argument that Aristotle was a Platonist, an argument that was widely accepted in the Hellenistic period. In this context, Porphyry wrote a book entitled *On the One School of Plato and Aristotle*. Therefore, in his *Introduction*, Porphyry avoided to delve into a problem (i.e., the ontology of genera and species) with regard to which Aristotle's arguments are different from Plato's theory of ideas.

In what follows, I shall study the aforementioned ontological problem, which Porphyry failed to investigate in his *Introduction*. In his *Phaedo*, Plato formulates his theory of ideas as follows: "if a person says to me that the bloom of color, or form, or any such thing is a source of beauty, I leave all that, which is only confusing to me, and . . . hold and am assured in my own mind that nothing makes a thing beautiful but the presence and participation of beauty," and he goes on as follows: "I stoutly contend that by beauty all beautiful things become beautiful . . . this principle will never be overthrown . . . by beauty beautiful things become beautiful" (100c–e). In addition, Plato clarifies his method as follows: "this was the method which I adopted: I first assumed some principle which I judged to be the strongest, and then I affirmed as true whatever seemed to agree with this, whether relating to the cause or to anything else; and that which disagreed I regarded as untrue" (100a). Furthermore, in his *Timaeus*, Plato makes the following distinction: "What is that which is existent always and has no becoming? And what is that which is becoming always and never is existent? . . . [T]he one of these is apprehensible by thought with the aid of reasoning . . . whereas the other is an object of opinion with the aid of unreasoning sensation" (27d–28a). As I argued in my book *The Metaphysics of World Order*, "according to Plato, reducing a collection of phenomena to an idea is equivalent to understanding their unity into a 'whole' which is a universal signification or value (idea)."[123]

On the other hand, Aristotle argues that Socrates never claimed that universals (genera and species) are self-subsistent. Thus, departing from Plato's thesis about the nature of universals, Aristotle writes in his *Metaphysics*: "There are two innovations which may fairly be ascribed to Socrates: inductive reasoning and general definition . . . whereas Socrates

---

123. Laos, *The Metaphysics of World Order*, 13.

regarded neither universals nor definitions as existing in separation, the others gave them a separate existence, and to these universals and definitions of existing things they gave the name of ideas."[124] Furthermore, Aristotle clarifies his own perspective as follows: "we must observe that some causes can be stated universally, but others cannot. The proximate principles of all things are the proximate actual individual and another individual which exists potentially. Therefore the proximate principles are not universal."[125] In the previous section of his *Metaphysics*, Aristotle, goes on as follows: "it is the particular that is the principle of particulars; 'man' in general is the principle of 'man' in general, but there is no such person as 'man,' whereas Peleus is the principle of Achilles and your father of you."

In *Metaphysics*, 1038b, Aristotle expounds his variant of Platonism as follows: "The universal also is thought by some to be in the truest sense a cause and a principle[;] . . . it seems impossible that any universal term can be substance." In the same section of his *Metaphysics*, Aristotle elaborates on the previous argument as follows: First of all, "the substance of an individual is the substance which is peculiar to it and belongs to nothing else; whereas the universal is common; for by universal we mean that which by nature appertains to several things." Thus, Aristotle is concerned with the following question: "Of what particular, then, will the universal be the substance?" His answer to the previous question is the following: "Either of all or of none. But it cannot be the substance of all; while, if it is to be the substance of one, the rest also will be that one; because things whose substance is one have also one essence and are themselves one."

Secondly, Aristotle elaborates on the following argument: "substance means that which is not predicated of a subject, whereas the universal is always predicated of some subject. But perhaps although the universal cannot be substance in the sense that essence [or nature] is, it can be present in the essence, as 'animal' can be present in 'man' and 'horse.'"[126] His response to the previous argument is the following: "Again, it is impossible and absurd that the individual or substance, if it is composed of anything, should be composed not of substances nor of the individual, but of a quality; for then non-substance or quality will be prior to substance or the individual. Which is impossible."

124 Aristotle, *Metaphysics* 1078b27–34.
125. Ibid. 1071a17–22.
126 Ibid. 1038b.

82   Methexiology

In Plato's philosophy, the reality of the world of ideas constitutes the supratemporal truth of beings, and the existence of beings stems from *methexis*, precisely, from their participation in the world of ideas. In other words, in the context of Plato's philosophy, the reality of the world of ideas is not a product of intellectual abstraction, but everything takes place with relation to the reality of the world of ideas. In order to understand better Plato's theory of ideas, let us consider, for instance, the following question: "What is bravery?" From the perspective of Plato's theory of ideas, when one asks this question, one does not seek to define the concept of bravery (as Aristotle will do later), but one aims at projecting the multitude of the empirical forms of bravery (e.g., "a brave man," "a brave woman," "a brave lion," etc.) into the unity of the idea of bravery as a universal spiritual reference.[127] Thus, by perceiving the unity of the idea as a universal spiritual reference, Plato perceives the spiritual unity of various empirical forms, and this is the essence of Plato's dialectic.[128]

A "concept" is an abstraction or generalization. Abstraction was originally discovered by Aristotle. Plato's ideas are not abstractions, since the scope of Plato's dialectic was to take a synoptic view, in the context of which a multitude of phenomena refer to the unity of the corresponding idea; in other words, out of many, there emerges the one. In the context of Plato's philosophy, species and ideas declare the visible, rational form of the life-giving and all-encompassing "One," and, in the context of the *theoria*[129] of the "One" (i.e., metaphorically speaking, by gazing at the life-giving and all-encompassing "One"), the truth of idea is identical to the reality of substance. In other words, according to Plato, "truth" and "reality" are mutually inseparable.

On the other hand, Aristotle perceived the abstract character of concepts, and, from this perspective, he argued that Platonic ideas bring about a pointless doubling of the world. However, Aristotle and Plato agree that the object of knowledge does not consist in intellectual abstractions, but in the universal. Aristotle argues that being exists according to its substance (i.e., its actual matter), and the "material" cause (or mode of being) is supplemented by a formal (in Greek, *morphikōn*) cause

---

127. By the term "reference," I mean a relation that obtains between certain sorts of representational tokens (e.g., names, mental states, pictures) and objects.

128. Plato, *Phaedrus* 265d, and *Republic* 537c. Moreover, see Laos, *The Metaphysics of World Order*, 12–13.

129. The Greek word *theoria* means "gaze"; it is etymologically derived from the Greek words *thēa* ("view") and *horān* ("to see").

(or mode of being) which is due to the species; in this case, the term "species" is mainly a synonym for the Platonic term "idea."

According to Aristotle's *Physics*, *Categories*, and *Metaphysics*, form is predicated of matter as subject, substantial individuals are hylomorphic compounds (i.e., compounds of matter and form), and one can always analyze a hylomorphic compound into its predicates and the subject of which they are predicated. The role of form in this hylomorphic context is the topic of Aristotle's *Categories* Z.7–9. Form is the principle of determination which accounts for the species of beings. Matter is the principle of potentiality, whereas form is the principle of actuality. According to Aristotle, whether we are thinking of natural objects (e.g., plants and animals) or artifacts (e.g., houses), we do not produce the matter (to suppose that we do leads to an infinite regress) nor do we produce the form (we cannot create form out of nothing), but we put the form into the matter, and, thus, we produce the compound.[130] Furthermore, according to Aristotle, both the matter and the form must pre-exist,[131] but the source of motion in both cases (what Aristotle calls the "moving cause" of the coming to be) is the form. In artistic production, the form is found in the soul of the artisan ("the art of building is the form of the house,"[132] and "the form is in the soul"[133]). For instance, the builder has in mind the plan for a house, he knows how to build, and, ultimately, he "enmatters" that plan by putting it into the materials out of which he builds the house. In natural production, the form is found in the parent ("the begetter is of the same species as the begotten, not one in number but one in form—for man begets man"[134]). Even though Aristotle substitutes species for Plato's transcendent ideas, thus articulating a hylomorphic philosophy, he argues that knowledge is a mental function, and that the mind is immortal[135] and arises from the outside[136] (in Greek, *thyrathen*). Since, according to Aristotle, the mind arises from the outside, it is not confined to its own products (i.e., intellectual abstractions), but it can achieve *Good*, which refers to knowledge for knowledge's sake, and it seeks the cause of being, in general. Therefore, Aristotle's theory of being remains Platonic.

130. Aristotle, *Categories* 1033a30–b9.
131. Ibid., 1034b12.
132. Ibid., 1034a24.
133. Ibid., 1032b23.
134. Ibid., 1033b30–32.
135. Aristotle, *On the Soul*, III, 5.
136. Aristotle, *On the Generation of Animals*, II, 3.

In addition to the material and the formal causes, Aristotle acknowledges two more causes, specifically, the efficient cause and the final cause. The efficient cause refers to the event that accounts for being, i.e., to the event that has produced and controls the existence of being. The final cause refers to the event at which being is aimed, and which is fulfilled by the existence of the given being. Hence, no being exists independently, since its existence is due to a factor that transcends the given being; the only exception, Aristotle contends, is the "prime mover," which is the cause of itself and the first of all substances. According to Aristotle, the "prime mover" is a logical necessity, since there cannot be an infinite regress in essentially subordinated causes. The *telos*, or purpose, of being, which can be regarded as the reversal of being's dependence on an efficient cause, is the existential vindication of being. The *telos* of being exists within being, and the non-fulfillment of the *telos* of being implies that such a being has no reason to exist, it is irrational and purposeless. In his book *On the Soul*, Aristotle argues that the soul is the formal, the efficient, and the final cause of the body.

The aforementioned ontological issues, which clarify the relation between Plato's philosophy and Aristotle's philosophy, were not addressed by Porphyry in his *Introduction*. However, in his *Commentary on Porphyry's Introduction*, Boethius, a sixth-century AD Roman philosopher, addresses the problem of the nature of universals: "Porphyry bears in mind that it is an introduction he is writing, so he keeps to the style of a textbook. This is why he says he avoids the tangles of deeper questions and limits himself to a few reasonable conjectures about the simple ones."[137] Boethius mentions that these deeper questions that Porphyry promises not to discuss in his *Introduction* are the following: (i) "Everything comprehended by the mind is either based in the real world, in which case the mind conceptualizes it and represents it to itself intellectually, or else it is not, in which case the mind represents it to itself through an empty image." (ii) "If genus and species are said to be immaterial, we come down to another urgent problem demanding a solution: do they exist immanently in bodies themselves, or might they also exist as immaterial substances over and above bodies?"[138]

In his *Commentary on Porphyry's Introduction*, Boethius accepts that "it must not be thought that a concept is false simply because it is

---

137 Boethius, *Commentary on Porphry's Introduction* I.158–61.

138. For more details, see Chadwick, *Boethius*.

not an exact representation of its objects . . . someone who does this by compounding is deceived (e.g., when they think centaurs exist because they have joined a horse and a human)," but he argues that "someone who does it by analyzing, abstracting, and taking them [concepts] out of the things in which they exist, not only is not deceived, but is the only person who can discover what is genuinely true."[139] In his previous argument, Boethius failed to bear in mind the difference between a "concept" (which is a product of intellectual abstraction, and, hence, can be known through analysis and syllogism) and a Platonic "idea" (which transcends the intellect, and can be known through methexis, i.e., through one's participation in its reality). By failing to understand the difference between intellectual abstraction and participation in Platonic ideas, Boethius cannot understand the spiritual core of Plato's philosophy. Additionally, by not paying enough attention to Aristotle's argument that the mind arises from the outside, and, therefore, it is not confined to its own products (i.e., intellectual abstractions), Boethius cannot understand that, even though Aristotle substitutes species for Plato's transcendent ideas, Aristotle's theory of being remains Platonic. Thus, in his *Commentary on Porphyry's Introduction*, Boethius argues as follows: "In one sense, genera and species do actually exist, but in another sense they are conceived: they are indeed immaterial, but they exist in sensible things in conjunction with sensible characteristics; on the other hand, they are conceived of as self-subsistent, and not as having their being in other things."[140] Having a grossly misguided understanding of Plato's and Aristotle's philosophies, Boethius maintains that our mind needs to overcome the fallacies that are caused by "compounding" (*per compositionem*) and to contemplate pure species *through abstraction* (as opposed to methexis). Finally, Boethius argues that he does not consider it fitting for him "to judge between the opinions of these two [Plato and Aristotle], for that is in the province of deeper philosophy."[141]

Boethius and the well-known Christian theologian and philosopher Augustine of Hippo[142] (354–430 AD) confused Aristotle's general

139. Boethius, *Commentary on Porphry's Introduction* I.165–66.

140 Ibid. I.166–67.

141. Ibid. 11.11.

142. Augustine of Hippo is venerated as a saint in both Eastern and Western Christianity. However, the Eastern Orthodox Church does not accept some of Augustine's teachings, because they reflect his Manichean background. According to the Manicheans, who were a gnostic sect, there are two principles in the world: one of the light

concepts (universals) with Platonic ideas, i.e., they were assuming that Aristotle's universals were radically separate from the material world, but, contrary to Plato, they were treating Platonic ideas as if they were logical substances. The Neoplatonic distinction between the sensible world and the intelligible world dominated in Boethius's scholarly work, which exerted significant influence on the West during the early Middle Ages.[143] Until the thirteenth century AD, Boethius's scholarly work was the major channel through which the Latin West was accessing Greek philosophy; however, that channel was molded and determined by the characteristics of Latin culture. The difference between Greek culture and Latin culture corresponds to the difference between philosophy (Greeks) and law (Latins).[144] As a result, the primary pursuit of the Greek East is the ontological wholeness, or perfection, of the human being, whereas the primary pursuit of the Latin West is the historical self-affirmation of the human being, since Greek philosophy expresses a quest for metaphysics, whereas the Latin legal tradition expresses a quest for rhetorical power. Traditionally, the Greek East is focused on the integration of the world into the divine economy, whereas the West fights against the world, in the sense that, under the influence of its own Neoplatonic tradition, the West "exiles" God to intelligible spheres, and, thus, ultimately, by abandoning the world to the utilitarian plans of individuals who seek their historical self-affirmation, the West espouses the logic of worldly necessities, transforming spirit into historical power. The espousal of the

---

(spirit) and one of darkness (matter). Marriage, the Manicheans maintain, is of the devil's law, because the birth of children only continuously imprisons souls in new bodies. Moreover, with regard to Christ, Manicheans believed that Christ had taken upon himself nothing human in the incarnation, and that his crucifixion, death, and resurrection never actually took place. Even though, in his early 30s, Augustine of Hippo converted to Christianity, he maintained a Manichean-like dualistic way of thinking. Nevertheless, the ongoing influence of the gnostics' dualism on Augustine's thought was likely not something he was aware of (at least, not something he would have accepted as true), and it was present only as a significantly modified form of the dualism.

143. Chadwick, *Boethius*.

144. The intellectual roots of Roman law can be traced back to the book *Dodecadeltos* (in Latin, *Duodecim tabularum*), which was written by the Greek philosopher and jurist Hermodorus, who was born in Ephesus, in the fifth century BC, and he was a student of the famous Greek philosopher Heraclitus. However, whereas ancient Greek jurisprudence was always placed within a broader metaphysical framework in order to serve the goal of *theoria*, i.e., the ontological integration and perfection of man, Roman law, gradually, gave primacy to the pursuit of practical, managerial goals over the pursuit of spiritual goals.

logic of worldly necessities, which leads to the transformation of spirit into historical power, is the essence of secularization.

By assuming, in Neoplatonic fashion, that Aristotle's universals were radically separate from the material world and by construing Platonic ideas as if they were logical substances, the West has proclaimed that individual consciousness is a foundation of truth. The previous distinction (i.e., the distinction between Aristotle's universals and the material world) is founded on the Neoplatonic and Augustinian concept of man as a union between two totally distinct substances, namely, an immaterial soul and a material body. Moreover, in the context of Western culture, the previous distinction is associated with a broader distinction between the sensible world and the intelligible world; from the latter distinction, which underpins Western mysticism, Augustine of Hippo infers that the human soul knows only through an inward experience and not through its relation to the body, and that the salvation of man comes after one's soul has ascended to the intelligible world.

In his *De ordine*, Augustine defines reason (*ratio*) as "a mental operation capable of distinguishing and connecting things that are learned."[145] Additionally, in his *Soliloquies* I.6:12—8:15 and *De immortalitate animae*, 6.10, Augustine follows the terminology of Cicero's philosophy of law and describes reason as the "look" or "gaze" (*aspectus*) of the soul that may be oriented, through the body, toward the corporeal world or, alternatively, inward and upward toward intelligible reality. If Augustine is certain of anything, it is the rationality of the soul. In *De ordine* II, he describes reason as a discursive movement of the soul, and he thrice considers the exact relation between reason and the soul.

Augustine makes the distinction between superior reason (*ratio superior*), which gives knowledge of the eternal and incorporeal and underpins wisdom, or intellectual knowledge (*sapientia*), and inferior reason (*ratio inferior*), which gives knowledge only of the temporal and corporeal and underpins sense knowledge (*scientia*).[146] Whereas the Orthodox church fathers, particularly the Hesychasts (to whom I refer extensively in chapter 4), maintain that the glory of God in the experience of humanity's deification has no similarity whatsoever with any kind of created knowledge, the Augustinian theologians believe that they are united with the uncreated ideas of God's intellect of which creatures

---

145 Augustine, *De Ordine* II. 1.30.
146. Augustine, *De libero arbitrio* II.9

are supposedly copies. In other words, the Augustinian theologians treat God's wills as if they were logical substances in God's intellect, and, therefore, they give rise to a kind of theology that begins in rationalism and culminates in mysticism. In contradistinction to the Orthodox church fathers, Augustinian Neoplatonism searches for mystical experiences of supposed transcendent, ideational realities by liberating the mind from the confines of the body. On the other hand, as I explain in chapters 4 and 5, from the perspective of the Orthodox church fathers, particularly the Hesychasts, Orthodox theology is "secret" (in Greek, *mystikē*), in the sense that it consists in an ontologically founded mystical experience of human deification: the experience of humanity's deification through our participation in God's uncreated energies transcends any kind of created knowledge and propositional language.

In medieval Western Europe, the Augustinian distinction between superior reason and inferior reason led to the argument that inferior reason does not lead to truth, because the propositions that are based on inferior reason stem from the use of discursive reasoning in order to analyze and organize sensible things. Later on, during the medieval history of Western Europe, Augustine's superior reason was identified with the intellect, and, therefore, in the twelfth century AD, Bernard of Clairvaux, a French abbot and the primary builder of the reforming Cistercian monastic order, made the distinction between understanding through faith (*intellectus fidei*) and judgment based on discursive thinking (*judicium rationis*).[147] After the aforementioned developments in the intellectual history of Western Europe, and given that the rationalism of Western spirit stems from the decision to acknowledge the certainty of consciousness as a criterion of truth, the individualism of the Western spirit, which I have just delineated, gave rise to a quest for the control of reason by an authority whose declared purpose would be to ensure that man would always be aware of rational truth. The previous quest for the control of reason was one of the main issues of scholasticism, which I shall methodically study in chapter 2.

Scholasticism—namely, a rationalist method and, generally, a rationalist philosophy that dominated teaching by the academics ("scholastics," "schoolmen") of medieval universities in Western Europe from about 1100 to 1700—followed and developed further the aforementioned rationalist legacy of Boethius and Augustine. Therefore, as I shall explain

---

147. Storrs, *Bernard of Clairvaux*.

in detail in chapter 2, even though the history of scholasticism is inextricably linked to the Vatican's attempt to impose itself as the supreme authority on reason, scholasticism signals the emergence of a peculiar rationalist kind of humanism, in the sense that, according to scholasticism, God is the supreme being, and the human being can access the supreme being syllogistically, particularly, through natural theology, which consists in speculating about God in a manner similar to man's speculations about the natural world and its structure. Even though many scholastic philosophers emphatically argue that the Pope is the final authority on reason, and, hence, that the Pope's authority should guide natural theology, scholasticism, in general, and natural theology, in particular, ignore the methexiological character of Plato's theory of ideas, which I shall study further in chapters 2 and 3. In other words, scholasticism signals an attempt of the Western individual to assert his epistemological autonomy from God, and, therefore, scholasticism, involuntarily, opened the way to modern philosophy, in the context of which philosophical consciousness explicitly and completely asserted its autonomy from both God and the Papacy.

In the seventeenth century, René Descartes (Latinized: Renatus Cartesius), the acknowledged father of modern philosophy, attempted to reverse scholastic ontology, which was founded on the aforementioned peculiarly Western, Neoplatonic interpretation of Aristotle's metaphysics. Descartes was not an atheist, but, starting from Galileo's principle about the validity of mathematical proof, and arguing that philosophy can provide valid knowledge if it follows the deductive method of mathematics, he elevated the logic of *evidentia* into a criterion of truth,[148] and he proposed a geometrical theory of reality. Moreover, Descartes formulated a physical theory, in the context of which phenomena are explained only through the geometry of space and the laws of motion in a given space. Thus, Descartes proposed a soul–body dualism, arguing that the body's movements depend on formal biological processes and that the essence of body is extension while the essence of soul is thought. In other words, in the context of Cartesianism, the soul is not capable of movement and cannot give force to bodies, since it is assumed that it is essentially unrelated to the body. In Descartes's philosophy, metaphysics plays only an

---

148. According to Descartes's principle of *evidentia*, a thing is true if it is evident in consciousness, and, thus, in a fashion of mathematical axioms, one can formulate the first "evident" ideas, from which one can deduce universal laws; hence, the universe reduces to a mechanistic system.

auxiliary role, in the sense that it underpins Descartes's attempt to mathematize everything. Since he assigns primary significance to the principle of thought (*cogito*), Descartes—in contradistinction to ancient Greek metaphysical philosophers—appeals to metaphysics not in order to seek the prime principle, but in order to find ontological underpinnings for the rational study of physical problems.

In his *Metaphysical Meditations*, Descartes argued that being is present both in itself, i.e., independently of consciousness, and in consciousness, which, in its turn, is exactly the consciousness of being, and it underpins being.[149] Through the previous argument, Descartes and his "school" (namely, Nicolas Malebranche, Baruch Spinoza, and Gottfried Wilhelm von Leibniz) founded modern ontology. Reacting against the ontological excesses of Leibniz[150] and especially of Christian Wolff,[151] Immanuel Kant, in his *Critique of Pure Reason*, acknowledged the necessity

---

149. Laos, *The Metaphysics of World Order*, 58–60.

150. In his *Monadology*, Leibniz argues that the activity of soul corresponds to "monads," which are immaterial, unextended, self-determining, and purposive substances (forces). Moreover, according to Leibniz, every monad is a process of evolution, it animates matter, it has perception and appetition, and it realizes its nature with an inner necessity. In his theological essays, Leibniz argues that God created the monads, and He transcends all monads, but man, even though he is a limited monad, can maximize the qualities which every monad possesses to a certain degree, and, in this way, man can achieve a partial knowledge of God, since, Leibniz contends, God is suprarational but not contra-rational. In Leibniz's philosophy, monads are united with regard to their existential *telos*, and, in this way, Leibniz sought to synthesize Descartes's ontology and biblical teleology, but, according to Leibniz, monads are mutually distinct and separate, and, therefore, they are entities-in-themselves. In Leibniz's philosophy, the knowledge of the whole, or God, concerns each monad individually as a conscious entity, and, therefore, ultimately, Leibniz's philosophy advocates and intensifies the individualism of the Cartesian ego. Laos, *The Metaphysics of World Order*, 62–63.

151. Christian Wolff redefined philosophy as the science of the possible, and, more or less, his philosophical work is a common-sense adaptation of Leibniz's monadology (Jolley, ed., *The Cambridge Companion to Leibniz*). Thus, according to Wolff's *Ontologia*, the task of the philosopher is to provide "the manner and reason" of every possible thing, since, according to Wolff, everything, whether possible or actual, has a "sufficient reason" for why it is rather than not. In section 56 of his *Ontologia*, Wolff defines "sufficient reason" as that from which it is understood why something is or can be. In the "Preface" to his *Critique of Pure Reason* (2nd ed.), Kant argued that Wolff is "the greatest of all dogmatic philosophers." Wolff's "strict method" in science, Kant argues, is based on "the regular ascertainment of . . . principles, the clear determination of . . . concepts, the attempt at strictness in . . . proofs, and the prevention of audacious leaps in inferences" (quoted in: Winkler, "Kant, the Empiricists, and the Enterprise of Deduction," 41).

of the thing-in-itself, but he argued that the thing-in-itself is not knowable, and he accepted only its transcendentality.[152]

In his *Phenomenology of Spirit*, Georg Wilhelm Friedrich Hegel, the major representative of German romantic idealism, proposed an alternative solution to the old, Parmenidean-like, ontological controversy.[153] According to Hegel, the thing-in-itself, namely, being, is the idea (universal reason) which, by giving rise to a contradiction to itself, moves away from itself in order, ultimately, to return to itself enriched by its adventure. Through his dialectical method, Hegel sought to synthesize the perception of being and the perception of becoming. According to Aristotle, the transition from potentiality to actuality indicates a principle of becoming that consists in the actualization of an ontological program (entelechy), but, on the other hand, according to Hegel, the transition from the "in-itself" to the "for-itself" through the "outside-itself" indicates a principle of becoming that consists in a process of alteration that resembles Heraclitus's model of the world and is actualized in a clearly organized way, which is the core of Hegel's secular teleology. Thus, ultimately, in Hegel's philosophy, being is identified with historical becoming, and history takes the place of God.[154]

Until now, the verbal form "to be" (in Greek, *einai*) and the present participle "being" (in Greek, *on*) have been used indiscriminately, but they correspond to different realities, and, more specifically, to different, yet complementary, aspects of reality itself. The difference between the verbal form "to be" and the present participle "being" has been emphasized by the philosophy of existence, known also as existentialism. The intellectual roots of existentialism can be traced back to the works of Augustine of Hippo and Blaise Pascal, but its pioneer in the context of modern philosophy is Søren Kierkegaard,[155] while Martin Heidegger[156] is the most prominent representative of existentialism. Whereas Aristotelian ontology emphasizes the essence of being (i.e., that of which a thing consists), what is most important in existentialism is not the essence of being, but its presence, its existence, the event that, somehow, it exists and is before me, or independently of me, or that it is me. In other words, from the perspective of existentialism, what is significant is that I am

152. Laos, *The Metaphysics of World Order*, 74–81.
153. Ibid., 81–87.
154. Ibid., 85.
155. Ibid., 94–98.
156. Ibid., 101–6.

consciously aware of my own existence and of that which exists outside myself; in the former case (i.e., when I am consciously aware of my own existence), objects exist not only "in themselves" but also "for myself," just like me. The previous distinction has been emphasized by Jean-Paul Sartre[157] under the obvious influence of Hegel's ontology.

The argument that essence and presence are not necessarily identical to each other follows from the fact that one can conceive of essence independently of its reality. For instance, let us consider a myriagon, which is defined as a polygon with ten thousand sides; this geometrical figure is practically non-existent in nature. By defining a myriagon, we declare its essence, without, however, imposing its existence. Similarly, by defining the mythical creature chimaera (according to Greek mythology, it was a monstrous fire-breathing hybrid creature, usually depicted as a lion, with the head of a goat arising from its back, and a tail that might end with a snake's head), we declare its essence, but we do not impose its existence. Therefore, at the level of human consciousness, essence and presence are not necessarily identical to each other. However, in the Bible, the statement "I am that I am" (Exod 3:14) means that God is substantially present; this is an exceptional case in which God, who is absolute, reveals Himself.

According to existentialism, existence precedes essence, not so much in the temporal sense as in the sense of importance. What is most important in existentialism is the event of the emergence of existence out of non-existence; in fact, existentialists assign primary importance both to the previous process of emergence itself and to the reality of non-existence out of which existence emerges. Thus, an existentialist is ultimately preoccupied with the "archaeology" of existence, and, more particularly, he seeks to find the reason for the emergence of existence out of non-existence and to investigate if existent reality emerges of itself for the sake of existence, or if, as Karl Jaspers[158] has argued, it is thrown out of its original Encompassing (*Umgreifende*), which is a transcendent and obscure reality (the Absolute Being) within which existence is formed, and from which it is nurtured, before being "thrown into the world"; in the languages of mythology and science, at the precise moment of existence and non-existence, the previous Encompassing is called chaos.

However, the aforementioned existentialist theories are not complete. Apart from seeking to find the reason for the emergence of

157. Howells, ed., *The Cambridge Companion to Sartre*.
158. Jaspers, *Reason and Existenz*.

existence out of non-existence, one must try to clarify both the process of the creation of existence and the precise moment of the transition from non-existence to existence ("borderline situation"), hence clarifying also if the reason for the emergence of existence out of non-existence is directly related to the moment of the transition from non-existence to existence; if the reason for the emergence of existence out of non-existence is directly related to the moment of the transition from non-existence to existence, then that particular moment is immensely significant, and its conception helps us to interpret the very event of existence, that is, the presence of being.

From the perspective of the philosophy of methexis, the ontological questions that we have discussed until now can be elucidated by studying the concept of *hypostasis*, which was originally used in the fourth century AD by the Greek church father Gregory of Nyssa in order to explain the doctrine of the Holy Trinity. In general, the Greek church fathers explain the doctrine of the Trinity by using concepts of classical Greek philosophy. For instance, in his treatise *On the Holy Spirit*, Basil the Great[159] explains the important role of the Holy Spirit as follows: "And He [the Paraclete = Holy Spirit], like a sun joining itself to your purified eye, will show you in himself the image of the invisible. And in the blessed vision of the image [i.e., the Son = Logos], you shall behold the unspeakable beauty of the Archetype [Father = Nous or Mind]" (9:23). Based on Basil's theological essays, Gregory of Nyssa stresses that the three Persons are "hypostatic," that is, essentially equal and the same; the only way to tell them apart is their mutual relations.

The concept of hypostasis was methodically studied by John of Damascus[160] in his book *An Exact Exposition of the Orthodox Faith*, where he defines "nature" as the principle of motion and repose, and, on this ground, he identifies the nature of a subject with its substance. However, he adds that, according to some pre-Christian philosophers, such as Aristotle, in contrast to substance, which is simple being, nature is substance

---

159. Basil the Great (also known as Basil of Caesarea) was a fourth-century AD Bishop of Caesarea in Cappadocia, Asia Minor. He is a saint in both Eastern and Western Christianity. Basil, Gregory of Nazianzus, and Gregory of Nyssa are collectively referred to as the Cappadocian fathers. The Cappadocian fathers worked methodically in order to synthesize Christianity and Greek philosophy or, more precisely, in order to expound the Christian doctrines by using concepts of Greek philosophy.

160. John of Damascus was a Syrian Christian monk and priest, who died at his monastery, Mar Saba, near Jerusalem in 749 AD. His fields of interest included theology, philosophy, music, and law. He is a saint in both Eastern and Western Christianity.

that had been made specific by essential differences so as to have, in addition to simple being, being in such a way. Thus, substance *qua* substance, to which belongs simple being, is amounted to unqualified subject. On the other hand, "nature" as substance that had been made specific by essential differences relates to qualified substance, which is specified by the essential difference, i.e., it has not only being in the former sense, but also being in such a way according to its essential differences.

Furthermore, in his book *An Exact Exposition of the Orthodox Faith*, John of Damascus introduces the term "hypostasis" in order to clarify the Trinitarian formula: in this case, "hypostasis" means the existence of an individual substance in itself (i.e., an individual that is numerically different). Consequently, according to the consensus of the early church fathers, nature *qua* species is a common thing, which is predicated of hypostases and has its existence in them, while hypostasis is a particular thing in a numerical sense, as an individual of some kind. Hence, according to John of Damascus, hypostasis not only possesses common as well as individual characteristics of the subject, but also exists in itself, whereas nature does not exist in itself, but is to be found in hypostasis. The previous definition of the hypostatic mode of existence implies that Christianity's Holy Trinity, being a communion of three hypostases, is not conceptualized in the same way as the God of general, abstract "monotheism." Christianity stresses God's personhood (i.e., God's hypostatic mode of existence), whereas general, abstract monotheism stresses merely the unity of God's nature.

Through the distinction between "hypostasis" and "nature," the Greek church fathers, and especially the Cappadocian fathers, explain how it is possible for God to assume the human nature without losing or degrading His deity. God's hypostatic mode of existence implies that God's nature does not constrain Him, that is, God's existence is characterized by absolute freedom. In particular, according to the New Testament, in the case of Jesus Christ, the same hypostasis of the Logos personalized both the divine nature and the human nature. Thus, according to 1 John 2:23, "No one who denies the Son has the Father; whoever acknowledges the Son has the Father also."

In his treatise *On the Holy Spirit: Against the Macedonians*, Gregory of Nyssa stresses that the Holy Trinity should not be understood as three separate Gods (e.g., Creator, Redeemer, Sanctifier). As Hans von Balthasar has argued, after the Cappadocian Fathers, "it is no longer possible to infer Divine Persons on the basis of different regions of the world . . . [for] there is a 'common operation' which links their divine essence."[161] In order to explain the meaning of the Christian Trinitarian formula, one may put forward the following simile: Let us consider the poet T. S. Eliot. The poetry of T. S. Eliot is his "logos" (word); Eliot's logos proceeds from Eliot's "nous" (mind); and Eliot's logos provides its readers with his "spirit," i.e., with a special culture that makes them feel that they participate in Eliot's personal world. Eliot's spirit remains with the readers of Eliot's logos even when they do not have his poems before them. Similarly, we may argue that God the Father is the Nous of God, God the Son is the Logos (Word) of God, and the Holy Spirit is the Spirit of God. However, in the case of the Holy Trinity, the Nous of God (Father), the Logos of God (Son), and the Holy Spirit are not attributes or functions of a being, but they are three Hypostases of the same divine Nature.

The aforementioned Trinitarian formula leads to the following ontological conclusions: God does not exist as a pure individual, i.e., as an isolated being; but He exists as a communion of three hypostases. Thus, as John D. Zizioulas has argued, "communion" is an ontological category that describes God's mode of existence.[162] In addition, communion comes from the three hypostases of God, i.e., it is founded on concrete and free persons. By analogy, since, according to the Bible, man is the image of God, "communion" is an ontological category that describes human personhood: no human being can exist without communion, i.e., no human being can exist as a pure individual, and communion comes from hypostases, i.e., from concrete and free persons. In general, a "person" (or "hypostasis") is an individual-in-communion, i.e., human personhood is impossible without communion, and any kind of communion that suppresses or eliminates individuality ("otherness") is inhuman and ungodly.

From the perspective of the philosophy of methexis, which is focused on the hypostatic mode of being, the term "soul" refers to a being that bears and manifests the life-energy in a personal (hypostatic) way; hence, the soul is the essence of "personhood," and not a naturally immortal substance. The previous argument is in conformity with the following arguments of the Greek church fathers: the soul is created by God, and, thus, it is God's grace that makes it immortal. In the second century AD, Justin Philosopher and Martyr[163] writes in his book *Dialogue with*

161. Von Balthasar, *Presence and Thought*, 19.
162. Zizioulas, *Being as Communion*.
163. Justin (103–65 AD) was an early Greek apologist and martyr. He is venerated as a saint by many Christian denominations, including the Eastern Orthodox church

Trypho 4-6, "if the world is begotten, souls also are necessarily begotten. ... They are not, then, immortal? ... No; since the world has appeared to us to be begotten. ... If, then, it [the soul] is life, it would cause something else, and not itself, to live, even as motion would move something else than itself." In the same book, Justin continues as follows: "Now, that the soul lives, no one would deny. But if it lives, it lives not as being life, but as the partaker of life; but that which partakes of anything, is different from that of which it does partake. Now the soul partakes of life, since God wills it to live."

The soul not only "pervades" (in Greek, *chorousa*) the "entire body" (in Greek, *hōlou ... tou sōmatos*), as Maximus the Confessor writes, but also every member of the body responds to the presence of the soul, though the soul is incorporeal.[164] In contrast to radically dualist theological and philosophical arguments—according to which the soul is a substance that is naturally immortal and exists in the mortal human body distinct and separate from it and unmarked by any essential interaction with the body—the Greek church fathers emphasize that the two substances that make up the human being—namely, the body and the soul—are different from each other without being separate, and they are united without being confused; thus, according to Maximus the Confessor, every action and every movement of the human being is simultaneously an act of his soul and his body.[165] Moreover, in the context of the philosophy of methexis, and in accordance with Aristotle's argument that the soul is the entelechy of the body, the integral union of the body and the soul is characterized by a hierarchy of interaction, in the sense that the soul precedes the body in that interaction, not only in the temporal sense but also in the sense of importance.

---

and the Roman Catholic church.

164. *Patrologia Graeca*, Vol. 91, 1100AB. Maximus the Confessor (ca. 580–662) was a Christian monk, theologian, and scholar. He methodically and systematically supported the Council of Chalcedon's position that Jesus Christ had both a human and a divine will, fighting a heresy called Monothelitism (for Greek meaning "one will"). Following an Asian tradition of transcendentalism, Monothelitism was an attempt to "reduce" the humanity of Christ by arguing that Christ had only one will, particularly, a divine one. Maximus the Confessor is a saint in both Eastern and Western Christianity.

165. Maximus the Confessor, "Peri Theologias kai tes Ensarkou Oikonomias" ("Regarding Theology and the Incarnate Economy"), 90.

2

Access to Being

"To be" and "being" are concrete situational realities, and the extent to which one's mind has access to them depends on the manner in which one can experience them. The most common way for consciousness to obtain this kind of experience is related to methexis. Methexis is one of the most ancient concepts in the history of philosophy. In fact, the history of methexis as a relation (and, particularly, as an event of participation) experienced by consciousness is older than the history of the definition and the use of methexis as a formal concept in the context of philosophy. The achievement of methexis was the purpose of the great ancient mystery traditions, such as the Osiris Mystery (in which Osiris symbolizes the drama of the human soul that has descended from the world soul symbolized by Isis) and the Mysteries of Eleusis (where Demeter symbolizes the world soul, and Persephone symbolizes the human soul). Moreover, according to Kabbalistic *midrashim* (i.e., mystical Jewish traditions), the "history" of Israel as chronicled in the Torah is a symbolic history of the human soul and its mystical rebirth through methexis in the Absolute, which was achieved after the children of Israel (souls), led by Moses (divine Logos), had passed through the Red Sea (chaos). Moreover, Jesus Christ himself emphasizes methexis as follows: "Remain in me, and I will remain in you" (John 15:4). Thus, in Acts 17:27–28, we read the following: "God . . . is not far from each one of us. For in him we live and move and have our being." In general, in the context of the so-called ancient mentality, ontology is founded on methexis, which is based on the assumption that there is a kind of continuity among beings, ontological states, and conscious experiences.

The development of philosophy helps to understand the relation between the objects that are experienced by consciousness in the context of methexis and the idea that consciousness expands toward the direction of those objects, which are embraced and, ultimately, assimilated by consciousness. From the perspective of ancient philosophizing of consciousness, methexis is achieved through a series of distant and obscure "prime causes" (i.e., supernatural forces) which operate according to a complicated system of preferences that is known only by concrete initiated conscious beings, namely, the magi, who are also capable of intervening in the operation of the world by controlling the previous forces in conformity with the intentionality of human consciousness.[1] The previous mentality is characterized by creativity and spiritual freedom, in the sense that—even though it admits that humanity cannot create out of nothing (since species is not a human creation)—it favors and encourages the intervention of human consciousness in the operation of the world, and it is expressed by being crystallized in the context of myth, which is also the major underpinning of magic. Thus, in this context, philosophers are as religious as they are rational, scientists are as rational as are mystics, and psychologists are as much spiritual healers as are scientific therapists.

Methexis is of decisive importance not only in the context of the so-called ancient mentality, but also in the context of a purely philosophical mentality. Originally, Platonism and, later on, Neoplatonism were the major philosophies through which perceptions of methexis were developed and disseminated among the philosophers of the ancient world. The acceptance of the concept of methexis is the most important expression of a dynamic conception of reality; this dynamic conception of reality opposes the static conception of being, according to which being is a closed world engrossed in itself. The concept of methexis implies a continuous, dynamic relation among ontical realities and among the conscious beings that express or seek ontical realities. Methexiological perception is based on the thesis that every being (and every situation) is related to other beings (and to other situations), and it remains "open" to them in order to participate in them and, ultimately, with them and through them, to

---

1. According to ancient Zoroastrian and Hellenistic traditions, "magus" (plural: "magi") means a wise man. Moreover, in the New Testament, we read that magi traveled thousands of miles to worship Jesus Christ for who he was (Matt 2:1–2, 11), thus disclosing the essence of true worship: we should worship God because he is perfect and almighty Creator of the universe, worthy of the best we have to give.

participate in the unique cosmic reality from which each and every being is individually derived. The previous methexiological perception is in conformity with the following biblical passages: John 1:3, where we read that all beings and things were made through the divine Logos; Matthew 22:37–39, where Jesus Christ says: "Love the LORD your God with all your heart and with all your soul and with all your mind," and "Love your neighbor as yourself"; Luke 10:36–37, where Jesus Christ clarifies that everyone must become a psychically open "neighbor" to everyone else.

There are two varieties of methexiological relations: an essentialist (and mainly passive) one and a teleological (and more active) one. The essentialist variety of methexis refers to the original attributes that are maintained by a being or a situation, and, therefore, it emphasizes the common origin of the beings or the situations under consideration. A characteristic example of the previous essentialist perception of methexis can be found in Plato's *Symposium*, where Aristophanes describes the mythical beings from which the two genders, namely, male and female, were descended "as each person was cut in two," and he mentions that the two genders tend to resynthesize their previous common existence through *eros* (holy love passion).[2] The teleological variety of methexis refers to an attempt to improve one's existential state by pursuing and fulfilling the purpose of one's existential program, i.e. one's *telos*. A characteristic example of this kind of methexis is any collective attempt to achieve moral or scientific goals; those who participate in a collective attempt to achieve moral or scientific goals endorse a common set of values and interests.

Through his theory of ideas, Plato has shown that teleology is the quintessence of spirituality and the core of philosophical life. He argues that the telos, or purpose, of our existence is our methexis, or participation, in the pure being (i.e., the Absolute Good) and our unification with it.[3] Moreover, he maintains that "the only way to acquire lasting knowledge" is to "bring together the disconnected subjects . . . and take a comprehensive view of their relationship with each other and with the nature of reality."[4] In Plato's philosophy, idea and species display the visible rational form of the life-giving universal One, and the *theoria* of, or mental gaze at, the life-giving universal One leads us to the conclusion

---

2. Plato, *Symposium* 189c–193e.
3. Plato, *Republic* 585b.
4 Ibid. 537c.

that the truth of the world of ideas is identical to the essence of reality. Thus, according to Plato, a dialectical philosopher is "synoptic" (or "comprehensive"), in the sense that he reduces a multitude of phenomena to the archetypal "one," instead of analyzing phenomena themselves.

According to Plato's *Phaedrus*, truth is the event of the soul's transcendent movement toward the transcendent sphere of being (i.e., toward the Absolute Good).[5] The subject/object dichotomy is something irrelevant to Plato's theory of philosophical vision, because, according to Plato, philosophical vision consists in the philosopher's methexis, or participation, in the object of philosophical vision, i.e., it is based on "seeing," or "gazing," and not merely on "being aware of." Therefore, in his *Republic*, Plato inveighs against "mimesis,"[6] because it leads to an abstraction of truth from sensible data, whereas, for Plato, truth consists in participating in the transcendent sphere of being.

Even though Aristotle discovered abstraction and substituted species for Plato's transcendent ideas, nowhere in his *Metaphysics* Λ (Book Lambda), does Aristotle argue that God, i.e., the Absolute Being, is a form. In *Metaphysics* Λ, Aristotle understands God as energy, life, "nous" (mind) or "noesis" (mental energy), and, in Λ9, he emphasizes that God is a kind of noesis that is simply noesis of the divine reality itself and of nothing else, which seems to yield no positive content to the description of God. Hence, in *Metaphysics*, Λ, Aristotle endorses apophatic theology, and he treats apophatic theology as the culmination of his ontology, thus paving the way to the apophatic theology of the Greek church fathers, particularly the Hesychasts. Additionally, in *Metaphysics* Λ, Aristotle paves the way to the Hesychasts' argument about the essence–energies distinction, by arguing that God is somehow a cause of the sensible world, but God seems to be directly a cause only of the outermost heaven, and everything else that is produced by God is a consequence of heavenly motions. Aristotle maintains that God is an efficient cause only by being a final cause, i.e., by being the ultimate and transcendent source of the significance of the beings and things in the world. The previous Aristotelian arguments about God's relationship with the world are very similar to arguments that have been put forward by the Hesychasts, and they underpin a methexiological attitude toward the problem of knowledge.

---

5. Plato, *Phaedrus* 76–77.

6. The Greek term "mimesis" carries a wide range of meanings, which include imitation, representation, and mimicry.

From a purely philosophical viewpoint, access to being is inconceivable without the use of a concrete method. In general, philosophical methods can be divided into two categories: the *a priori* methods and the *a posteriori* methods; the first were playing a dominant role in philosophy until the eighteenth century AD, whereas the latter played a dominant role in the development of philosophy after the eighteenth century. The common characteristic of the *a priori* methods is that they are based on original hypotheses that are accepted as axiomatic and deductively produce series of syllogisms that lead to guaranteed specific conclusions, which, as much as it is possible, are flawlessly related to the propositions that precede them in the given series of syllogisms. The more coherent a philosophy is, the higher its chances of being imposed are. However, often, hypothetico-deductive systems exhibit logical "cracks," and, therefore, they are less solid than initially assumed.

Among the *a priori* philosophical methods, some were created in ancient times, others were created during the medieval times, and others were created during the modern era. In chapter 1, it was made clear that the Presocratic philosophers' general model consists in axiomatically accepting a principle as the prime principle of the world and in assuming that all particular realities are deducible from that principle. Socrates and the sophists were the first to extricate philosophy from the intellectual shackles of the previous cosmological, physicalist/ontological dogmatism: the sophists indicated the reasonableness of particular doubts about the general validity of their predecessors' philosophical achievements; Socrates sought an undeniable criterion of philosophical truth through the method of maieutic, which was originally developed by Socrates himself, and it was expounded by Plato in his *Symposium*. Besides the controversies between Socrates and the sophists, both sides have played a decisive role in shifting philosophical enquiry from the world to the human being.

In his first dialogues, Plato expounded Socrates's method of maieutic—according to which, truth cannot be taught directly as a transmission of knowledge from an instructor to a learner, but instead the learner learns truth by interacting with an instructor and through his own experience—in conjunction with the method of Socratic irony, which consists in admitting (pretending) that you are ignorant and willing to learn while exposing someone's inconsistencies by close questioning. However, Plato developed his own philosophical method, which he called dialectic. In Plato's dialogues, it is clear that Plato perceives dialectic as a form of internal dialogue that is motivated by the philosophizing soul's pursuit of truth in order, ultimately, to achieve existential perfection.[7] On the other hand, when a Latin scholar, such as Augustine of Hippo, seeks the reason (*ratio*) of the world, he mainly seeks to collect, define, and organize various elements into a consistent whole, specifically the world.

Plato's dialectic has two complementary aspects: an ascending aspect and a descending one. According to the ascending aspect of Plato's dialectic, by classifying things into genera and species, philosophical enquiry proceeds from one concept to another until the philosopher's mind perceives the ultimate causes of things, and, therefore, the philosopher manages to know the truth of phenomena through their corresponding ideas. According to the descending aspect of Plato's dialectic, philosophical enquiry proceeds from ideas, in which the philosopher's mind has already managed to participate, to the interpretation of phenomena.

Plato's myth of the cave is a parable narrated by Plato in his *Republic* (Book 7, section 7) in order to illustrate "our nature in its education and want of education."[8] Imagine, says Plato, a cave in which prisoners are chained since their birth in such a way that all they can see are shadows thrown on a wall in front of them. They would have the illusion that these shadows were reality. If, however, one of them were freed, and he managed to emerge into the sunlight, he would acquire a new kind of knowledge and he would realize how limited his vision was in the cave.

In his presentation of the myth of the cave, Plato discerns four different types of "seeing," which are four different types of knowledge and four different states of consciousness, or existential conditions: (i) Illusion, or conjecture (in Greek, *eikasia*): it provides only the most primitive and unreliable opinions. Illusion is the level of consciousness at which one establishes arbitrary correspondences between reality and the things that are present in one's consciousness. At this level of consciousness, a person confuses reality with desires. (ii) Belief (in Greek, *pistis*): it is an experiential form of knowledge that enables one to discern between the images of things and the prototypes, but, at this level of consciousness, a person has not developed scientific consciousness, yet. (iii) Rule-based reasoning, or logic (in Greek, *dianoia*): at this level of consciousness, a person can achieve systematic knowledge of the objects of consciousness through a disciplined application of the understanding. By the term "science,"

---

7. Plato, *Theaetetus*, 154d–e, *Charmides*, 166c–e, *Philebus*, 38c–e, *Sophist*, 263e, and *Laws*, 893a.

8. Plato, *Republic*, 514a.

we mean an intentional and methodical enterprise whose purpose is to identify the reason of beings and things, and logic is a way of expressing a person's need to explain the itinerary of the scientific thought to other persons by using a formal language. (iv) Intelligence (in Greek, *noesis*): it is the supreme (*ne plus ultra*) level of consciousness, and it corresponds to the knowledge of the Absolute Good. In particular, at this level of consciousness, a person participates in the world of ideas, and, because, according to Plato, ideas constitute the life of God's essence, those who participate in the world of ideas attain to existential perfection. This level of consciousness requires a different philosophical method. According to Plato, the philosophical method that leads to this level of consciousness is dialectic, and it is a logical as well as metalogical method: it is logical in the sense that the knowledge of the Good presupposes that one's consciousness has progressed from the first level of knowledge to the third level of knowledge (logic); it is metalogical in the sense that, in order to ascend to this level of consciousness (intelligence), one must be aware of the limits of logic and to have acquired a kind of knowledge that is derived from an experience of enlightened intuition. Hence, as we read in Plato's *Republic* 476b, as well as in the entire Platonic dialogue *Phaedrus*, the relationship between the philosopher and the Good is not only a cognitive one, but also an erotic one.

According to Plato, humans can attain to a personal experience of the Absolute Good, but they cannot logically deduce the Absolute Good from any deterministic series of syllogisms. Thus, Plato emphasizes that the knowledge of the Absolute Good presupposes not only the ability to give an account, but also a psychic cleansing or cure. The metaphysical kind of knowledge that corresponds to intelligence is what Plato has in his mind in *Phaedrus*, where he describes the soul journeying in "that place beyond the heavens" where "true being dwells, without color or shape, that cannot be touched."[9] Additionally, in his *Republic*, Plato argues that one has cured his soul if he has "attained to self-mastery and beautiful order within himself, and ... harmonized these three principles [the three parts of the soul: reason, the emotions, and the appetites] ... linked and bound all three together and made himself a unit, one man instead of many, self-controlled and in unison."[10] Since, as we read in *Republic* 585b, the purpose of our existence is our participation in the

---

9 Plato, *Phaedrus* 247c–e.
10 Plato, *Republic* 443d–e.

pure Being (the Good) and our unification with the Good (i.e., the Good-in-itself), psychic cleansing is a necessary presupposition of our transformation into the corresponding absolute principle; for "it cannot be that the impure attain the pure."[11]

Plato's concept of "intelligence" (*noesis*) is a kind of spiritual intuition, and there is a striking resemblance between Platonic *noesis* and the kind of spiritual intuition about which we read in the Bible, particularly, in Luke 11:33–36, Mark 9:3ff., and Matthew 6:22 and 17:1. The kind of spiritual intuition that is mentioned in these biblical passages is the core of Hesychasm. Michael Psellus (Michael Psellōs; 1018–ca.1081), a Hesychast and Neoplatonic philosopher, has written extensively on the nature of light emanating from Christ during Christ's Transfiguration. He describes the relation between God's activity and man's as follows: at midday, the sun is always shining, but only those who have healthy eyes are capable of gazing at it; by analogy, only those who have a mental eye purified in their soul are capable of participating in God.[12]

In the context of classical Greek philosophy, cognition does not produce knowledge by itself, and, whenever knowledge is produced by cognition alone, it is identified with imagination. According to classical Greek philosophy, knowledge is intimately associated with a process whereby the mind receives and processes sensible data. In particular, in Plato's *Timaeus*, the soul, like the body, is characterized by "that sensation which we now term 'seeing'"[13]; and, in Aristotle's *On Sense and the Sensible* 438b10, the soul operates as the center of sensation. Hence, the classical Greek philosophy of vision is focused on a consciousness-independent light that enables one to see an image without the mediation of mental representations. Since, according to Plato's and Aristotle's theories of vision, an image can be seen independently of (and prior to) images formed in the mind (mental representations), it follows that, in the context of classical Greek philosophy, knowledge is obtained when a conscious being moves outside itself in pursuit of the consciousness-independent reality of the idea, and not through mental representations. In other words, in the context of classical Greek philosophy, knowledge is based on a vision that is prior to conceptual thinking, and it consists in one's participation in the light of the idea.

11. Plato, *Phaedo* 67b.
12. Psellus, *De Omnifaria Doctrina*.
13 Plato, *Timaeus* 45d.

As I argued in chapter 1, even though Aristotle substituted species for Plato's ideas, he endorsed the transcendent purpose of Plato's philosophy. Thus, in his *Physics* V.265a, Aristotle writes that God is the direct object of the universal eros that characterizes the eternal physical beings (i.e., the celestial spheres), which imitate the perfection of the divine mode of life through their harmonious motions. In addition, in his *Metaphysics* 1072b, Aristotle argues that "God is a living being, eternal, most good; and therefore life and a continuous eternal existence belong to God; for that is what God is." In *Nicomachean Ethics*, Aristotle—who places God, as the ultimate source of the significance of beings and things in the world, on the top of his metaphysical system—argues that the communion between God and humans takes place through the perfection of the human mind and the mental vigilance that is caused by mental pleasure.[14]

In his *Poetics*, Aristotle argues that mimesis, as a natural inclination of the human being, is a creative act, not because it passively represents something, nor because it maintains a form, but because it "enmatters" species, and, hence, it discloses the absolute purpose of being, i.e., the real truth of being. Thus, in *Poetics* 50a15, Aristotle understands mimesis as "the constitution of things" (in Greek, *he ton pragmāton systasis*).

If, in the context of mimesis, humanity could create species—as sophists and modern philosophers claim—then human creative activity would be of a purely imaginary nature, and, therefore, every statement about real truth, i.e., about the Absolute, would be cognitively insignificant, since, in that case, only sensible stimuli and products of the subject's intellect would be cognitively significant. The faculty of imagination develops because the intellect (i.e., the faculty of reasoning and understanding objectively, especially with regard to abstract matters) cannot perceive the Absolute in an objective way; however, imagination cannot create species. Imagination is a natural function of consciousness that is not constrained by the world, and, more generally, it does not submit to the principle of reality. Therefore, imagination can perceive things that may only apparently represent the reality of the world, and it can even perceive things that may not represent the reality of the world at all. Imagination endows the things that it perceives with new significances, and it reorganizes them into new historical forms, utilizing elements of its external existential conditions (e.g., latent societal trends and changes)

---

14 Aristotle, *Nicomachean Ethics* 1177a.

that are not historically crystallized forms, yet. Hence, imagination is a kind of visionary perception that assigns its own logical forms to the sensible world, which is relative and impermanent, in order to accommodate the absolute world. In other words, imagination reshapes empirical data into mental images in order to disengage them from the semantics of the empirical world and to transform them into members of a new world of significations that has been instituted by imagination itself.[15] But, since it is characterized by subjectivity, imagination does not have universal significance. Therefore, the activity of imagination is unstable, and, for this reason, imagination is compelled to overcome the lack of universal significance by resorting to other (i.e., external) sources of significance.

In contrast to Platonic ideas, imagination does not consist in establishing a relation between a varied and changeable world and a stable meaning, but it simply depicts empirical data through mental images. Similarly, in the context of logic, empirical data are intellectually "depicted" (i.e., organized) by causal relations. The empirical world is stable only with regard to the meaning of its existence, since its effective and final cause is the "absolute" (God). On the other hand, at the level of representations, the empirical world is always unstable, since the physical world and history are subject to change, and conscious states are subjective. Therefore, the world of imagination is necessarily unstable. Because the world of imagination is constituted of images, it cannot be the only source of the significance of being, and it depends on an external source of significance.

Imagination can assign significances to beings and things, and it can change the significances of beings and things, but it cannot create significance out of nothing. Images endow significances with logical shapes, i.e., they transform meaning into something sensible, and, therefore, they enable consciousness to assign meaning to sensible objects. But the formation of a universally acceptable image presupposes the universality of the corresponding meaning, i.e., it depends on significance. Therefore, significance always transcends the limits of its image, and this is the limit of imagination. Even if we accept the Aristotelian and Kantian argument that imagination creatively unites sense and understanding (in the sense that imagination provides cognition with mental images of sensible things which are subject to synthetic reasoning), the creativity of imagination is

---

15. Castoriadis, *The Imaginary Institution of Society*.

not original, because it depends on a concrete prior significance. In other words, significance precedes imagination.

Species *qua* truth is not an imaginary creation, but it is disclosed by the ultimate, suprahistorical purpose of beings, i.e., it is a divine creation, as it is indicated by Plato's example of the three beds: a carpenter's task is to create an empirical bed, which is an imitation of the idea of a bed, a painter's task is to create an image of an empirical bed, and God's task is the creation of the real bed-in-itself, i.e., the idea of a bed.[16] When human creative activity imitates God, it is *poiesis*, and, in this sense, it can be understood as the transition from non-being into being, since it produces a meaningful world from formless matter.

In the context of methexiology, a being or a world of beings A is significant if it refers to a reality X that transcends A, and, particularly, the significance of A consists in its relation to the reality X. Furthermore, in the context of methexiology, and according to my argument that significance precedes imagination, the significance of significance (i.e., the source of significance) is God. Thus, humans can be united with the source of their significance by participating in God, whereas, if they try to be united with the source of their significance through their discursive reason and selfish sentiments, they will, ultimately, be confined to the realm of imagination. For this reason, as the Orphic Mysteries and Plato maintain, the union of the soul with the source of the significance of being, i.e., with God, presupposes "initiation," i.e., a process of psychic cleansing or cure.

On the other hand, as I argued in chapter 1, in the Middle Ages, many Western scholars were assuming, in Neoplatonic fashion, that Aristotle's universals were radically separate from the material world, and they were treating Platonic ideas as if they were logical substances, thus giving rise to Western rationalism. In the context of Western rationalism, consciousness is confined to its own creations, and, since Western rationalism construes Platonic ideas as if they were logical substances, the rationalist variety of methexis consists in a series of abstract concepts which are hierarchically arranged according to their degree of generality; according to the Western rationalist variety of methexis, the degree of generality is assumed to be equivalent to the degree of reality. This

---

16. Plato, *Republic*, 597b–c.

rationalist variety of methexis was solidified by Thomas Aquinas, the major representative of scholastic philosophy.[17]

In his book *Scripta super libros sententiarum*, Thomas Aquinas argues that superior reason (*ratio superior*), which is identified with intellectual truth, is the knowledge of God. According to Thomas Aquinas, God knows all things in One (i.e., in Himself) and, therefore, He does not need any methodologies, syllogisms, analyses or syntheses, whereas humans know only under particular conditions and through particular mental processes. In his *Scripta super libros sententiarum* III.31, Thomas argues that, "in the present life, it is true what the Philosopher [Aristotle] says, namely that, without images ['phantasmata'], the soul could neither develop science nor revise the things that it already knows; since images are for the intellect what sensibilia [i.e., sensible data] are for the senses." Therefore, Thomas Aquinas discarded Augustine's qualitative distinction between superior reason and inferior reason. In his book *Summa Theologica*, Aquinas substituted Augustine's qualitative distinction between superior reason and inferior reason with a distinction between the supernatural end and the natural end of human life. According to Aquinas, the supernatural end of human life is the object of theology and is based on faith, whereas the natural end of human life is the object of philosophy, and, due to reason, the knowledge of the natural end of human life can be achieved by man himself.

The continuity of faith and reason, of grace and nature, is central to Aquinas's philosophical and theological system. For Thomas, there is only one truth—namely, the divine truth—and the soul unites the sensible world with the intelligible one. He maintains that the soul is essentially different from the body, and, even though it is not self-existent, it is hierarchically the supreme intellectual creature of God, and it is immortal, immaterial, and capable of knowing the intelligible realm. However, according to Thomas, because the soul is united with the body, the soul cannot know non-corporeal beings directly, but it can only know them through reason, in the context of which general concepts are distanced from objects, specifically, through abstraction, which is a process whereby higher concepts are derived from the use and classification of concrete, individual forms.

17. Thomas Aquinas (1225–1274) was an Italian Dominican priest and one of the most influential medieval philosophers and theologians. In the Roman Catholic church, Thomas Aquinas is venerated as a saint (in 1323, Pope John XXII pronounced Thomas Aquinas a saint).

According to Aquinas, in the sensible world, the universal (general concept) cannot exist as such, apart from the individual; it is immanent in the individual as the essence specifically common to all members of the same species. This essence constitutes the thing specifically what it is. Therefore, he argues that knowledge starts from the sensible world (i.e., he disagrees with Augustine's argument that inferior reason leads to false knowledge) and culminates in superior reason, and that, in this way, man attains to the knowledge of the universal, i.e., he can logically discern species. Furthermore, Thomas argues that there is a group of truths, such as the mysteries of the Trinity and the Incarnation, quite incapable of justification by reason. In this case, Thomas Aquinas argues that faith, which is a gift from the Creator, perfects the finite nature of man, but this does not reduce the significance or power of human reason. According to Thomas, the grace that confers faith comes from the outside, but, since it comes from the Creator who is responsible for the existence of humanity, faith is intrinsic to the nature it perfects. Hence, Thomas Aquinas claims that we are impelled to comprehend the mysteries of faith through reason. From the aforementioned arguments of Aquinas, it is clear that his philosophical and theological system carries on Boethius's misinterpretation of classical Greek philosophy, and it indicates that Thomas Aquinas was not only ignorant of Plato's and Aristotle's quest for an experiential ("erotic") knowledge of God, but also he was disregarding the difference between knowing God and knowing *about* God, a difference that is explicitly mentioned in Matthew 15:9, where Jesus Christ repeats the prophet Isaiah's criticism of hypocrites: "These people honor me with their lips, but their hearts are far from me. They worship me in vain; their teachings are but rules taught by men."

In medieval Western Europe, apart from Thomas Aquinas, many other advocates of philosophical realism—such as the ninth-century Irish Neoplatonic philosopher Johannes Scotus Eriugena, author of the book *De divisione naturae* (*On the division of nature*), and Anselm of Canterbury,[18] author of the book *Proslogion*—were philosophizing as logicians, in the sense that—due to their fragmented and profoundly misguided knowledge of Plato's and Aristotle's philosophies—they were assuming that the logical and the real orders are exactly parallel, and that the human intellect, the seat of logic, is an ontologically sufficient

---

18. In 1093, Anselm of Canterbury (ca. 1033–1109) was enthroned as Archbishop of Canterbury. In the Roman Catholic church, he is venerated as a saint, and, in 1720, he was named a doctor of the church by the same church.

foundation of theology. In a sense, the previous philosophical realists were adapting the idea of God to the requirements of their intellect, and, in this way, they were forming the impression that they had understood God.

Having erroneously construed Plato's ideas as if they were logical substances, the scholastics' philosophical realism implies that general concepts, called "universals" by the scholastics, constitute the authentic reality, whereas individuals belong to the world of imperfect phenomena. In other words, according to the scholastics' philosophical realism, the "human being" as a general concept is more real than me as an individual; hence, one's life and relation with the world are (and should be) subject to rules and axioms that are superior to any significance that one may have as an individual.

Logical structures are always authoritarian and coercive, since, according to logic, the degree of generality is equivalent to the degree of reality, and the more general concept imposes its authority on the less general one "from above." According to the scholastic philosophical realists, universals are logical substances separate from the sensible world, and the behavior of the individual (i.e., the empirical representative of the human species) must conform to the commands of the universal. In other words, according to the scholastic philosophical realists, the duty of the individual is to learn the commands of the universal and to try to comply with them, since they are more real than the individual. Thus, the individual's life is meaningful only if and to the extent that it complies with the commands of the universal. In other words, man is real to the extent that he negates his existential otherness for the sake of the universal.

The scholastics' realist arguments imply that society must be structured in such a way as to serve the corresponding universal, which, in this case, is the "kingdom of God" (perceived as the most general concept of society). From the previous perspective, the Pope is logically the person who has the supreme authority and duty to disclose and impose the commands of the universal. Thus, in medieval Western Europe, philosophical realism was a philosophical weapon with which the Vatican attempted to consolidate its authority. Due to the scholastics' philosophical realism, the Pope managed to impose his *"plenitudo potestatis,"* i.e., his overlordship. On the other hand, as I argued in chapter 1, for Plato, ideas are not logical concepts, but the energies of the Absolute Good, and, therefore, Plato's ideas neither command humans "from above" nor underpin authoritarian regimes, but they call humans to participate in them through a process of psychic cleansing or cure. Additionally, as I argued in chapter 1, even though Aristotle discovered abstraction, he did not discard the methexiological character of Plato's philosophy, and, thus, he argued that the mind is immortal and arises from the outside (*thyrathen*).

In medieval Western Europe, the major opponent of philosophical realism was nominalism, whose founders are Roscelin, an eleventh-century monk of Compiègne, and William of Occam, a thirteenth-century English Franciscan friar and philosopher. Because Roscelin's and William of Occam's knowledge of classical Greek philosophy was not better than that of their realist opponents, they attempted to fight against philosophical realism by advocating a radical form of individualism. Thus, Roscelin argues that *universalia sunt nomina*, i.e., the universals (general concepts) are names; universals are not things, but they are merely words (*flatus vocis*), which are used for taxonomic purposes.[19] Moreover, according to William of Occam, only individuals exist, rather than supra-individual universals, and universals are products of abstraction and do not exist independently of the human intellect.[20] Because nominalism emphasizes abstraction and the operations of the individual's intellect, while the scholastics' philosophical realism maintains that general concepts are substances, many medieval Western scholars formed the impression that nominalism is founded on Aristotelianism, and that the scholastics' philosophical realism is founded on Platonism; however, as I have already argued this impression is wrong.

At the political level, the scholastics' philosophical realism underpins the Papacy's absolutism and, generally, authoritarian regimes, whereas nominalism underpins civil society (known also as the "bourgeois" society). Nominalism was the major philosophical weapon of the medieval civil class (known also as the "bourgeoisie") against the Papacy's absolutism. Already in medieval Western Europe and in the Renaissance, civil society instituted its own "church," namely, the "university," its own "priesthood," namely, university professors striving for scholarly pontification, and its own "saints" and "heroes," namely, technocrats and accomplished businessmen. Thus, medieval nominalism was

---

19. A taxonomic scheme is a particular classification ("the taxonomy of . . .") arranged in a hierarchical structure or classification scheme. Of Roscelin's writings there exists only a letter addressed to Abelard.

20. Laos, *The Metaphysics of World Order*, chapter 2.

a major philosophical underpinning of a liberal educational movement that emerged at the University of Paris in the thirteenth century, and it encouraged the development of empiricism. In 1210 and in 1229, major riots took place at the University of Paris, and, eventually, on April 13, 1231, after two years of negotiations, Pope Gregory IX issued the Bull "Parens scientiarum," which guaranteed the University of Paris independence from local authority, whether ecclesiastical or secular, placing it directly under Papal patronage. Moreover, in 1251, new fierce riots took place at the University of Paris, and they were settled in 1261, when it was decided that the University of Paris would continue allowing monks to become members of its faculty, but no monk would be allowed to teach at the school of arts,[21] which thus was given the right to maintain a liberal intellectual environment. In medieval Western Europe, nominalism was an outlet for the oppressed civil class, and it paved the way to the individualism of modern philosophy, whose pioneer is Francis Bacon, and whose acknowledged founder is Descartes.

Rationalism is a theory according to which knowledge is innate, independent of experience and self-confirming. Hence, the opposite of rationalism is empiricism, i.e., a theory according to which knowledge is derived from experience. In the sixteenth century, Francis Bacon, an English philosopher, statesman, scientist, and jurist, articulated a systematic study of the empirical method. In his *Novum Organum Scientiarum*, Bacon argues that classic induction proceeds at once from sensible data and particulars up to the most general propositions and then works backward (via deduction) to arrive at intermediate propositions; thus, Bacon maintains, a serious problem with this procedure is that one contradictory instance suffices to falsify the conclusions. For this reason, Bacon proposed a different inductive method, according to which the philosopher must proceed regularly and gradually from one axiom to another, so that each axiom (i.e., each step up "the ladder of intellect") is thoroughly tested by observation and experimentation before the next step is taken (i.e., each confirmed axiom becomes a foothold to a more general axiom, and the most general axioms represent the last stage of the process). By the term "experience," Bacon does not refer to everyday experience, but he prescribes a different approach to experience: his empirical method is

---

21. At the school of arts, students were studying the "trivium" (i.e., grammar, rhetoric, and logic) and the "quadrivium" (i.e., music, arithmetic, geometry, and astronomy).

to correct and extend sensible data into facts by setting up tables.[22] By the term "table," Bacon refers to a compilation of observational data. Bacon prescribes the following tables: the table of essence and presence (which enables the investigator to survey all known instances where the nature of the phenomenon under investigation appears to exist), the table of absence in proximity (which enables the investigator to survey all known instances where the nature of the phenomenon under investigation is not present), and the table of degrees (which enables the investigator to categorize the instances of the nature of the phenomenon under investigation into various degrees of intensity). Thus, Bacon assumes that, from lower axioms, more general ones can be derived by induction, and, from the more general axioms, Bacon strives to reach more fundamental laws of nature, which lead to practical deductions as new experiments or works.

Even though Bacon's empirical method clarifies the importance of investigating phenomena that are objects of human experience, it separates the objects of human experience from their telos (i.e., their transcendent purpose), and, therefore, from Bacon's perspective, in the sensible world, only two kinds of forces operate: the natural laws and the selfish desires of human consciousness. There is a clear difference between Bacon's understanding of experience and Plato's understanding of experience. In the context of Plato's theory of ideas, knowledge is not founded on bodily sensations, but, as I have already argued, this does not mean that it is founded on representations created by the subject's mind; instead, according to Plato's philosophy, knowledge is founded on a peculiar mental *sensation*.[23] Thus, according to Plato, the mind does not reproduce an external object through a visualization/conceptualization process, nor does it create mental models of external objects, but it knows an external object by participating in the corresponding idea. For this reason, in his *Republic*, Plato argues that those artists who wield art in order to transform truth into a mental representation should be exiled from the ideal republic.

Descartes understood the significance of Bacon's empirical method, and he attempted to reverse scholastic ontology. In the field of mathematics, Descartes proposed the analytical method, and he articulated a kind of geometrical philosophical method that is *a priori*, and, yet, its foundation is not an arbitrary external (i.e., consciousness-independent)

---

22. Peltonen, ed., *The Cambridge Companion to Bacon*.
23. Plato, *Timaeus*, 27d–28a.

object, but conscious experience itself. According to Descartes, all things, including the sensible world, have an inner essence or form, whose presence explains the structure of things as they ordinarily appear. Moreover, Descartes takes for granted that, when the form is known, it exists in the mind of the knower; in other words, in the context of Cartesianism, the knower is identified with the known. Whereas Aristotle maintains that the knowledge of the form is given by real definitions of species concerning genus and specific difference, Descartes maintains that the essence of the world is given by the laws of geometry together with the principle that, in any change, quantity of motion is conserved (according to Descartes's geometrical philosophy, the previous conservation principle follows from the unchanging nature and stability of God the Creator). Two factors that expedited the formulation of criticisms against Descartes's method were Spinoza's mechanistic world-conception, which is based on Descartes's geometrical method, and the ontological excess that characterizes Leibniz's interpretation of Cartesianism.

In the history of modern philosophy, Cartesianism signals the first major philosophical shift from the study of the world to the study of the human subject. The second major philosophical shift from the study of the world to the study of the human subject in the context of the so-called modernity was due to Kantianism. Kant was impressed by David Hume's empiricism, which was formed in the context of English philosophers' elaborations on Bacon's method.[24] In the field of philosophical research, Kant's "critical" and, in reality, ambivalent attitude toward *a priori* and *a posteriori* methods (since, according to Kant, *a priori* intuitions and concepts provide some *a priori* knowledge, which, in its turn, provides the framework for *a posteriori* knowledge) underpins the two major directions that have been followed by modern philosophy ever since, namely, idealism and positivism. According to "idealism," in its modern sense, philosophy is founded exclusively on inner experience (before Kant, Descartes had already highlighted the previous concept of idealism, but Descartes did not negate the objective extension of consciousness). On the other hand, "positivism" is founded exclusively on what is regarded as certainly knowable, and, simultaneously, it discards every object that is associated with transcendentality, which is regarded as inaccessible to the human mind. Moreover, there are mixed philosophical methods, which aim at synthesizing or, at least, combining idealism and realism.

24. Laos, *The Metaphysics of World Order*, 63–70.

Hegel's dialectic—usually presented in a threefold manner, precisely, as comprising three dialectical stages of development: a thesis, giving rise to its reaction, an antithesis, which contradicts or negates the thesis, and the tension between the two being resolved by means of a synthesis—is simultaneously a method of philosophical research and a model of the process according to which, Hegel maintains, reality develops and tends toward a state of integration and wholeness. Because of the previous twofold use of the term "dialectic" by Hegel, the Hegelian dialectic is characterized by vagueness. In addition, because of the vagueness of the Hegelian dialectic, a similar kind of vagueness characterizes also those theories which are influenced by Hegelianism, and it is, to a large extent, responsible for the latters' determinism and prophetism. For instance, "scientific materialism," including both "dialectical materialism" and "historical materialism," has not managed to clarify if it is a method of philosophical research or if it only refers to particular objective processes which are interpreted by it, and, therefore, from a purely philosophical perspective, it is confusing.[25] Similarly, even though they seek to follow an *a posteriori* method, several variants of positivism, especially Auguste Comte's positivism, make the mistake of philosophically depending on an *a priori* model of a threefold advancement of human affairs, such as Comte's law of three stages,[26] whose roots can be traced back to the beliefs of Gerardo di Borgo San Donnino, an Italian thirteenth-century friar and follower of the millenarian ideas of Abbot Joachim of Fiore. Thus, ultimately, Comte's positivism failed to provide a sustainable philosophical

---

25. Heyer, *Nature, Human Nature, and Society*. Dialectical materialism is the world outlook of Marxism–Leninism, and historical materialism is the extension of the principles of dialectical materialism to the study of social life. Marx inverted Hegel's dialectic by arguing that "the ideal is nothing else than the material world reflected by the human mind and translated into forms of thought" (Marx, *Capital*, 25). In his book *A Contribution to the Critique of Political Economy* (written in 1859), Marx reformulated the determinism and the prophetism of Hegel's dialectic from a materialist perspective by arguing that "it is not consciousness of men that determines their being, but, on the contrary, their social being that determines their consciousness" (Smelser, ed., *Karl Marx*, 5).

26. In his book *The Course in Positive Philosophy*, Comte formulated the law of three stages, according to which society as a whole and each particular science develop through the following mentally conceived stages: (i) the theological stage (which, according to Comte, refers to explanation by personified deities), (ii) the metaphysical stage (which, according to Comte, refers to explanation by impersonal abstract concepts), and (iii) the positive stage (which, according to Comte, refers to scientific explanation based on observation, experiment, and comparison).

method, and it merely provided theoretical underpinnings for the development of mysticism.¹

In the twentieth century, positivism gave rise to neopositivism, which is founded on the thoughts of the so-called Vienna Circle, i.e., an association of philosophers gathered around the University of Vienna in 1922, chaired by Moritz Schlick. The Vienna Circle admitted no third category of significance besides that of *a priori* analytical and *a posteriori* synthetic statements; in particular, Kant's category of synthetic *a priori* statements was banned as having been refuted by the progress of science itself, since the theory of relativity proved that what had been held to be an example of a synthetic *a priori* system of statements, namely, Euclidean geometry, is not the global geometry of physical space. Hence, the Vienna Circle rejected the knowledge claims of metaphysics on the grounds that they are neither analytic and *a priori* nor empirical and synthetic.

The Vienna Circle's mentality is characterized by formalism, according to which any scientific discipline can be reduced to a system of formulas with symbols and of rules for the production of formulas from an axiomatic system. In the context of formalism, scientific existence and scientific truth are identical to the production from a given axiomatic system. David Hilbert, the acknowledged father of mathematical formalism, has argued as follows: "If the arbitrary posited axioms do not contradict one another or any of their consequences, they are true and the things defined by them exist. That is for me the criterion of truth and existence."² In order to apply the formalist program to geometry, Hilbert decided to develop a model of geometry based on real numbers, because the axioms of analytic geometry can be reduced to those of real numbers. Hence, the

---

1. Comte proposed a new religion of humanity; in particular, he articulated a catechism based on the worship of reason and humanity, he proposed replacing priests with a new class of scientists and industrialists, and he even developed a new solar calendar replete with positive "saints," i.e., great figures in Western European history in the fields of science, religion, politics, philosophy, industry, and literature.

2. Quoted in Laos, *Topics in Mathematical Analysis and Differential Geometry*, 95.

problem of the consistency[3] and the completeness[4] of geometry shifted to that of the real numbers and, finally, of natural numbers (on which the reals are based).

The strongest demonstration of the falsehood of the formalist viewpoint is due to the Austrian logician and mathematician Kurt Gödel. In 1931, Gödel proved the following incompleteness theorem: "In every consistent formal system Φ which contains the system of natural numbers, there exist propositions Π such that neither Π nor $\neg\Pi$ (the negation of Π) can be proved in Φ, i.e., there exist undecidable propositions."[5] Thus, because of Gödel's incompleteness theorem, "no matter which ω-consistent axiomatic system we choose, there exist propositions Π such that neither Π nor $\neg\Pi$ is provable by means of the given axioms."[6] Gödel himself drew an important corollary from his incompleteness theorem: in order to prove the consistency of any language adequate for arithmetic, one must go outside that language. In 1931, Gödel proved the following inconsistency theorem: "The consistency of any formal system Φ containing the system of natural numbers cannot be proved in the system itself."[7] In other words, according to Gödel's inconsistency theorem, "a mathematical system cannot be proved except by methods more powerful than those of the system itself."[8]

The aforementioned theorems of Gödel do not suggest that we should advocate agnosticism, but they imply that truth transcends any formalist program (including, of course, first-order logic, higher-order logic, i.e., type theory, intuitionist type theory, etc.).[9] Furthermore, in 1936, the American logician and mathematician Alonzo Church proved the following theorem: "There exists no efficient method by means of which one can determine which propositions of a consistent formal sys-

---

3. The absence of contradiction in an axiomatic system is known as consistency.

4. An axiomatic theory is said to be complete if each statement in the theory is capable of being proven true or false.

5. Laos, *Topics in Mathematical Analysis and Differential Geometry*, 96.

6. Ibid., 98. By the term "ω-consistent theory," Gödel refers to a collection of statements that is not only syntactically consistent (i.e., it does not prove a contradiction), but also avoids proving certain infinite combinations of sentences that are intuitively contradictory.

7. Ibid., 99.

8. Cohen, *Set Theory and the Continuum Hypothesis*, 3.

9. Henkin, "Completeness in the Theory of Types"; Lambek and Scott, *Introduction to Higher Order Categorical Logic*.

tem Φ containing the system of natural numbers are provable in Φ."[10] Gödel's and Church's theorems imply that the truth of mathematics is a metamathematical question, and that logic (i.e., the science of formal principles of reasoning or correct inference) can organize or formalize other scientific disciplines, but it cannot fully organize or formalize itself.

One of the most influential members of the Vienna Circle was the Austrian-British philosopher Ludwig Wittgenstein, a paradigmatic representative of analytic philosophy.[11] According to Wittgenstein's *Tractatus Logico-Philosophicus*, language, thought, and the world are all isomorphic, and philosophical problems arise from misunderstandings of the logic of language. However, Wittgenstein's linguistic formalism and Hilbert's mathematical formalism have been shattered by the aforementioned theorems of Gödel and Church. Moreover, even though analytic philosophy has helped philosophers to develop particular methods of clarifying linguistic forms that express mental processes, it tends to lead to a philosophical stalemate, since, in essence, it repeats, in a more technical manner, Kant's fruitless attempts to define the presuppositions of the presuppositions of philosophy, whose rationalist investigation may continue indefinitely (i.e., it may give rise to an infinite regress).

In addition to the aforementioned philosophies, other philosophies that were faced with difficulties when they attempted to form *a posteriori* methods are pragmatism and Bergsonism. According to pragmatism, whose most prominent representative was William James, truth, understood as the agreement between reality and its image that is present in consciousness, is not a static relation but a process that is due to the functions of consciousness, so that reality undergoes changes because of the fact that consciousness refers to reality.[12] The previous thesis is shared by every philosophy of action. However, in this way (i.e., by advocating the previous pragmatic thesis), philosophy ceases to be scientific, and, furthermore, it ceases to be a worthy cause, precisely, it becomes contradictory and self-defeating: if we adhere to pragmatism, then no conclusion of any philosophical investigation should be accepted, because, according to pragmatism itself, reality is continually being created due to the functions of consciousness, and, therefore, the conclusions of any philosophical investigation are meaningless.

10. Laos, *Topics in Mathematical Analysis and Differential Geometry*, 98–99.
11. Sluga and Stern, eds, *The Cambridge Companion to Wittgenstein*.
12. Brandom, *Perspectives on Pragmatism*.

Pragmatism is based on the philosophies of William James, Charles Pierce, and John Dewey, and it attempts to combine the rationalist thesis that the mind is always active in interpreting experience and observation with the empiricist thesis that revisions in our beliefs are to be made as a result of experience.[13] According to pragmatism, theories are underdetermined by the evidence, and, therefore, scientists have to choose between a number of theories that may all be compatible with the available evidence. Hence, as William James has put it, truth is "only the expedient in the way of belief," meaning that we need to adjust our ideas as to what is true as experience unfolds. Pragmatism, then, defines what is true as what is most useful in the way of belief (a utilitarian epistemology). However, pragmatism is ultimately self-defeating. Even though pragmatism appears to reflect a dynamic attitude toward reality and epistemology and to be a progressive epistemological stance, it is profoundly narrow-minded and assigns a deeply passive role to the human spirit. By stressing the adaptation of our ideas to an unfolding experience, pragmatists ignore the dynamic continuity between the reality of the historical world and the reality of consciousness, a dynamic continuity that allows conscious beings to impose their intentionality on historical reality, instead of merely adapting to a reality that is external to their consciousness. Conscious beings are not merely obliged to look for methods of adaptation to historical reality, but they can utilize and restructure historical reality according to their intentionality.

During his attempt to form an *a posteriori* method, Henri-Louis Bergson, whose philosophy has exerted an important influence on the final formation of pragmatism, faced important difficulties, too. According to Bergson, the only reality is duration, and the conception of duration can be achieved through intuition. Bergsonian intuition is always an intuition of duration, and it consists in entering into the thing, rather than going around it from the outside. For this reason, Bergson calls intuition "sympathy."[14] Bergsonian intuition is an *a posteriori* method,

---

13. Misak, ed. *Pragmatism*.

14. Bergson, *The Creative Mind*, 159. According to Bergson, our experience of sympathy begins with our putting ourselves in the place of others. Moreover, Bergson argues that intuition enables us to transcend the divisions of the different schools of philosophy like rationalism and empiricism or idealism and realism. Bergsonism and pragmatism maintain that the antinomies of philosophical concepts and positions result from the habitual way human intelligence works. According to Bergson, intuition reverses the habitual working of intelligence, which is analytic (synthesis being only a development of analysis), and this reversal of habitual intelligence is called "the turn

but its only difference from the *a priori* methods is that its object, which is an inner experience, is identified with consciousness. At this point, it becomes clear that inherent in Bergsonism is an inverted Cartesianism, which is an antinomy, since Bergson formulates his anti-rationalist and anti-Cartesian arguments in a rationalist and Cartesian way. However, Bergson's most important philosophical achievement is that he realized and emphasized that the major object of philosophical enquiry lies beyond the phenomena from which scientific knowledge starts, and, contrary to Kant's arguments, it is accessible to consciousness. At this point, it becomes clear that Bergson's intuitionist *a posteriori* method has important similarities with Edmund Husserl's phenomenological *a posteriori* method.[15]

The term phenomenology has been coined by Hegel. In the context of Hegel's philosophy, phenomenology refers to Hegel's conception of the itinerary of spirit, which is actualized in history. According to Hegel, "spirit" is "the subject that has returned to itself," and "this subject exists as a people, and its spirit is the national spirit."[16] On the other hand, according to Husserl—who starts from a Cartesian position combined with scholastic views—phenomenology consists in a continuous attempt of consciousness to remove from reality all those acquired features that conceal its core and to gaze at pure essences (*Wesenschau*).[17] In other words, Husserl's phenomenological consciousness tends to look past the empirical facts, and it neglects the existential otherness of the person in favor of the abstract universal. Therefore, Husserl's phenomenology should not be confused with classical Platonism, since, as I have already emphasized, Plato's ideas are not concepts (abstract generalizations), and the knowledge of Plato's ideas consists in a peculiar spiritual sensation which presupposes psychic cleansing. Phenomenology has exerted an important influence on existentialism, and the latter has adopted phenomenology as its method.

In the twentieth century, phenomenology was applied in the study of the most distant elements of reality whose knowledge precedes the essence of reality; these elements constitute the structure of reality. In the context of modern philosophy, the term "structure" refers to an inner

---

of experience"; Bergson, *Matter and Memory*, 184–85.

15. For an extensive introductory discussion of the principal works of the classical phenomenologists, see Moran, *Introduction to Phenomenology*.

16. Laos, *The Metaphysics of World Order*, 84.

17. Ibid., 98–101.

reality that is being organized and reorganized by itself, and it is conditioned by its own order, which also constitutes its own core. The term structure has originally been used in physics, biology, and linguistics; ethnology, sociology, and philosophy have borrowed this term from linguistics. The acknowledged father of structural linguistics is Ferdinand de Saussure. In Ferdinand de Saussure's *Cours de Linguistique Générale* (compiled by Charles Bally and Albert Sechehaye from notes on lectures given by Ferdinand de Saussure at the University of Geneva between 1906 and 1911), linguistic analysis is focused not on the use of language (called *parole*, or speech), but on the underlying system of language (called *langue*), and, therefore, this approach examines how the elements of language relate to each other in the present, i.e., synchronically rather than diachronically.[18]

Heidegger, the most prominent representative of existentialism, attempted to break with the thought of his predecessors in the history of modern philosophy and to eliminate the metaphysical foundations of the modern subject. In Heidegger's philosophy, Being is the openness of a relation to otherness, being (*Sein*) is constitutively being-with (*Mit-Sein*). Therefore, in Heidegger's philosophy, Being is a principle without ontological substance, the most proper problem of Being is the other, and the Present exists as a structure and not as subjective consciousness. The previous arguments of Heidegger seem to express a methexiological quest, but this is not true. As I have already argued, methexiology, being founded on the metaphysical principles and pursuits of Plato, Aristotle, and the Hesychasts, is focused on the communion between the human being and the Absolute (God), and this communion is a personal methexiological experience, in the context of which man is open to the "Other" (God), he participates in the "Other" (God), and, therefore, he achieves to improve his existential conditions and to become ontologically integrated and whole through non-temporal means. On the other hand, Heidegger proposes a profane and time-dependent method of transcending one's existential conditions.

Heidegger is aware of the philosophical problems that his predecessors faced throughout the history of modern philosophy, and he argues that the previous stalemate can be overcome by understanding Being[19]

---

18. Harris, *Reading Saussure*.

19. In the context of Heidegger's philosophy, the word Being with capital B indicates Heidegger's analysis of being as activity, i.e., as the cause of individual entities (beings with small b). For more details, see Heidegger, *Basic Writings*.

as otherness, which discloses the truth of a new possibility of existence through a direct and unmediated awareness of the Present. Therefore, Heidegger tries to remove every element associated with the consciousness of the external world from the ego, because, even indirectly, such elements connect the ego with a transcendent reality. According to Heidegger, the Present should be understood as the structure of existence, and not as consciousness of existence, and, furthermore, for him, the Present is the event on which the understanding of Being is founded. In this way, Heidegger believes that he has achieved to eliminate the thinking subject of Western metaphysics, whose paradigmatic representatives are Kant and Descartes. But, contrary to Heidegger's expectations, the subject cannot be eliminated in the previous way, because, in a rather subconscious way, the subject participates in every philosophy whose most proper problem is the subject. In particular, in his philosophy, Heidegger eliminated the subject as a syllogistic, or representational, certainty, but, ultimately, the subject is restored in Heidegger's philosophy, because Heidegger's endeavor is to substitute the "ego" with the "I am." In the context of Cartesianism, the power of the subject is founded on Descartes's resolution "cogito ergo sum" (I think therefore I am). In the context of Heidegger's philosophy, the subjectivism of the Cartesian "cogito" is replaced with the subjectivism of the Heideggerian "I am," and, thus, the modern subject (even indirectly, or subconsciously) is still present in Heidegger's philosophy. The ego as individuality (otherness) is the core of the reality of the manifestation of the Heideggerian Being in the Present (*Dasein*). It is exactly for the previous reason that Heidegger's philosophy (which, to a large extent, can be considered as a form of inverted Cartesianism) is an integral part of modern Western philosophy and philosophically alien to Plato, Aristotle, and Hesychasm.

In contrast to Heidegger's philosophy, Plato, Aristotle, and the Hesychasts understand *theoria* as the entelechy of philosophy, and, as Aristotle writes in his *Metaphysics* Λ.1–9, *theoria* (wisdom, or first philosophy) is not concerned with the learning, knowledge, or discovery of truth, but it is an active orientation of the mind toward a truth with which the mind is already familiar, i.e., it is an active orientation of the mind toward the divine reality. Thus, Aristotle equates pleasure with the energy of *theoria* and not with the acquisition of knowledge. Furthermore, according to Aristotle's *Metaphysics* (Book Lambda), *theoria* is superior to "knowledge," exactly due to the fact that the first is concerned with the divine reality, whereas the latter is exhausted in human reason. Thus, *theoria* is achieved through man's "mental eye" (and is related to spiritual intuition), whereas knowledge is merely founded on and derived from the subject. The "subject" is a historical being filled with reason and will, and, more precisely, a historical actor capable of acting on the basis of reason and will. In order to obtain an integrated understanding of methexiology's approach to being and *theoria*, one must study the modes of being—both God's modes of being (since, as I have already argued God is the source of the significance of being) and man's modes of being; this will be my task in chapter 3.

3

The Modes of Being

As I argued in chapter 2, the verbal form "to be" and the present participle "being" correspond to different concrete presences: the present participle "being" refers to a system consisting of qualities that can be identified and attributed to it; the verbal form "to be" refers to a situation of which a being partakes in an absolutely positive way (hence, we call it a real being), or in an absolutely negative way (hence, we call it a real non-being), or in any other possible way that corresponds to an intermediate ontological degree. Each degree is a mode of being. In his *Sophist* 254d–e, Plato discerns the following *summa genera*: motion, rest, "the same," "the other," and relation (between them), which Aristotle would call categories of being, and which correspond to modes of being. Aristotle argues that being exists according to its substance, according to its form, according to the relation between substance and form, according to its time, according to its space, according to its activity, and according to its passivity. In the context of methexiology, the logos of being is simultaneously the effective and the final cause of being, and truth is the disclosure of the logos of being.

According to Plato, "real beings" are the ideas, which are universal and transcendent realities to which phenomena are reducible; between the real being (i.e., the idea) and the real non-being (i.e., the phenomenon) there are intermediate ontological levels, at which the being of things is confirmed to different degrees. Thus, Plato's theory of ideas should not be regarded as an idealist philosophy in the modern sense of the term, because, as I argued in chapter 2, in the context of modern philosophy, "idealism" refers to all those philosophies that emphasize the extension of consciousness in the real world. On the other hand, according to the terminology of modern philosophy, Plato's theory of ideas is a realist philosophy, in the sense that, according to Plato, ideas are realities *par excellence*, i.e., they are independent of consciousness. For the same reason, Hegel's reference to the Idea—which he defines as universal reason, which manifests itself in nature, in individuals, in right/law, in morality, and in custom—should not be regarded as a variety of idealism, because Hegel attributes reality to the Idea.[1] However, Plato's ontology can, arguably, be characterized as a partially idealist philosophy, not on ontological grounds, but on epistemological grounds, because, according to Plato's *Meno*, *Republic* VII, and *Symposium*, ideas are accessible to consciousness; more specifically, they are inherent in the soul, and, through the exercise of memory, they emerge into the forefront of consciousness, so that one comes to know reality itself.

As I mentioned in chapter 1, according to Aristotle, being exists according to its substance, which is the material mode of being, and the material mode of being, which is a quantitative attribute, is supplemented by the formal mode of being, which is a qualitative attribute, and it is due to the species. In addition to the previous two modes of being, Aristotle has also discerned the effective and the final modes of being. For instance, let us consider a bronze pot: bronze is the pot's material cause, the pot's formal cause is the element that makes it a pot and not, for instance, a statue, the pot's effective cause is the craftsman who has created it, and the pot's use is its final cause and its purpose.

The aforementioned four modes of being are not the only ones. In chapter 1, I mentioned that Aristotle has also discerned "being potentially" and "being actually." In order to understand the potential mode of being and the actual mode of being, one must clarify another mode of being, that is, the relation between substance and form. In the language of modern philosophy, the relation between substance and form is called the structure of being, and it is the program of a being that tends toward a state of integration and wholeness in accordance with its final cause. The structure of being determines the rational, free, and unique arrangement of the internal and the external elements of being, whose coexistence is clearly expressed through and according to the corresponding structure.

---

1. Laos, *The Metaphysics of World Order*, 83.

Moreover, structure enables being to adapt to changes without changing itself.

According to Aristotle, form is the sensible surface, or constitution, of a thing, and it corresponds to its definition. In order to refer to the outline of a thing, Aristotle uses the term *schema* (shape), and he emphasizes the conceptual difference between the terms "form" and "shape." If Aristotle had identified "form" with "shape," he would be compelled to accept "shape" as the effective cause of being and to discard truth as species. However, because, as I argued in chapters 1 and 2, the scholastics' approach to classical Greek philosophy was conditioned by problematic indirect sources[2] (such as Boethius's *Commentary on Porphyry's Introduction*), scholasticism, contrary to Aristotle, discarded truth as species, because it interpreted form as a substantial mode of being, i.e., as a principle that is opposite to matter, and it postulated that the existence of being is due to its form, thus reducing shape to form. According to Aristotle, form is the energy, or the life of matter, but scholasticism assigns individual spiritual substance to form, and, therefore, it maintains a sharp distinction between form and matter. In other words, from the perspective of scholasticism, form is not a universal attribute of being, but it is merely an individual attribute, and, ultimately, it is subjugated to individual sensation, which, having ceased to be an image of its object, is merely a consequence of the intentionality of consciousness.

In Aristotle's philosophy, form is equated with species, and it is an enhypostatic (i.e., personalized) natural symbol; it is neither an unsubstantial nor a self-subsistent symbolic representation. By contrast, in the context of scholasticism, form is autonomous from the substantial mode of being, and it becomes a kind of "sign" (i.e., a symbolic representation), which is a product of thought and an underpinning of individuation, clearly separate from impersonal matter. Thus, ultimately, in the context of Western civilization, form ceased to have a consciousness-independent dimension, it became associated only with the subject, and the subject started creating one's own forms. Because of the logical reformulation of form, i.e., because of the total separation of form from matter, in the context of Western civilization, form became a garment of thought (i.e., the content of form was reduced to thought), whereas, in the context of

---

2. Until about 1125, medieval Western thinkers had access to only a few original texts of ancient Greek philosophy, mainly a portion of Aristotle's logic, and, they were intellectually confined to a few problematic textbooks and translations of ancient Greek philosophical books.

classical Aristotelianism, form was a garment of life. Moreover, because of the logical reformulation of form, what is significant to the Western subject is not the truth of the thing *per se*—since, for the Western subject, "reality" and "truth" are distinct and separate from each other—but the subject's representations (*conceptus*, or *intellectio rei*), precisely, the form that the subject's imagination gives to the matter of the inner and the external worlds.

According to Thomas Aquinas, knowledge presupposes a "correspondence between the thing and the intellect" (*adaequatio rei et intellectus*), and he calls the previous correspondence "truth." Such a truth may be a formal one or an essential one; a truth is said to be formal if it refers to the consistency between different logical terms, and it is said to be essential if it refers to the agreement between sensible or mental objects and the meanings that they represent in the subject's consciousness. Therefore, from Thomas Aquinas onward, the West has been dignifying the creation of forms as an expression of individual consciousness. The culmination of the previous tendency was the so-called modern Western philosophy, which, in the second half of the twentieth century, started exhibiting self-destructive tendencies in the context of the so-called postmodernity, which is characterized by an unrestrained abstraction of form.[3]

In contradistinction to the Western thought, Aristotle argues that physical beings (the celestial spheres), conforming to the universal eros, imitate the divine mode of life through their physical motion, which is "perfect and eternal," i.e., cyclical.[4] Man, in his turn, can reach existential fullness through his participation in the world. In his *Republic* 500c, Plato argues that geometry, to which physical bodies conform, ensures that these perfect beings, in imitation of the divine mode of life, are righteous to each other. By contemplating the order and the harmony of the universe, ancient Greek philosophy discovered a manifestation of causal necessity and simultaneously a manifestation of divine justice, whose infinite creative and destructive power consists in a combination of opposite forces and, hence, in the eternity of the universe.

Plato, in his *Laws* A638b, and Aristotle, in his *Politics* 1289b25, argue that justice is like life, in general: it saves whatever it can be preserved, and it destroys whatever it is destined to be eliminated. Additionally,

---

3. Laos, *The Metaphysics of World Order*, chapter 3.
4. Aristotle, *Physics* 265a25.

Plato argues that justice preserves the existence of the world, since it is the source of "law and order that are marked by limit," and, for this reason, sometimes, the role of law and order is lifesaving, while, other times, it is destructive.[5] This dual role of justice—which is simultaneously creative and destructive—lies at the core of ancient Greek tragedy. As we read in Aeschylus's *Choephoroe* 595, and in Sophocles's *Antigone* 372, man is a worrisome and awesome being because of his overweening *phrenes* (mind), precisely, because of his *hubris* (extreme pride or self-confidence), which urges him to disturb and endanger the relations that constitute the cosmic order. The tragic element of life emerges when the human will, due to its arbitrariness and excesses, conflicts with justice, thus bringing about *nemesis* (divine retribution), as in the cases of Eteocles and Oedipus. When man does not adhere to justice, he experiences his own destruction, because, as Heraclitus has argued, law, whose presence is eternal, exterminates *hubris*. In other words, in the context of ancient Greek tragedy, *catharsis* (purification or cleansing) is the means through which cosmic equilibrium and a sense of eternity are restored.

From the perspective of ancient Greek philosophy, *theoria*, "theoretical life," is the noblest ideal of life. According to ancient Greek philosophy, *theoria* means direct knowledge of the eternal being and union with it. Moreover, theoretical life means love of wisdom (i.e., it is the philosopher's life), and wisdom is the beginning and the result of the enquiries of that philosophizing consciousness which gazes at and familiarizes itself with the totality of the being of the world, and, together with the gods, it experiences mental pleasures. Aristotle argues that the human mind is not only active but also receptive, and that man can access the deity through the perfection of the human mind and through the mental vigilance that is caused by *eudemonia* (a state of having a good indwelling spirit and being healthy and prosperous).[6]

However, the aforementioned *theoria*, or theoretical life, was, philosophically, the terminal point of ancient Greek philosophy. Ancient Greek philosophers realized that the highest level of *eudemonia* is theoretical life, precisely, a state in which one's mind is open to infinity, but they also realized that, without the finite and perishable material body, the mind is inviable; therefore, ultimately, ancient Greek philosophers became aware of a tragic chasm between the "absolute" and the "relative,"

---

5. Plato, *Philebus* 26b.
6. *Nicomachean Ethics* 1177a20–21 and *Metaphysics* 1072b18–24.

or between "universality" and "particularity." In the context of ancient Greek philosophy, the more the human mind moves toward the Absolute, which transcends the perishable and relative realm, the more painful the awareness of the weak and perishable nature of the human being becomes. Aristotle argues that theoretical life may "be held to be the only activity that is loved for its own sake" (since "it produces no result beyond the actual act of *theoria*, whereas from practical pursuits we look to secure some advantage, greater or smaller, beyond the action itself"), but he also argues that man cannot live continuously in a state of pure *theoria*, since man's nature is composite (being composed of mind and body), and, thus, man mainly lives in accordance with the logic of "human life" and not in accordance with "theoretical life."[7] In other words, the human spirit is oriented toward the *eudemonia* of the mind, but man, as a mortal being, lives in a historical society and socializes with other men. Thus, the more man experiences the *eudemonia* of the mind, the more intensely he feels the pain of death. Additionally, Aristotle argues that, on the one hand, the existence of the human being is vindicated when man, through his mind, is united with the ultimate cause of the world, namely, with God, who is pure energy and intelligence, but, on the other hand, humans cannot bridge the chasm between man and God by their own means and capabilities.[8] Hence, faced with the previous irrationality of life, man's spirit cannot find peace, since human life is divided between theoretical life (the realm of spiritual freedom and mental *eudemonia*) and practical life (the realm of material necessity and historical action).

Furthermore, the ancient Greek concept of *theoria* was the major philosophical underpinning of both the individuation and the socialization of the ancient Greek person, in the sense that the experience of *theoria* was a source of a dual sense of individual value and communion. However, ancient Greek philosophers were contemplating God and the world with regard to their essences, and they were identifying essence with its presence, so that they were bringing God under the domination of the world's essence, and they were identifying freedom with the causal necessity that pervades the world's essence. Ancient Greek philosophy attempted to deduce the knowledge of God from the knowledge of the cosmic order (e.g., in Plato's *Timaeus*, the "Demiurge" is subject to the cosmic order), and ancient Greek psychology was founded on the thesis

---

7. Aristotle, *Nicomachean Ethics* 1177b.
8. Ibid.

that the soul is an immortal substance living within a mortal body. Therefore, even though ancient Greek philosophers were highlighting human freedom of will, their notion of freedom of will could not transcend the cosmic order, and, therefore, it could not lead to real spiritual freedom. By the term "real spiritual freedom," I do not refer to one's egoistical self-affirmation. In the context of methexiology, as I understand and propose it in this book, "real spiritual freedom" means that one surrenders his ego to God in order to participate in God's freedom through God's uncreated grace. From the perspective of ancient Greek philosophy, the soul's freedom is naturally determined (i.e., it is necessarily harmonized with the cosmic rhythm), and, therefore, it is imperfect, and it gives rise to a tragic sense of irrationality.

By discovering *theoria*, the ancient Greeks arrived at an awareness whose consequences were philosophically and psychologically unbearable to them. Ancient Greek philosophy discovered the life of the spirit, but it could not ensure the unity of spiritual life, since, according to Aristotle's *Nicomachean Ethics* 1178a9–1179a16, human life is divided between theoretical life and practical life. Moreover, even though classical Greek philosophers were aware of the soul's freedom of will, they could not overcome the antinomy between the soul's freedom of will and the cosmic order. Therefore, ancient Greek philosophy arrived at a stalemate. In order to overcome the previous stalemate, to which it arrived as a consequence of its own achievements, ancient Greek philosophy was vitally in need of a logos (that is, of an effective and final cause of being) which would be substantially free from the logic of the material world, and, simultaneously, could be united with the material world. The Christian faith, which is founded on the doctrine of the Incarnation of the divine Logos, provides ultimate answers to ancient Greek philosophy's ultimate questions, and, for this reason, the ancient Greek world was Christianized, and ancient Greek philosophy underpins the theology of the Greek church fathers.

Classical Greek culture, particularly the philosophies of Plato and Aristotle, gave birth to philosophical theology, as an alternative to both Jewish prophetic theology and ancient mystery cults. Therefore, the Christianization of the ancient Greeks was an event of immense historical significance, and it prescribed the domination of Christianity in the Roman Empire, since the Greek culture was the dominant cultural force in the Roman Empire. The importance of the Christianization of the Greeks has been emphasized by Jesus Christ himself: according to

John 12:20–23, when Andrew and Philip informed Jesus that there were some Greeks who would like to see and worship him, he replied as follows: "The hour has come for the Son of Man to be glorified." Moreover, Clement of Alexandria argues that "the same God that furnished both the Covenants was the giver of Greek philosophy to the Greeks, by which the Almighty is glorified among the Greeks."[9]

Methexiology is founded on the philosophies of Plato and Aristotle and on the works of the Greek church fathers. For this reason, it emphasizes that God exists at three different levels, which are three modes of being: at the level of His essence, at the level of His hypostases, and at the level of His energies. As regards His essence, God is *totally unknowable and inaccessible* to humanity. God's essence is uncreated, whereas the essence of creation (i.e., of the created world, including the essence of the human being) is created, and, therefore, at the level of the essence of being, there is an ontological discontinuity between God and every other being. In other words, humans cannot be united with God's essence. God's essence is *totally inconceivable*. Since God's essence transcends any possible characterization, and since, in respect of God's essence, God is neither finite nor infinite, the only argument that a human being can put forward with regard to God's essence is that God is a kind of inconceivable nothing, the positive void from which the significance of every being and thing is derived.[10] Hence, in the Bible, in Isaiah 55:9–10, we read: "For my thoughts are not your thoughts, neither are your ways my ways, declares the LORD. As the heavens are higher than the earth, so are my ways higher than your ways and my thoughts than your thoughts." Furthermore, in respect of the total unknowability of God's essence, and since God is not constrained by any substantial mode of being, God should not be regarded as *a* "being," and, indeed, He should not be regarded as the "Supreme Being," either (since God is the source of "being," and, therefore, He is naturally *above* "being"). In respect of the total unknowability

---

9. Clement, *Stromata* VI.5–6.

10. The Hesychasts argue that the only thing that humans can think and say about God's essence is that it is a kind of inconceivable nothing, and, in this way, they emphasize that humans can only access God's mode of being by *transcending human reason*. In the Jewish *Kabbalah*, Kether (literally, "Crown"), i.e., the purest level of existence, is a subtle being of which human thought can grasp nothing, and it is designated as "Ain," which, in Hebrew, means nothingness; Scholem, *Major Trends in Jewish Mysticism*. Avoiding speculation about parallel development, the similarities between the Hesychasts' teachings about the transcendence of God's essence and the Kabbalists' teachings about the transcendence of Kether are too obvious to be ignored.

of God's essence, God can be perceived only as the positive void from which the significance of every being and thing is derived, i.e., as the *ex nihilo* Creator of every being.

At the level of God's hypostases, God exists as a communion of three hypostases, namely: Nous (Mind), Logos, and Spirit; this is the Trinitarian doctrine, which I expounded in chapter 1. God himself is present in Himself;[11] the three divine hypostases are naturally, totally, eternally, and inextricably joined to each other, and they are totally and essentially present in each other, since they are connatural to each other, without, however, being confused. God the Father is the first Nous, as the *ex nihilo* Creator of everything, and His Logos is connatural to Him and coeternal with his Spirit. The divine Nous is hypostatically different but not separate from the Logos or the Spirit, because the divine nature is undivided, and the three hypostases are united without being confused. Thus, even though the divine Nous naturally begets (or generates) the Logos, He is not separate from the Logos, because He is not separate from Himself. The Holy Spirit proceeds from the divine Nous and is present in, coeternal with and connatural to the Logos. Thus, the Holy Spirit is hypostatically different but not separate from the divine Nous. A hypostatic union between God and humanity (i.e., a union of God's nature and human nature in one hypostasis) occurred only once, namely, in the person of Jesus Christ, the Incarnate Logos of God;[12] therefore, Jesus Christ is the Person (i.e., the person *par excellence*) through whom God's love was manifested in the historical, material world.

The Orthodox church's doctrine of the Holy Trinity was officially declared by the First Council of Nicaea (i.e., the First Ecumenical Council), in 325 AD. According to this doctrine—which is philosophically underpinned by the Greek philosophical notion of hypostasis, properly

11. John 5:26.

12. The following biblical passages emphasize the divine nature of Jesus Christ: Matthew 3:13–17; 11:27; 16:16–17; 17:5; 20:19; 22:41; 28:20; Mark 1:9–11; 9:3; 10:34; Luke 1:35; 3:21–22; 4:3–9; 18:33; John 1:1–14; 14:9; 1 John 2:23; 5:20; Revelation 5:6, 8, 13; 12:10; 19:16; 21:6; 22:13; Romans 1:3; 9:5; Galatians 4:4; Ephesians 4:13; Philippians 2:6; Colossians 1:12; 2:9; Hebrews 1:1; 2:5; 5:5; James 1:1; 2:1; 4:12; 2 Peter 1:1, 3, 16; 3:2; Jude 5, 14, 21. The following biblical passages emphasize the human nature of Jesus Christ: Matthew 1:20–23; 4:3–4; Mark 14:35–36; Luke 23:45; 24:36–43; John 1:14; Romans 1:3; 7:3; 9:5; 2 Corinthians 5:21; 8:9; 13:4; Galatians 2:17; 4:4; Philippians 3:10; Colossians 1:24; 1 Timothy 3:16; Hebrews 1:5. Moreover, references to the historical Jesus Christ can be found in several historical books written by Roman historians, namely: Tacitus, *Annales* 15:14; Suetonius, *Vita Neronis* 16:2, and *Vita Claudii* 25:4; Plinius, *Epistle* 10:96; Josephus, *Antiquities of the Jews* 28:33.

interpreted by the Greek church fathers in the context of the New Testament[13]—any given trait must be common to all Persons of the Holy Trinity, or else it must be unique to one of them. In particular, according to the Orthodox church's Triadology, fatherhood is unique to the Father, begottedness is unique to the Son, procession is unique to the Holy Spirit, and Godhood is common to all.

On the other hand, in the ninth century AD, Charlemagne, an illiterate and megalomaniac king of the Franks, convened a local church council in Aachen in 809–10, where he affirmed the doctrinal innovation of the *Filioque* (Latin for "and from the Son") as regards the procession of the Holy Spirit. According to the original Nicene Creed (as adopted in 325 AD by the First Ecumenical Council), the Holy Spirit proceeds from the Father (divine Nous), and the term "proceeds" signifies the particular personal relationship between the Holy Spirit and the Father and not an authoritarian hierarchy. As a consequence of the doctrinal innovation of the *Filioque*, the Holy Spirit becomes a subordinate member of the Holy Trinity, and the Holy Trinity becomes an authoritarian Neoplatonic-like hierarchical system. The argument that the trait of being the source of the Holy Spirit's procession can be shared by only two Persons of the Trinity, namely, by the Father and the Son, implies that those two Persons are superior to the third Person, and, therefore, the balance of unity and diversity is overturned. In 810, Pope Leo III rejected the doctrinal innovation of the *Filioque*, but, in 1014, at the request of the German King Henry II, who had come to Rome to be crowned Emperor, Pope Benedict VIII—who owed to Henry his restoration to the Papal throne after the deposition of Antipope Gregory VI—approved the inclusion of the *Filioque* in the Latin Creed used in the church of Rome.

The reasons for the approval of the doctrinal innovation of the *Filioque* by medieval Western churches were the following: First, as I have already argued, medieval Western rationalism was based on Boethius's Neoplatonism, and it was treating Platonic ideas as if they were logical substances, thus equating the degree of generality with the degree of reality. Because of the previous misinterpretations of classical Greek philosophy by medieval Western scholars, and because, until the eleventh century AD, medieval Western Europe had poor access to classical

---

13. In the New Testament, explanations of the Holy Trinity can be found in Mark 1:10–11; John 15:26; and Acts 1:4–5. Moreover, in Matthew 28:19, Jesus Christ's words affirm the reality of the Holy Trinity. The role of the Holy Trinity in salvation is mentioned in Romans 5:5–6.

Greek philosophy, the initiators of the doctrinal innovation of the *Filioque* drew an analogy between the Holy Trinity and their own rationalist Neoplatonic thought. In particular, implicit in the doctrinal innovation of the *Filioque* is an analogy between the Persons of the Holy Trinity and logical concepts endowed with substance, so that, from the perspective of the advocates of the doctrinal innovation of the *Filioque*, the Father somehow corresponds to a logical substance that is more general than the Son, the Son somehow corresponds to a logical substance that is more general than the Holy Spirit, and, therefore, the Holy Spirit somehow corresponds to a logical substance that is subordinate to the Father and the Son. The second reason for the approval of the doctrinal innovation of the *Filioque* by medieval Western churches was that the New Testament and the Nicene Creed were originally written in Greek, and many medieval Western theologians were unable to understand the difference between the Greek concepts *ekporēvete*, meaning "proceeds," and *pēmbete*, meaning "is sent." According to the original texts of the Nicene Creed and the New Testament, particularly, John 15:26, the Holy Spirit *ekporēvete* (i.e., proceeds) from the Father and *pēmbete* (i.e., is sent) through the Son. The third reason for the approval of the doctrinal innovation of the *Filioque* by medieval Western churches was Charlemagne's and other German kings' intention to disparage Byzantine spirituality and control the Christian church, in general.[14] Thus, the *Filioque* clause was one of the major causes of the Great Schism (also known as the East–West Schism) in 1054 AD. However, in the twentieth century, several Western churches officially admitted that the *Filioque* clause was a mistake. The Lambeth Conference called on the churches of the Anglican Communion to shed the *Filioque* from future copies of the Book of Common Prayer, first in 1978 and then again in 1988 and 1998. Moreover, the 1994 General Convention of the Episcopal church resolved to delete the *Filioque* from the Nicene Creed in the next edition of the Prayer Book.

Apart from the levels of His essence and His hypostases, God also exists at the level of His energies. At the level of God's energies, God exists in His actions, and He is knowable to humans through His natural energy. In particular, when we use such terms as God's providence, God's love, God's goodness, God's omnipresence, God's omniscience, God's omnipotence, etc., we refer to God's energies. The presence of God in His energies is substantial, i.e., God is substantially present in His energies.

---

14. Meyendorff, *The Orthodox Church*.

Thus, the presence of God in His energies should not be interpreted as the active presence of a cause in its consequences. In contradistinction to created beings, God's energies are not consequences of the divine Cause. God's energies have not been created out of nothing, but they emanate, ceaselessly and eternally, from the essence of the Holy Trinity. In other words, God's energies and God's essence are equally divine, but, whereas God's essence is totally inaccessible to humans, we can participate in God's energies. God's energies disclose the mode of God's being, apart from God's essence. Humanity's participation in God's energies is the pure, real theology, and it consists in the deification of man through God's energies, which are collectively referred to as God's uncreated grace.

The term "to create" refers to God's energies, whereas the term "to generate" refers to God's essence. The distinction between God's essence and God's energies corresponds to the distinction between the progression of the three divine Persons and the creation of the world. All created beings are consequences of God's energies. The sensible universe, being a created reality, neither emanates from God's essence nor unfolds from its own essence. If created beings were identical to divine energies themselves, then either created beings would be uncreated, which is absurd, or God would not have energy prior to created beings, which is an irreverent thought that diminishes God's creativity. God has been active and omnipotent before all ages. Therefore, created beings are not God's energies, but consequences of God's energies. God's energies are uncreated and coeternal with God. Moreover, God's energies cannot be known through speculations about God's essence, but, on the contrary, God's energies inform us that God's essence exists, without, however, revealing what God's essence actually *is*. Hence, we know God not through His essence, but through His providence.

In Christianity, personhood (hypostasis) takes precedence over essence, and, therefore, God is not constrained by His essence, He is free from every essential determination, because He exists personally (hypostatically), and He is the Creator of everything out of nothing (*ex nihilo*). As I have already mentioned, from the perspective of ancient Greek philosophy, the soul's freedom is naturally determined. On the other hand, from the perspective of the Greek church fathers, particularly the Hesychasts, freedom is a matter of personal choice, and it is experienced through one's relationship with God and with his fellow-humans, i.e., through the transformation of a natural individual into an ecclesiastical person, where "ecclesiastical person" means a person in communion with his fellow-humans and with God in the context of the mystery of Eucharist.

Cyril of Alexandria has argued that "the divine nature is ineffable and cannot be comprehended by us in its fullest possible form, but only in what it accomplishes and effects."[15] Similarly, in his *Letter* 234 to Amphilochius, Basil the Great writes about the distinction between the essence and the energies of God: let us consider the question, "Do you worship what you know or what you do not know?" If one answers that he worships what he knows, then others would reply to him, "What is the essence of the object of worship?" Then, if one confesses that he is ignorant of the essence, the others would turn on him again and say, "so you worship you know not what." Therefore, in his previous letter, Basil the Great argues that "the word 'to know' has many meanings," and he explains that "we say that we know the greatness of God, His power, His wisdom, His goodness, His providence over us, and the justness of His judgment; but not His very essence." In other words, Basil the Great argues, humans cannot know the absolutely transcendent essence of God, but this does not mean that they are ignorant of God, since they can know His "operations," which "come down to us," even though "His essence remains beyond our reach."

Maximus the Confessor uses the concepts of infinity and God's ontologically grounded freedom in order to explain and defend the doctrine of the unknowability of God's essence. In particular, in his *Mystagogia* 5, Maximus the Confessor argues that "the wonderful grandeur of God's infinity is without quantity or parts, and completely without dimension, and offers no grip to take hold of it and to know what it is in its essence." Moreover, talking about the nature of the infinity, Maximus the Confessor argues as follows: "if no kind of essential difference can exist from eternity as the infinite's other, then the infinite can be in no way receptive of duality."[16] Therefore, no concept can be assigned to God's essence. However, in his *Mystagogia* 5, Maximus emphasizes that, even though no created being can circumscribe the Creator or be on par with Him, the "divine activity" (i.e., God's energy) is not divided from the one God, but God is "shared without division," and this reflects the "simplicity and indivisibility" of God's natural energy.

---

15. Cyril of Alexandria, *Commentary on John* 3.2 (*Patrologia Graeca*, Vol. 73, 259D–260A). Cyril of Alexandria was the Patriarch of Alexandria from 412 to 444 AD and a prolific writer. He is venerated as a saint in both Eastern and Western Christianity.

16 Maximus, *Ambiguum* 10; *Patrologia Graeca*, Vol. 91, 1185A.

The created world exists within a spatio-temporal framework. In general, humans perceive time as a succession of states through which being passes. Thus, time seems to be intimately related to being itself, and, for Aristotle, it is one of the modes of being. In contrast to eternity, which is the continuous substratum of the movement of being, time (i.e., a means by which the movement of being is measured) is not continuous, but it consists of segments that are infinitely divisible by consciousness. Thus, time is not so much an aspect or dimension of the reality of the world as a measuring instrument used by consciousness when the latter attempts to determine reality. However, Isaac Newton construes time as an undeniable objective reality according to which consciousness relates to the world. Moreover, Kant argues that time is an *a priori* schema according to which consciousness both locates the world within the realm of consciousness and assigns a knowable constitution or order to the world.[17]

In his psychological treatises, the epistemologist Jean Piaget has shown that the conception of time develops within consciousness and in parallel with the latter: initially, the conception of time does not refer to a unified time, but to a collection of particular conceptions of time, which are different from one another, and each of them performs different functions in consciousness; consciousness refers to a particular conception of time when it wants to integrate a particular experience into it, and the previous particular conceptions of time are gradually united only during later stages of development.[18] In a sense, Piaget's theory of time is an extension of Bergson's theory of time, which is based on comparing time with duration. According to Bergson, duration is the only undeniable reality, and it constitutes both the substratum of the reality of consciousness and the substratum of the reality of the world; however, unlike eternity, duration is not infinite, and one can perceive duration through a logical concept, just as one can perceive the practical substitute of duration, namely, time, through a conceptual alteration.[19]

In the context of Bergsonism, duration is a continuous flow that can be perceived neither logically nor empirically, but only through intuition, which is a function of consciousness that enables the human mind to enter into the thing, rather than go around it from the outside. Thus,

---

17. Kant, *Critique of Pure Reason*.
18. Piaget, *The Child's Conception of Time*.
19. Bergson, *The Creative Mind*.

consciousness is aware that it is duration, that it is the consciousness of the duration of existence, and that, since it is duration, it is part of reality. From Bergson's perspective, time is a concept that is always formed *a posteriori* as a consequence of a synthesis between the concept of divisible time and the consciousness of (indivisible) duration, i.e., time is totally artificial, in the sense that it is created by the consciousness that wants to overcome difficulties by analyzing them according to Descartes's method and, hence, by making them measurable.

The "arrow" of time is not uniform; the velocity of time varies, e.g., sometimes, it is very fast, while other times, it is almost imperceptible. Thus, time is subject to contraction and expansion. The previous fact can be interpreted in two ways: there are different types of time (e.g., astronomical time, biological time, and historical time); the elasticity of time allows consciousness to distort time. Moreover, there is a new dimension, a "now-experience," which belongs to both time and the consciousness of time, and it is distinct from the concepts "before" and "after."

Husserl has highlighted the now-experience (i.e., the extension of the living presence into the future) and he has argued that "protention" (i.e., an extension of the now—an extension of intuition into the future) is often part of intuition, in the sense that, in the case of a given experience, one frequently has intuited expectations as well. In the context of Husserl's philosophy, one's protentions are almost always fulfilled, because his expectations are based on past experience, but, furthermore, intuited expectations show how intuitions themselves can rest in the future aspect of one's temporality. Therefore, Husserl has argued that one's act of intuition and one's protentional temporality are mutually interrelated.[20] In other words, in Husserl's philosophy, the consciousness of time is possible because of the intentionality of consciousness, i.e., because, according to Husserl, consciousness is the consciousness of its contents, which, thus, become conscious experiences. From Husserl's perspective, the intervention of consciousness in the flow of reality consists in the conscious affirmation of the presence of experiences in consciousness. However, if one endorses a Bergsonian approach to intentionality, then the role of consciousness is more active, in the sense that, in the context of a Bergsonian approach to intentionality, consciousness not only affirms the presence of its experiences in itself, but also it causes their presence.

---

20. Brough, "Husserl and the Deconstruction of Time."

Whereas time can be perceived as the set of all points through which reality passes successively, space can be perceived as the set of all points over which reality is extended simultaneously. The first scientific theory of space is due to ancient Greek geometricians, whose results have been methodically expounded by Euclid. According to Euclidean geometry, space is three-dimensional and isotropic (i.e., invariant with respect to direction). The Euclidean perception of space, modified by the fact that it was associated with the concept of gravity, was enriched and completed by Isaac Newton.[21] However, in contradistinction to Newton's realism, Kant endorses an idealist approach to space (and time), in the sense that he argues that space is an *a priori* schema of consciousness, and that, through this schema, the intellect can articulate synthetic statements about the sensible world, whereas sense-perception is fragmented.

In 1854, in his seminal research paper "On the Hypotheses which Lie at the Foundations of Geometry,"[22] the German mathematician Bernhard Riemann introduced the idea of "a multiply extended magnitude out of general notions of quantity," and he showed that "a multiply extended magnitude is susceptible of various metric relations," where, by the term "metric," mathematicians mean a rule for measuring distance; Riemann, in particular, studied n-dimensional spaces whose intrinsic geometry is determined by a quadratic formula ("metric") for the infinitesimal change in distance dx. Such a structure is now called a Riemannian manifold. Different manifolds yield different geometries, depending on their dimensions and on their metric. In other words, Riemann proved that mathematicians can define infinitely many different geometries, thus showing that the classical Euclidean–Newtonian geometry is not the only possible geometry and that the Euclidean space is not an *a priori* schema of consciousness.

In the early twentieth century, Albert Einstein—based on Riemannian geometry and guided by the research works of the mathematician Constantin Carathéodory and of the physicist Max Planck—arrived at the conclusion that, in reality, statements about space and time, distances and duration, are relative. In particular, Einstein proved that mass and energy are equivalent according to the following famous equation:

---

21. Hollingdale, *Makers of Mathematics*.

22. Riemann read this research paper on June 10, 1854 for the purpose of his "Habilitation" with the philosophical faculty of Göttingen; Riemann, "On the Hypotheses which Lie at the Foundations of Geometry," 411.

$$E = Mc^2$$

where E stands for "energy," M stands for "mass," and c stands for the speed of light, and, also, that space and time are relative (and, in a sense, interchangeable) according to the following famous equation:

$$s^2 = -t^2c^2$$

where s stands for "space," t stands for "time," and c stands for the speed of light.

Thus, Einstein's theory of relativity gave rise to the conception of a four-dimensional space whose fourth dimension is time.[23] Given that, according to Einstein's general theory of relativity, the physical world in which we live is four-dimensional and non-Euclidean (precisely, Riemannian), whereas, for physiological reasons, our cognition does not allow us to perceive four-dimensional non-Euclidean spaces or entities, the following question emerges: what is the three-dimensional Euclidean physical world that our cognition perceives? According to Einstein's special theory of relativity, the three-dimensional Euclidean physical world that our cognition perceives is the projection of the four-dimensional non-Euclidean physical world onto our familiar three-dimensional Euclidean space, which is a creation of our consciousness, and, therefore, it is a distorted and consciousness-dependent image of the actual physical world.

Bergson attempted to transcend the relativistic studies of spatial reality and of temporal reality by discerning between conceptual or perceived time and real duration. Following Bergson's philosophy of space, the Russian-French psychiatrist Eugène Minkowski combined the study of the four-dimensional space with the study of consciousness, and he argued that the entire physical reality is directly related to the reality of consciousness, and that consciousness itself determines both the relations that pervade consciousness and the relation between consciousness and existence. In his book *Lived Time*, Minkowski argues that schizophrenia is "characterized by a deficiency of intuition and of lived time and by a progressive hypertrophy of the intelligence and spatial factors."[24]

In the twentieth century, the philosophical debates about space were related to the development of a continuous cosmological model that underpins wave mechanics and of a discrete (non-continuous)

---

23. Hollingdale, *Makers of Mathematics*.
24. Minkowski, *Lived Time*, 272.

cosmological model that underpins quantum mechanics. According to the discrete (non-continuous) cosmological model that underpins quantum mechanics, electromagnetic energy is absorbed or emitted in discrete packets, or quanta, whereas the continuous cosmological model that underpins wave mechanics conceptually secures the principle of continuity by stating that energy travels through space in the form of waves. The wave–particle duality—that is, the concept that the same phenomenon (particularly, elementary particles or quantic entities) exhibits the properties of not only particles, but also waves—addresses the inability of the classical concepts "particle" and "wave" to fully describe sub-atomic phenomena. In the context of modern philosophy, Bergson leans toward the continuous cosmological model that underpins wave mechanics, whereas the French epistemologist Gaston Bachelard[25] leans toward the discrete (non-continuous) cosmological model that underpins quantum mechanics, arguing that there is a dynamic continuity between knowing consciousness and known object.

Furthermore, the history of modern philosophy of space is intimately related to the history of a fairly new branch of mathematics that is called topology. Topology—whose most important pioneers are the eighteenth-century Swiss mathematician Leonhard Euler and the French mathematician and epistemologist Henri Poincaré (1854–1912)—is the abstract study of the concepts of "nearness" and "continuity."[26] This is done in the first place by picking out in classical geometry the fundamental properties of nearness and postulating them. For instance, if E is an n-dimensional Euclidean space and p a point in it, the "neighborhood" of p can be thought of as a set of points near p and entirely surrounding p. In a more mathematically rigorous language, we can define a neighborhood of p as any set U such that U contains an open solid sphere of center p. Topologists are interested in those properties of a thing that, while they are "geometrical," they are the most important, in the sense that they will survive distortion and stretching. Thus, for instance, the roundness of a circle is not a topological property (since one can unite the ends of a bit of string and make it into a circle, and then, without disconnecting or cutting it, he can make it into a square), but the fact that it has no ends is a topological property. Moreover, from the perspective of topology, what is (topologically) important in a straight line is not the fact that it is straight

---

25. Bachelard, *The Poetics of Space*.
26. Laos, *Topics in Mathematical Analysis and Differential Geometry*, chapter 2.

(since it does not have to remain straight), but the fact that it is continuously connected along itself. In other words, topology is concerned with the (topologically) invariant in things, and, for this reason, it treats things in groups, or "sets." When one shape or curve can be distorted into another without disconnecting what was originally connected (e.g., without making a cut or a hole) and without connecting what was not originally connected (e.g., without joining the ends of a previously unjoined string, or filling in a hole), they are said to be homeomorphic to each other; for instance, a square can be homeomorphically distorted so as to get rid of its four angles and be transformed into a circle. Mathematical physicists study our physical space-time topologically, and this means that, in the context of modern physics, our physical space-time is subject to several homeomorphic distortions.

In cosmology, space-time is considered to have the structure of a four-dimensional manifold, called the "World." A topological n-manifold, in general, "is constructed from domains in n-dimensional Euclidean space, pieced together by homeomorphisms."[27] Points of the four-dimensional manifold that cosmologists call the World are called "events." Events are determined by their four coordinates in local charts. Local charts on a manifold can be regarded as local frames of reference in space-time. Since a manifold admits all atlases equivalent to a given atlas, we realize that the very concept of space-time includes all possible classes of reference frames which are consistent with it (some classes of reference may prove to be preferable only *a posteriori*, i.e., when the space-time under consideration is endowed with additional postulates which must of course have physical grounds). The previous remarks led Albert Einstein to argue that "time and space are modes by which we think."[28]

In the four-dimensional manifold that cosmologists call the World, a space-time distance is defined between two neighboring points

$$x_i = (x_0, x_1, x_2, x_3) \text{ and } x_i + dx_i = (x_0 + dx_0, \ldots, x_3 + dx_3)$$

and for an arbitrary coordinate system (x_i); its square

$$ds^2 = \sum g_{ij} dx_i dx_j$$

is a quadratic form in the differences of the coordinates of the neighboring points. The four-dimensionality of the World is an empirical fact; in general, by the term "dimension," physicists refer to the number of the

---

27. Donaldson, "The Geometry of 4-Mnifolds," 43.
28. See Laos, *Topics in Mathematical Analysis and Differential Geometry*, 536.

The Modes of Being 143

degrees of freedom of a physical system. A classical observer using his means of measuring space (rulers) and time (clock) can establish a local coordinate system where

$$x_0 = ct$$

(t, standing for "time," is recorded on his clock, and the speed of light c is used in order to convert temporal units to spatial ones), and x_1, x_2, x_3 are Cartesian coordinates in the observer's physical space. At the eightieth Assembly of German Natural Scientists and Physicians (Cologne, September 21, 1908), the German mathematician Hermann Minkowski argued that it is impossible to notice "a place except at a time, or a time except at a place," and he defined a World point as "a point of space at a point of time."[29] In addition, in his previous research paper, Hermann Minkowski noticed that the variations dx_1, dx_2, dx_3 of the space coordinates of a substantial point correspond to time element dx_0, so that we come up with a curve in the World, called a "World line," which is an image of the career of the substantial point. The World line of an observer is the observer's own stream of time, and his clock counts off the values of the integral $\int \sqrt{ds^2}$ along the World line, i.e., its length.

The special theory of relativity regards space-time as a four-dimensional space whose geometry is determined by a certain group of transformations. The general theory of relativity went a step further by abandoning the concept of a homogeneous space-time and asserting that space-time is, globally speaking, non-homogeneous; space-time may be regarded as homogeneous only locally. In fact, the general theory of relativity is a theory of gravitation which explains how gravitation determines the global structure of space-time. In the theory of gravitation, the notion of curvature plays a major role. The fundamental equations of Albert Einstein relate directly the quantities that determine the curvature of space-time to the quantities that characterize the distribution of the motion of matter.

Let us try to mark a point of the World on the World line of a particle of mass m. This cannot be done without an error at least equal to the so-called Schwarzschild radius for the given mass m; the Schwarzschild radius (also called the gravitational radius) is the radius of a sphere such that, if all the mass of an object were compressed within the sphere, the escape velocity from the surface of the sphere would be equal to the speed of light. Hence, the higher the level of accuracy we obtain, the smaller

29. Ibid., 537.

the mass of the particle under consideration must be. However, quantum mechanics, which studies the world of the very small, leads to a different conclusion. In quantum mechanics, a state of a micro-particle subjected to a potential field is described by a complex-valued wave function, known as the psi-function. In the context of quantum mechanics, the Heisenberg uncertainty principle (according to which, neither the momentum nor the position of a particle can be predicted with arbitrarily great precision, and the uncertainties in the two quantities play complementary roles) and the fact that all velocities are upper bounded by the speed of light imply that the indeterminacy position is not less than h_0/mc, where h_0 is the Planck constant h divided by 2π, m is the mass of the particle under consideration, and c is the speed of light; hence, from this perspective, the higher the level of accuracy we obtain, the bigger the mass of the particle under consideration must be. This is a characteristic example of the intriguing way in which quantum principles interfere with the notion of a point of the World as an elementary event. In other words, the study of the relation between the models of the classical World and the principles of quantum mechanics (which refer to the world of the very small) leads to the conclusion that the basic rules for the description of matter do not agree with one another.

The aforementioned developments in the fields of modern philosophy and modern science lead to the conclusion that neither realism nor idealism—as modern philosophers understand them—is a general theory of reality. Modern philosophical realism is founded on the following syllogism: since experience provides human consciousness with images of a reality that seems to be external to human consciousness, it naturally follows that an external reality is the cause of perception; therefore, on the basis of the principle of causality, a mind-independent reality exists necessarily. On the other hand, modern idealism is founded on the following syllogism: if the nature of reality were different from the nature of consciousness, then it would be impossible for humans to know reality; therefore, the representatives of idealism emphasize the principle of identity, while the representatives of philosophical realism emphasize the principle of causality.

The endorsement of realist views is encouraged and philosophically justified by the unquestionable awareness that the world is somehow different from consciousness. Indeed, if the world were not somehow different from consciousness, then consciousness would not try so hard to know the world, and the self-knowledge of the human being would be equivalent to cosmology. On the other hand, the endorsement of idealist views is encouraged and philosophically justified by the unquestionable awareness that, from a certain perspective, the structure of the world is not fundamentally different from the structure of consciousness. Indeed, if the structure of the world were absolutely different from the structure of consciousness, then it would be impossible for consciousness to obtain even partial knowledge of the world. Therefore, modern philosophy and modern science lead to the conclusion that the structure of the world and the structure of consciousness are not identical to each other, but they are united. In fact, the structural continuity between the reality of the world and the reality of consciousness underpins the imposition of the intentionality of consciousness on the world.

In a special collection of articles published in July 2005, *Science Magazine* and its online companion sites celebrated the journal's 125th anniversary with the publication of a list of 125 compelling puzzles and questions facing contemporary science. One of those questions was the following: *what is the universe made of?* Is it made of quarks, or gluons, or other elementary particles, or is it made of strings, quantum loops, dark matter, dark energy, etc.? None of the previous theories provides a global explanation of the universe. Moreover, the attempt to incorporate the quantum principle of uncertainty into the general relativity is very difficult (if possible), but it is the ultimate way through which one can reveal the underlying mechanisms of the physical world. As Michael Berry has argued, "quantum physics describes the world of the very small. Classical Newtonian physics describes larger scales. But in the border country between the two, rigorous mathematical descriptions are difficult to find, and chaos rears its head."[30] Another important question included in the aforementioned list of the *Science Magazine* was the following: *what is the biological basis of consciousness?* As I have already mentioned, the study of modern philosophy and modern science leads to the conclusion that consciousness is not an epiphenomenon of matter, nor is matter an epiphenomenon of consciousness, knowledge takes place in consciousness, and we imagine that the external world corresponds to our experience of it. In other words, our consciousness experiences a map of the world, but, as Alfred Korzybski has argued, "the map is not the territory."[31]

---

30. Berry, "Quantum Physics on the Edge of Chaos," 43.

31. Korzybski, "A Non-Aristotelian System and its Necessity for Rigour in Mathematics and Physics," 747.

From the perspective of methexiology, the world is a dynamic structural field of being,[32] and the logoi of beings exist potentially in the Logos of God; the logoi of beings exist actually when the corresponding beings are created in the world. Therefore, the highest form of knowledge of the world consists in the knowledge of the logoi (i.e., the effective and final causes) of the world and of the beings that exist in it. Given that God is absolute while the world is relative and subject to change and corruption, the following question emerges: *how does God relate to the world?* Intimately related to the previous question is the following one: *what is the relation between eternity and time?* First of all, classical Greek philosophers, primarily Plato and Aristotle, attempted to transcend the temporal reality and partake of eternity. Plato argues that, if a soul chooses the philosopher's life three times in a row, it flies to the transcendent realm, and it is freed from the temporal cycles of reincarnation.[33] Aristotle argues that time does not exist independently of the soul, and that the noetic faculty of the soul arises from the outside (*thyrathen*).[34] Therefore, from Plato's and Aristotle's perspectives, time is an image of eternity (i.e., of the "absolute"), and it is not identical to the cycle of physical becoming. In the context of classical Greek philosophy, the connection between time and eternity does not imply that time is a physical necessity (i.e., that time is produced by physical motion), but it implies that time is produced by the spiritual purpose, or entelechy, of beings (i.e., it is teleological).

From the perspective of methexiology, the aforementioned teleological conception of time has been modified and perfected by Christianity, since the latter is founded on the historical revelation of the telos, i.e., the existential purpose, of beings through Jesus Christ, the Incarnate Logos. The resurrection of Christ[35] is not a supernatural event, but a mystery. Gabriel Marcel has explained the difference between the terms "problem" and "mystery" as follows: a problem is something that one meets and finds complete before one, and which one can manipulate, but a mystery is a peculiar problem that "encroaches its own data," and it is

---

32. The world is not homogeneous, i.e., there are structural variations (e.g., an electron is something different from a proton). Additionally, the structure of the universe changes, since there is motion.

33. Plato, *Phaedrus* 249.

34. Aristotle, *Physics* 223a21–26; *On the Soul* III.5; *On the Generation of Animals* II.3.

35. For more details about Christ's resurrection, see the following biblical passages: Matthew 28:6; Mark 16:6; Luke 24:6–7.

"metaproblematic."[36] In contradistinction to a "problem," a "mystery" is something in which one is personally involved, and, therefore, the distinction between what is in one's consciousness and what is before one is not valid. Active faith (in contradistinction to passive faith and superstition), i.e., faith *qua* mystery, consists in a conscious acceptance of an ontological principle, precisely, of a presence, toward which one is free to be psychically transparent and open or psychically closed.

According to methexiology, the mystery of faith does not consist in one's trust in something that is perceivable through the senses, but it consists in an inner pursuit and discovery of a different (uncreated) world that is also present in our (created) physical world; this meeting between the two worlds—namely, between the divine (uncreated) world and the physical (created) world—takes place mysteriously within the soul of each person. For this reason, we read in the New Testament that there were no witnesses to Jesus Christ's resurrection, and, after his resurrection, Jesus Christ "appeared in a different form."[37] Through his ministry—which was characterized by mystery, discretion of judgment, and humility—Jesus Christ revealed that he is the perfect example of man's deification. Humans can really understand Christ only if they allow his birth to take place in their souls. In order to understand the mystery of Christ's resurrection, we need what Hermes Trismegistus[38] has called "spiritual vision," i.e., we must be freed from the logic of our physical and historical constraints. Thus, in Luke 12:11–12 and 24:25, we read that, in order to speak truly about Christ and to really understand the Bible, we need the grace, i.e., the uncreated energies, of the Holy Spirit.

A supernatural event—no matter how extraordinary it is, as an extreme manifestation of physical possibilities—keeps us confined to the logic of the natural world, because we approach it through our senses, and, therefore, we continue to exist according to the dictates of the natural world, and, as we read in Romans 8:13, "if you live according to the flesh," i.e., spiritually enslaved to the logic of physical and historical constraints, "you will die, but if by the Spirit you put to death the misdeeds of the body, you will live." Therefore, in contradistinction to Thomas Aquinas's and many other scholastics' use of the term "supernatural," Christ is not a supernatural being, but he represents a totally different, uncreated world

---

36. Marcel, *The Philosophy of Existentialism*, 19.
37. Mark 16:6, 12.
38. Copenhaver, ed., *Hermetica*.

that enters into our created, natural world through the mystery of the Incarnation. Christ brings us the light of a different world, thus signaling the dawn of a new era, as we read in 2 Peter 1:19: "we have the word of the prophets made more certain, and you will do well to pay attention to it, as to light shining in a dark place, until the day dawns and Phosphorus [i.e., the Morning Star] rises in your hearts." Without Christ's uncreated light, the human being is confined to created lights, namely, the physical light of the sun, the electric light, and the light of the human intellect. Moreover, without Christ's uncreated light, the human being's creativity is determined by the structural continuity between the reality of the world and the reality of consciousness, and, in this case, as the apostle Paul writes, "we see but a poor reflection as in a mirror."[39]

Christ's resurrection is a reminder of the human being's capability of transcending the logic of physical and historical necessities. Christ is the divine archetype of the human being, as Gregory the Theologian writes in his "First Oration: On Easter and His Reluctance": "I am glorified with Him . . . let us honor our Archetype."[40] Moreover, Maximus the Confessor argues that "God and man are examples of each other," and that "God makes himself man out of love for men as much as man deifies himself out of love for God."[41]

Based on Aristotle's concepts of being actually and being potentially, Maximus the Confessor has endowed methexiology with a cosmology founded on the principle of free will. Maximus the Confessor's cosmology starts from the principle that God is absolutely free, and, therefore, God creates without using any other resources apart from His own will. Hence, Maximus the Confessor stresses that the world and everything in it were brought into existence out of nothing (*ex nihilo*). Creation (i.e., the created world) is the actualization of the Creator's will (in Greek, *thēlema*), and the Creator's will is not constrained by any necessity, such as the laws of logic, the principle of causality (known in the Orient as the principle of "karma"), etc. In fact, this is the essence of God's hypostatic mode of being, which I explained earlier in this chapter. Therefore, as regards their essences, God and His creation are different, distinct, and separate from each other. However, Maximus argues that "a logos of angels preceded their creation, a logos preceded the creation of each of the

---

39. 1 Corinthians 13:12.
40. Included in Schaff and Wace, *A Select Library*, Vol. 7, 203.
41. Maximus, *Ambiguum* 10; *Patrologia Graeca*, Vol. 91, 1113 BC.

beings and powers that fill the upper world, a logos preceded the creation of human beings, a logos preceded everything that receives its becoming from God, and so on."[42] These logoi, which precede the beings and things in the world, do not exist actually before the creation of the corresponding beings and things in the world, since they are only wills (in Greek, *thelēmata*) of God. In other words, according to Maximus, the logos of a being is not a substance, but its effective and final cause, and, therefore, it does not subsist in itself, but it only exists potentially in God, as a yet unmanifested possibility. Additionally, in the Bible we read that God has all the forces of nature at His command and that He can manage them at will (Job 38:22–35).

Following Dionysius the Areopagite, Maximus the Confessor names the logoi of beings divine "wills" (in Greek, *theia thelēmata*). Therefore, in the context of Maximus the Confessor's cosmology, God is not related to the essences of the beings and things in the world, since the essences of the beings and things in the world are created, whereas God's essence is uncreated, but God knows the beings and things in the world as actualizations of His will, and for this reason, His knowledge is equivalent to an erotic relationship. Furthermore, according to Maximus the Confessor, the Logos of God is the One that gathers in Himself the multitude of logoi, since, as we read in John 1:3 and in Colossians 1:16, the world itself is made by Him. According to Maximus, "the one Logos is many logoi and the many logoi are One. Because the One goes forth, out of goodness, into individual beings creating and preserving them, the One is many. Moreover the many are directed toward the One and are providentially guided in that direction."[43] Using Aristotle's concepts of being potentially and being actually, Maximus explains that, within the Logos of God, all the logoi of the beings and things in the world exist potentially, and their actualization discloses the same work and presence of the Logos. In other words, in each created being, through its logos, the Logos of God is made present and manifested.

---

42. Maximus, *Ambiguum 7*; *Patrologia Graeca*, Vol. 91, 1080A.
43. Ibid. ; *Patrologia Graeca*, Vol. 91, 1081BC.

In contrast to Origen[44] and the gnostics,[45] who saw a decline in corporality and materiality, Maximus the Confessor writes that the creation of the world itself is a revelation of God's will, and the essence of this revelation is the presence of the Logos of God in the logoi of the created beings; this is an Embodiment of the Logos of God. In his *Questions to Thalassius* 15, Maximus the Confessor speaks about a triple embodiment of the Logos: in nature, in the Bible, and in the historical person of Christ.[46]

Furthermore, in contrast to Origen and Gnosticism, Maximus the Confessor's cosmology is highly dynamic. In fact, in order to refute Origen's and the gnostics' cosmological arguments, which reflect the Oriental spirit of passivity, Maximus the Confessor emphasized the movement of the created beings. Origen and many Oriental philosophies and religious systems argue that, between God and the soul of the created beings, there is a kind of connaturality (e.g., many gnostics argue that the human soul is a spark of the divine nature), as they are both in a state of repose or rest in the original Unity (the gnostics' One). But, Gnosticism maintains that for some reason (e.g., satiety) the state of the spirits (or "Aeons") changed, and they started moving until they came into a material life, from which they will (or must) return to the original Unity. In other words, according to Origen and Gnosticism, movement is the cause of sin. On the other hand, according to Maximus the Confessor, movement is a natural characteristic of all beings, because they tend toward some end. Maximus

---

44. Origen was an early Christian Alexandrian scholar and theologian (born ca. 185 AD). He was strongly influenced by the solipsistic philosophical traditions of Asia and Egypt, and, thus, his theological work was based on his belief that spirit is the only true substance. His solipsistic views were condemned at the Fifth Ecumenical Council, which took place in Constantinople in 553 AD.

45. Gnosticism (from Greek *gnosis*, which means "knowledge") refers to a set of religious beliefs and spiritual practices based on the doctrine of salvation by a peculiar esoteric knowledge that promises to "free" the soul from the material world. The roots of Gnosticism can be traced to non-Christian and pre-Christian Asian religious communities. In particular, Walter Bauer and Christian Lassen argue that Gnosticism is strongly related to the religions of India (Bauer, *Orthodoxy and Heresy*; Lassen, *Indische Alterthumskunde*). According to Lassen, the Indian elements in the gnostic "schools" were derived from Buddhism, which exerted a considerable influence on the intellectual life of Alexandria. R. A. Lipsius argues that the origins of Gnosticism are in Syria and Phoenicia (Lipsius, *Der Gnosticismus*). Adolf Hilgenfeld argues that Gnosticism is strongly connected with later Mazdaism, i.e., the worship of Ahura Mazda, who, in Zoroastrianism, is the source of all light and good (Hilgenfeld, *Die Ketzergeschichte des Urchristentums*).

46. *Patrologia Graeca*, Vol. 90, 297B–300A.

argues as follows: "The movement that is tending toward its proper end is called a natural power, or passion, or movement passing from one thing to another and having impassibility as its end. It is also called an irrepressible activity that has as its end perfect fulfillment."[47]

According to the aforementioned cosmology of Maximus the Confessor, which underpins methexiology, the existential perfection of man consists neither in returning to a primordial "womb" nor in renouncing the material world, but it consists in an end to be progressively achieved in the future. For this reason, according to Maximus, movement is related to the concept of "telos," or purpose: "nothing that came into being is perfect in itself, nor has a purpose in itself."[48] Moreover, he continues as follows: "If then rational beings come into being, surely they are also moved, since they move from a natural beginning in being toward a voluntary end in well-being."[49] Hence, the creation of the material world is not a negative event, but, on the contrary, it is the necessary context in which rational beings can exercise their freedom of will and pursue their existential perfection.

From the perspective of methexiology, as I understand and propose it in this book, and according to Maximus the Confessor's theology, "ideas," on which Plato's thought is focused, should not be regarded as causes of created beings existing potentially within God. In other words, "ideas" should not be regarded as determining factors of God's essence, and the latter should not be regarded as the prime cause of created beings. In contrast to the previous views—which were advocated by Augustine of Hippo and were taken further and generalized by Thomas Aquinas in the context of Western medieval theology—Maximus the Confessor and, generally, the Greek church fathers assert that "ideas" have a much more dynamic character, precisely, they have a *volitional* character. Because God's ideas are distinct from God's essence, it follows that neither the act of creation nor God's will is equivalent to any kind of determinism. Thus, as I have already mentioned, Maximus the Confessor emphasizes that God knows beings not as substances, but as actualizations of His divine will, and, for this reason, His knowledge is equivalent to love, and not to a "covering-law model."

---

47. Maximus, *Ambiguum* 7; *Patrologia Graeca*, Vol. 91, 1072B.
48. Ibid. *Patrologia Graeca*, Vol. 91, 1072C.
49. Ibid. *Patrologia Graeca*, Vol. 91, 1073BC.

Because God exists personally (hypostatically), and, thus, He is not an abstract substance, whose existence would be the ultimate source of cosmic determinism, humans can freely accept to be in a personal relationship with God, thus opening their souls to God and being transparent to God, or, alternatively, they may choose the path of solitary existence, which is the essence of "hell," since it means separation from God. Because God discloses Himself through His creative ideas-wills, particularly, through the logoi of the created beings, He can be known through His creatures, that is, indirectly, by humans. However, humans can also know God directly, that is, through the "secret" theoria (vision) of His uncreated energies, which are the splendor of His Face and His true glory (in accordance with Matthew 16:27–28); this is the manner in which God disclosed Himself during the Transfiguration of Jesus Christ (in accordance with Matthew 17:1 and Mark 9:3), and this is the manner in which God discloses Himself to the saints, in general, i.e., to those persons who choose the "theoretical life," in accordance with the methexiological epistemology that I will expound in chapter 4.

4

Epistemology and the Noetic Faculty of the Soul

AMONG THE FOUR MAJOR questions of philosophy as understood by Kant, the first one is: "What can I know?" According to Kant, the previous question (which is the essence of epistemology) is the most important philosophical problem, and it introduces us to all other philosophical questions. Indeed, if we have not first of all estimated and evaluated human cognitive capacities—through which one can acquire, assimilate, and criticize pieces of knowledge—we cannot know anything with certainty. Furthermore, in the context of epistemology, philosophers are concerned with the search for criteria and methods by which one can justify truth claims.

Kant has correctly criticized dogmatic rationalism by highlighting and emphasizing the fundamental difference between the object of consciousness and consciousness's reference to its object. In other words, Kant has emphasized that we should not confuse the thing-in-itself (i.e., the thing *per se*) with our cognitions about it. However, at a next level, consciousness's reference to its object can be regarded as an object of conscious investigation (i.e., we may reflect on our cognitions), and this process may continue indefinitely, thus giving rise to an infinite series of cognitions about one's cognitions. By analyzing cognitions about one's cognitions and then cognitions about one's cognitions about one's cognitions, etc., repeating this analytical process indefinitely, we confine philosophy to cognitions about philosophy and, even worse, to an analysis of propositions that have no real significance.

One can validly criticize dogmatic rationalism for reducing philosophy to a naïve system of speech games, but the overcritical attitude of analytic philosophy concurs with the overcritical attitude of nihilism, whose roots can be traced back to the thought of Friedrich Nietzsche. In his book *Beyond Good and Evil*, Nietzsche severely criticizes reason (i.e., a rational motive for a belief or action) and, particularly, instrumental rationality: instrumental rationality is focused on the most efficient or cost-effective means of achieving a specific end, but it does not itself reflect on the value of that end, nor is it concerned with goals of higher value, such as the advancement of human understanding and the improvement of the human condition. But, in contradistinction to analytic philosophy, which may, ultimately, lead to a philosophical "assassination" of philosophy, Nietzsche is not an unqualified enemy of reason; instead, he argues that reason, and, therefore, truth have not been adequately investigated by his predecessors in the history of philosophy.[1] According to Nietzsche, what philosophers actually do is to defend judgments which are equivalent to advocates' tricks or their own hearts' desires, and they present them in abstract forms and by means of arguments which they have articulated after (not before) the original conception of their ideas.[2] However, at this point, Nietzsche makes a mistake: the validity of a premise depends not on its "genealogy," but on its logic (i.e., on its consistency), and the logic of a premise, in its turn, depends on the fact that it can associate a multitude of data under a concrete perspective, and, therefore, transform them into a harmonious "whole." Hence—at least when one cares about the consistency of one's syllogisms and does not have the arrogance of Hegel to argue that one's philosophy signals the end of the history of philosophy—philosophers are not as dishonest as Nietzsche contends.

Consciousness is an outgrowth of life, but it is not an *a posteriori* one; it is potentially inherent in what Bergson has called "élan vital" (vital impetus), that is, in the tendency of a being to exist. Thus, consciousness exists even in instinct, which is a logic that governs the behavior of the simplest organisms, and in the processes according to which various forms of life adapt to their living conditions. Between instinct, which is the most elementary form of consciousness, and moral and contemplative

---

1. Nietzsche, *Beyond Good and Evil*, Aphorism 1.
2. Ibid., Aphorism 5.

consciousness, which is the most advanced form of consciousness, there are several intermediate stages in the development of consciousness.

The problem of consciousness is intimately related to the connection between the problem of the continuity of life and the problem of the discontinuity between the "absolute" and the "relative." The problem of the discontinuity between the "absolute" and the "relative" is derived from the difference between temporality (dependence on time) and atemporality (being independent of time). Everything that is measurable is subject to the jurisdiction of time, which is created by consciousness, since, through time, consciousness is capable of controlling reality according to consciousness's own relativity. Whatever transcends time introduces us to the realm of the "absolute."

A conscious shift from temporality to atemporality can take place through the substitution of the categories "before" and "after" with the categories "not yet" and "no more." The categories "not yet" and "no more" enable us to conceive of the edge of the temporal or relative realm, beyond which consciousness seeks the atemporality of the "eschaton" (i.e., the final and unmeasurable). Thus, as I argued in chapter 2, consciousness resorts to imagination. However, as I also argued in chapter 2, imagination cannot create species. Therefore, on the one hand, philosophy has accomplished the task of proving the reality of the Absolute on the grounds of ontological and moral evidence, but, on the other hand, the truth that philosophy has discovered in this way is unstable (due to the instability of imagination, to which I referred in chapter 2); philosophy has not managed to enter into the substance of the Absolute, and, ultimately, it leads to the conclusion that the source of the significance of being is not consciousness itself, but the Absolute, which, for this reason, is consciousness's primary object of pursuit. From the previous perspective, we can argue that philosophy contributes to the knowledge of the Absolute, but, with regard to this issue, philosophical reasoning is neither self-reliant nor self-sufficient, and it introduces us to the field of pure theology, which consists in an experience of one's participation in the Absolute (methexis).

However, it should be clear by now that, if epistemology were confined to the functions of consciousness, and if the human soul were identical with consciousness, then pure theology—being concerned with the Absolute and, hence, with the uncreated—would be impossible, since the faculties of consciousness can produce created knowledge (i.e., knowledge that is derived from created sources), whereas the Absolute is uncreated. For this reason, in the context of methexiology, as I understand and propose it in the present book, the human soul is not only the being of human consciousness, but also it is endowed with the mind (nous), which should be defined according to Hesychasm, that is, the mind should be defined as the repository of God's uncreated energies within the human being; hence, the mind is clearly distinct from the intellect, in the sense that the knowledge that is based on the intellect is derived from a created source (human reason), but the knowledge that is based on God's grace is derived from the uncreated energies of God, i.e., directly from God. Therefore, the mind should be clean and transparent, in the sense that no created source of knowledge should interfere with the mind. In other words, the mind should reach a state of emptiness, or inner stillness and freedom from passions, in order to operate as a pure repository of God's uncreated energies and to be filled with them.

The most important defender of the Hesychast tradition is Gregory Palamas (1296–1359), who is venerated as a saint in the Eastern Orthodox Church. According to Gregory Palamas, Hesychasm can be understood as a deep experience of communion and union with God through the "Jesus Prayer," which exists in several forms; the most familiar formula is: "Lord Jesus Christ, Son of God, have mercy on me, a sinner," but Gregory Palamas himself was fond of the following formula: "Lord Jesus Christ, Son of God, enlighten my darkness."

Hesychasm is a very old practice in the Greek East, but the first methodical exposition of the Hesychasts' method of prayer in the Greek sources dates only from the late thirteenth century AD, in the work *On Vigilance and the Guarding of the Heart* by Nicephorus the Hesychast, a monk of Mount Athos. Moreover, there is a closely similar description in a work entitled *Method of Holy Prayer and Attentiveness*, which is attributed to Symeon the New Theologian (949–1022 AD), a Byzantine Christian monk and poet, who is venerated as a saint in the Eastern Orthodox Church. In the previous texts, Nicephorus and Symeon the New Theologian describe the physical techniques that are used by Hesychasts as follows:

(i) The aspirant is to sit with his head bowed, and, according to Symeon the New Theologian's *Method of Holy Prayer and Attentiveness*, the aspirant should rest his beard on his chest and direct his bodily eyes together with the mind toward the middle of his belly, that is toward his navel. The navel controls the digestive tract, and it is related to liver, spleen, stomach, as well as to the alimentary canal and the generative organs. As Bhagavan Das has written, "it is worth noting that in Sanskrit literature the naval is often treated as more central . . . than the heart."[3] Other Hesychast texts suggest that the aspirant's gaze should be fixed on the place of the heart. The heart is also closely associated with the thymus; one of the most important roles of the thymus is the induction of central tolerance (a mechanism by which newly developing T cells and B cells are rendered non-reactive to self).

(ii) The aspirant's breathing rhythm is to be slowed down. In particular, in Symeon the New Theologian's *Method of Holy Prayer and Attentiveness*, we read that the aspirant should restrain the inhalation of his breath through the nose, so as not to breathe in and out at his ease.

(iii) As he controls his breathing, the aspirant is at the same time to search inwardly for the place of the heart. In particular, Nicephorus writes that the Hesychast is to imagine his breath entering through the nostrils and then passing down within the lungs until it reaches the heart, and, in this way, he is to make his mind remain with the breath within the body, so that mind and heart are united.

Through the aforementioned psychosomatic method of prayer, the Hesychasts want to teach that the mind (i.e., the repository of the Holy Spirit) should be freed from the influences of both the body and the discursive intellect, receptive to God's uncreated energies, and concentrated in the heart in order to transmute the human being, as a psychosomatic unity, into a spiritualized being in the image of God, and, thus, achieve the deification of man. From the previous perspective, when we read in the book of Genesis 1:26 that God created man in His image, we should understand that God endowed man with the mind, which is the image of God, since it is the repository of God's uncreated energies, known also as the uncreated grace of the Holy Spirit. There are similarities between the Hesychasts' notion of mind and the biblical term *neshamah*, which literally means breath, and it can be broadly understood as the "soul proper" and the ability to become partakers of God. In the Old Testament, there are several references to the *neshamah*, such as the following: Isaiah 30:33: breath of God as hot wind kindling a flame; 2 Samuel 22:16 and Job 4:9: as destroying wind; Job 32:8 and 33:4: as cold wind producing ice; 1 Kings 17:17, Isaiah 42:5, Job 27:3, and Daniel 10:7: breath of man;

3. Das, *The Science of the Sacred Word*, Vol. 1, 82.

Genesis 2:7 and Job 34:14 and 36:4: breath of life and God's breath in man; Isaiah 2:22: man in whose nostrils is but a breath.

In his *Triads in Defense of the Sacred Hesychasts* (known also simply as his *Triads*), Gregory Palamas argues that, through pure prayer, which, in essence, is a mental state of Christocentric stillness and spiritual freedom, one becomes, through an intimate knowledge of God within the heart, a true theologian. Additionally, in his *Triads*, Gregory Palamas argues that pure prayer gives rise to a peculiar joy of the heart at the coming of grace, and it leads to a peculiar vision of God, Who manifests Himself in what Palamas calls "uncreated light" (in Greek, *āktiston phos*), or divine radiation (in Greek, *theia ēllampsis*) of God. This light, he maintains, was the same light in which Christ appeared in Mount Tabor at the Transfiguration. It was also the divine light that, according to Acts 9:1–6, Paul experienced on the road to Damascus. In the context of the vision of God's uncreated light, the mind is freed from the influences of both the body and the discursive intellect, i.e., no longer do the physical and intellectual faculties exert any influence over the noetic faculty, and the mind is filled with divine grace. Additionally, in the context of the vision of God's uncreated light, the body, being controlled by the mind, which thus becomes the overseer of the body, is freed from the sin.

Hesychasm is very sensitive to symbolism, and Hesychasts often use a poetic language in order to refer to the experience of deification, which consists in an existential state in which man is unceasingly united with the source of the significance of being (i.e., with God,) and, therefore, he is a partaker of God's mode of being, which is freedom. By being unceasingly united with the source of the significance of being, man is freed from both the logic of the intellect and the logic of the instincts, and, in this way, he is in a state of unceasing prayer, in accordance with Jesus's Parable of the Persistent Widow (Luke 18:1–8), and with the apostle Paul's call to "pray unceasingly" (1 Thess 5:17). When humans "pray unceasingly"—that is, when they are unceasingly united with the source of the significance of being—they are historically active and responsible persons, but the purpose of their historical activity transcends history, and, thus, they are not subjugated to the logic of historical necessities, since they unceasingly refer ("pray") to the Absolute. On the other hand, if human historical activity is exhausted in the pursuit of historical goals—i.e., if the accomplishment of each and every historical task is merely a means to another historical task—then humans are subjected to the ratio of accounting, of instinctive passions, and of "efficiency indices" instituted by authoritarian political and business elites.

As I argued in the previous chapters, the scholastic representatives of philosophical realism, including Thomas Aquinas, having only a problematic and fragmented access to classical Greek philosophy, misinterpreted Platonic ideas as logical substances and, in the context of their interpretation of Christianity, they identified God's wills with logical substances. Therefore, they gave rise to a rationalist world-conception, known also as "natural theology," whose fundamental principles have been methodically expounded by Thomas Aquinas and can be summarized as follows: (i) Reason (*ratio*) governs the soul, and reason's indirect access to God is the greatest possible spiritual achievement of which the human being is capable. (ii) Love as an attribute of the human being is inferior to reason, because will is determined by the knowledge of the Good as a logical substance and, therefore, by reason. (iii) Freedom as an attribute of the human being is inferior to reason, because freedom necessarily depends on cognition, and, therefore, it is determined by reason. (iv) God's essence is identical with His energies, in the sense that the scholastic representatives of philosophical realism think of God as an unknowable essence or as an unknowable pure energy, and, therefore, they preclude man from knowing God directly. In other words, by discarding the Hesychasts' essence–energies distinction, the scholastic representatives of philosophical realism confine man to *created* sources of knowledge, and they even assert that the divine grace which, according to them, perfects reason is a "supernatural," yet created, gift of God to mankind. In the context of the previous rationalist world-conception, pure prayer is essentially impossible, since God is an inaccessible essence or pure energy. Man can speculate about an inaccessible essence or pure energy through his discursive intellect, but he cannot develop a personal relationship with an inaccessible essence or pure energy. Hence, if God is an inaccessible essence or pure energy, prayer reduces to an expression of romantic feelings to an imaginary fatherly figure.

In contrast to scholasticism, the Hesychasts emphasize that—while, with regard to God's and humanity's essences, any kind of direct knowledge of God by man is impossible (since God's essence is uncreated, but man's essence is created)—God's energies are uncreated, distinct from His essence (yet, an outgrowth of His essence), and accessible to human beings, in the sense that human minds, having been created in the image of God, can partake of God's uncreated energies, thus providing people with *an uncreated source of knowledge*. Therefore, in the context of Hesychasm, pure prayer is meaningful, and, in fact, it is the essence of pure theology.

Hesychasm was called in question and challenged during the decade 1337–47, in what is known as the Hesychast controversy. The attack on Hesychasm was launched by a learned Greek from southern Italy, Barlaam the Calabrian (ca. 1290–1348), who was influenced by the fourteenth-century rationalist schools of Western Europe. Barlaam was answered by a learned monk from Mount Athos, Gregory Palamas. Palamas's famous book *Triads in Defense of the Sacred Hesychasts*, which was probably written between 1338 and 1341, is comprised of nine treatises in the form of questions and answers. By early spring 1341, it was clear that the dispute between Gregory Palamas and Barlaam would need to be resolved by conciliar means. Six patriarchal councils were held in Constantinople between 1341 and 1351 to consider the issues. The dispute over Hesychasm came before a council held in Constantinople on June 10, 1341 and presided over by Emperor Andronicus III Palaiologos. This council lasted only one day, and it vindicated Gregory Palamas. However, Emperor Andronicus III died just five days after the council ended, and, thus, Barlaam hoped for a second chance to present his case against Hesychasm. John V Palaiologos, son of Emperor Andronicus III, succeeded his father in 1341, at age nine. The wife of Emperor Andronicus III Palaiologos was Empress Anna, the daughter of Count Amadeus V of Savoy by his second wife Maria of Brabant. Barlaam soon realized the futility of pursuing his cause, and he left for Calabria, where he converted to the Roman Catholic Church and was appointed Bishop of Gerace. After Barlaam's departure from Byzantium, the theologian Gregory Akindynos continued the legacy of Barlaam's theology in Byzantium and became the chief critic of Palamas.

A council held in Constantinople in August 1341 condemned Akindynos, but Akindynos and his supporters gained a brief victory at a council held in 1344, since the then Patriarch of Constantinople, John XIV (surnamed Kalekas), was opposing Hesychasm, in general, and Gregory Palamas, in particular. In November 1344, the Patriarch's synod excommunicated Gregory Palamas for heresy and vindicated Akindynos, even though the latter had been condemned as a heretic by the council that was convened in August 1341. Moreover, Empress Anna and Patriarch John XIV had Gregory Palamas imprisoned. Patriarch John XIV was an active participant in the Byzantine civil war of 1341–47 as a member of the regency for John V Palaiologos against John VI Kantakouzenos. The supporters of John VI Kantakouzenos were in favor of Hesychasm, whereas Patriarch John XIV and Empress Anna were spiritually closer to the West. In May 1346, John VI Kantakouzenos was crowned emperor at Adrianople, and, in February 1347, John VI Kantakouzenos having prevailed over his enemies, a new council declared Patriarch John XIV deposed, affirmed the resolutions of the council of 1341, and it excommunicated Akindynos and his followers. The new Patriarch of Constantinople, Isidore Buchiras, celebrated the triumph of Hesychasm by replacing several senior members of the ecclesiastical hierarchy with supporters of Hesychasm who were loyal friends of Gregory Palamas's. Moreover, Patriarch Isidore ordained Gregory Palamas as Archbishop of Thessalonica. In 1351, a new patriarchal council at Constantinople, known also as the Fifth Council of Constantinople, proclaimed that the Hesychast theological doctrines are the exclusive binding truth for the whole Orthodox church. After Gregory Palamas's death, the controversies around Hesychasm continued until 1368, when the then Patriarch of Constantinople, Philotheos, convened a last council on this matter, which proclaimed Gregory Palamas a saint.

The victory of Hesychasm in the Eastern Roman Empire signals that, for the Eastern Orthodox church, *grace precedes reason, mystery precedes rationality, hypostasis (personhood) precedes essence, and the purpose of the genuine church of Christ is the deification of humanity.* Therefore, the spiritual secret of Hesychasm is that the genuine church of Christ is a community of uncreated knowledge across time and above space, a spiritual community of persons capable of participating and progressing in the Holy Spirit's uncreated grace, a community of spiritually free persons pursuing their ontological perfection, beyond the state, beyond worldly religious authorities and institutions, and beyond the logic of physical and historical necessities. In this way, humans can achieve what the apostle Paul writes in Ephesians 4:23: to be unceasingly renewed in the spirit of their minds.

Apart from Gregory Palamas, another very influential medieval Hesychast who fought against Western rationalism was Symeon the New Theologian (949–1022 AD), a Byzantine Christian monk and poet who is venerated by the Eastern Orthodox church as a saint. Additionally, the Eastern Orthodox church has given the title of "Theologian" to only three saints, one of whom is Symeon the New Theologian (along with John the Evangelist and Gregory of Nazianzus). The title of "Theologian" was applied to Symeon not in the modern academic sense of theological studies, but to recognize someone who spoke about God from personal experience of God's uncreated energies. On the other hand, Western theology is not focused on personhood, but on logical substances (in the case of scholastic philosophical realism) or on subjective psychological functions (in the case of nominalism). Thus, Western theology cannot easily understand the difference of "religion" as an institutional and psychological issue from "revelation" as a divine call to authentic life, real being.

In the tenth century AD, in the Greek East, Symeon the New Theologian expresses a quest for a kind of faith that is spontaneous, comes from the inside, and it is not exhausted in conforming to conventional specifications. In contradistinction to the theology of Symeon the New Theologian, ritualism seems to declare that the clergy somehow exerts authority over God, who is assumed to have granted his omnipotence to church formalities. Thus, spiritually incompetent clergymen hide their incompetence behind ritualism. Ritualism underpins and secures the psychological authority of the clergy over the laity, and it maintains superstition.

The difference of the Orthodox Christian faith from academic theology can be understood by delving into Symeon the New Theologian's *Hymns of Divine Eros*, in which he contrasts the sense of divine illumination (i.e., a deifying experience) with abstract knowledge and with the argument that everything is explicable entirely within scriptural terms. Symeon the New Theologian's spiritual guide was Symeon the Studite, an influential monk of the famous Monastery of Stoudios in Constantinople during the tenth century AD. Symeon the Studite advised Symeon the New Theologian to read the book *On the Spiritual Law*, which was written by Mark the Ascetic, a Hesychast who lived in the fifth century AD and was a disciple of John Chrysostom's (Mark the Ascetic is also is venerated by the Eastern Orthodox church as a saint). Mark the Ascetic, like Plato, argues that the kind of wisdom that a man can achieve by participating in the Absolute presupposes not only the ability to give an account, but also a psychic cleansing or cure, and, therefore, he connects epistemology with ethics and psychotherapy.

Symeon the New Theologian read Mark the Ascetic's book *On the Spiritual Law*, and he was excited by the following statement that he found in that book: "seeking therapy, pay attention to your conscience and act as it dictates, and, thus, you will benefit yourself." Following Mark the Ascetic's previous advice—according to which "therapy" is the goal of spiritual life, and "paying attention to one's conscience" is the means to spiritual therapy—Symeon the New Theologian articulated a theology that is founded on the principle that a faithful person can be united with God even during his present life. In particular, Symeon argues that the purpose of ascetic life is to cure "spiritual illness," by which he means selfishness and the pathological attitudes that are associated with it, that is, the separation of man's will from God's will. Why does the essence of spiritual illness consist in the separation of man's will from God's will? Because, when man's spirit is selfish (i.e., committed to the service of its own will) it cannot actualize its God-given potential, which is to become a hypostasis that attains to universality by receiving the universal God. A really faithful person maintains an infinitely large psychological space in order to receive and accommodate God, whereas a selfish man is shrunk to and entrenched in his "ego," and he approaches everything and everybody from a utilitarian perspective.

Vaingloriousness, voluptuousness, and avarice are "symptoms" of selfishness that usually are not directly manifested, because they are usually hidden behind a socially acceptable principle of self-affirmation. For instance, I may behave in a saccharine way in order to take advantage of other persons, I may help others in order to affirm myself and/or to receive benefits, etc. However, even though others may not be aware of our hidden expediencies, and even though we may deceive ourselves by focusing on deeds and not on intentions, Mark the Ascetic argues that our secrets are known by God and by our conscience, and that God and our conscience bring correction to us.

Mark the Ascetic argues that, in the context of asceticism, the purpose of paying attention to one's conscience is the following: we resort to our inner judge, precisely, to our conscience, because "conscience is the natural Bible" and those who study it have an "experience of divine perception," and because our conscience knows our intentions, and, therefore, it can inform us about what is really good and judge dishonesty. Therefore, from Mark the Ascetic's perspective, the essence of asceticism consists in developing a moral theory that is focused not on our deeds themselves, but on the intentions that guide our deeds, and in accepting the master of the Good, namely, God, as the king of our intentionality. The previous thesis of Mark the Ascetic transcends every conventional recipe for moral behavior and ritual worship, and it underpins the theology of Symeon the New Theologian.

The era in which Symeon the New Theologian lived, that is, the tenth and the eleventh centuries AD, was characterized by the domination of rationalist theology over Western Europe. As regards the doctrines of Christianity, this new Western theology was made manifest through the doctrinal innovation of the *Filioque*. As I argued in chapter 3, the doctrinal innovation of the *Filioque* is intellectually rooted in the tendency of several Western theologians (including Augustine of Hippo and Thomas Aquinas) to interpret the revelation of God and, particularly, the Persons of the Holy Trinity according to the model of Neoplatonic ontological series that describe the descent of Logos into the world by identifying the divine essence with the divine energies and by identifying each Person of the Holy Trinity, individually, with the divine essence as if each Person of the holy Trinity were an energy of the divine essence, and, in this way, they reduced the energies of the Persons of the Holy Trinity to created symbols through which, according to Western theologians, humans can know God. For this reason, in the context of Augustinian theology, the only way in which humans can know God in this life consists in ecstasy, while unceasing prayer, to which I referred earlier in this chapter, is impossible. From the perspective of Augustine's Neoplatonism and according to the doctrinal innovation of the *Filioque*, the Holy Spirit, proceeding from both the Father and the Son, is an ontological "stage" that produces created symbols of God (created grace). Therefore, the doctrinal innovation of the *Filioque* and, generally, Western Christianity's Neoplatonism lead to the following conclusions: (i) humans cannot participate in God, but can only think about God; (ii) since the symbols of God's revelation, the divine signatures in nature, are created, God's grace is created, and, particularly, it consists in a psychological habit that guides the human will toward God. In the context of the previous Western theology, the deification of humanity (i.e., human participation in the Absolute, the "uncreated") is impossible, and, since humans are confined to the realm of created beings, the spiritual freedom of humanity is a shadow of itself.

The aforementioned Western theological tradition cannot understand the Hesychast teachings about the liberation of the mind from selfish passions, because, by arguing that God's grace consists in a natural habit (something created), the aforementioned rationalist theological tradition identifies the mind with the intellect, and, therefore, it treats a mind that is subjected to rational selfishness as if it were a divinely illumined one, and it dignifies technocracy, looking down upon those who, like Jesus Christ, are "humble in heart" (Matt 11:29) and upon those to whom Jesus Christ referred when he said, "Blessed are the poor in spirit" (Matt 5:3). Moreover, during the era of Symeon the New Theologian, a form of technocratic theology had already started developing in Byzantium, too. That Byzantine technocratic theology was based on knowledge derived from the study of books and formal definitions, and, even though it was outwardly maintaining all the characteristic elements of Eastern Orthodox Christianity, it did not have a strong bond with Orthodox spiritual life. Therefore, even though the previous Byzantine technocratic theology could not be accused of doctrinal deviations, which would trigger theological controversies, it was severely problematic as regards the maintenance of the Orthodox Christian way of life, that is, as regards the application of the Greek church fathers' teachings, which had been degraded into a system of theological formalism. During the era of Symeon the New Theologian, the theological elite of Constantinople was perceiving "holiness" not as the Christians' traditional way of life—which can be achieved by anyone who decides to follow the path of unceasing prayer, called *nepsis* by the Hesychasts—but as a historical phenomenon that belongs to the past, and, therefore, the practice of Christianity in the present was reduced to ritual worship and doctrinal accuracy. The previous trends of academic theology were rejected and severely criticized by Symeon the New Theologian. Moreover, Symeon the New Theologian attempted to reform Byzantine monasticism, since, by the eleventh century, monks had become subservient to the emperor and overly concerned with the acquisition of property, books, and artefacts, instead of following the path of unceasing prayer.

Symeon the New Theologian endured severe opposition from church authorities, and one of his most fierce enemies was the chief theologian of the emperor's court, Archbishop Stephen of Nicomedia, who had previously been a politician and diplomat. Under the influence of rationalist theology, Archbishop Stephen accused Symeon the New Theologian of obscurant enthusiasm and heresy for supporting personal direct experience of God's grace and for teaching that direct experience of God's grace gives monks the authority to preach and give absolution of sins, without the need for formal ordination (as practiced by his own teacher, Symeon the Studite). However, Symeon argues that the real heresy is to teach that man is incapable of having direct experience of God.[4] In contradistinction to Archbishop Stephen's theology, Symeon

---

4. *Discourses* 29.4; Hymn 27.125–32.

emphasizes not only the possibility, but also the necessity of personally experiencing God's uncreated grace. Furthermore, Archbishop Stephen found fault with Symeon for revering his spiritual father, Symeon the Studite, whom Archbishop Stephen attacked as unholy and sinful. In 1005, after an ecclesiastical trial, Symeon the New Theologian was forced to resign from his position as abbot of the monastery of Saint Mamas, near Constantinople, and, in 1009, he was sent into exile near Paloukiton, a small village near Chrysopolis, on the Asiatic shore of the Bosporus, where, with the economic assistance of one of his spiritual children, he renovated a deserted and ruined chapel that had been dedicated to Saint Marina, and he created his hermitage (religious retreat) there. Symeon spent the last thirteen years of his life in exile, remaining at the hermitage of Saint Marina, and he reposed on March 12, 1022. However, ultimately, the Eastern Orthodox church vindicated Symeon by canonizing him and bestowing upon him the title of "New Theologian," thus confessing that the Holy Spirit is the ultimate criterion of truth and the ultimate church authority.[5]

Symeon the New Theologian is interested in the kind of knowledge that underpins salvation (in Greek, *soteria*), meaning ontological fulfillment, and not in the kind of knowledge that merely satisfies man's natural curiosity. In the context of the Greek patristic thought, "salvation" does not mean a static, passive, and actually tedious state, nor an infinite extension of time. Furthermore, in the context of the Greek patristic thought, "hell" does not mean an eternal penalty in a legalistic sense. In particular, from the Hesychasts' perspective, "salvation" does not mean that one is "saved from" something (e.g., from a danger or from a penalty), but it means that one is integral, whole, precisely, that one has reached ontological fulfillment. In other words, "salvation" means the full actualization of one's existential potential. Thus, the Greek word *soteria* is derived from the Greek word *sōos*, which means integral, whole, healthy, and safe. Similarly, the English word "salvation" comes from the late Latin *salvationem*, which comes from *salvare*, which itself is derived from the Latin *salvus*, meaning "healthy" or "safe." Moreover, the proto-Indo-European root of "salvus" is *solwos*, the base of which is *sol-*, meaning "whole." Furthermore, from the perspective of the previous remarks, "holiness" means a struggle for ontological integration and wholeness, and the kind of knowledge that underpins salvation is a kind of practical spiritual therapy.

5. Meyendorff, *Byzantine Theology*, 75.

In his *Hymns*, Saint Symeon the New Theologian emphasizes the sense of God's uncreated light, and he maintains that God revealed Himself through the incarnation of His Logos in order to save humanity, and that humanity's salvation is impossible without the continuous presence of God; in Saint Symeon's own words, humans can know God only "by the vision of the Light which comes from Him." Man's spiritual freedom is founded on and stems from the continuous unity between man and God, and, therefore, in his *Hymns*, Saint Symeon writes the following: "By what boundless mercy, my Savior, have you allowed me to become a member of your body? . . . How is that you have clothed me in the brilliant garment, radiant with the splendor of immortality, transforming all my members into light?"[6] Additionally, in his *Hymns*, Symeon the New Theologian expresses his gratitude to God by writing the following: "I thank you that you have become one spirit with me, without confusion, . . . you the God of all. And that you have become everything for me . . . I express my gratitude to you because for me you have become unsetting light and non-declining sun."[7]

Symeon the New Theologian clarifies exactly what he means by the "total salvation" of humanity in his fifteenth hymn, which Dionysios Zagoraios, an eighteenth-century Orthodox Christian priest and monk, silenced and excluded from his 1790 edition of Symeon the New Theologian's complete works, because Symeon the New Theologian's fifteenth hymn is too provocative for narrow-minded pietists. In particular, in his fifteenth hymn, verses 121, 127–28, 141–79, 226–27, and 235–38, Symeon the New Theologian emphasizes God's presence and energy within and outside the world by using images of physical love related to wedding, nudity, and sexual intercourse. In fact, from the perspective of Symeon's fifteenth hymn, Christ's church is a symbol of the spiritual wedding between man and his archetype, namely, Christ. In the context of the church mystery, man walks barefoot (i.e., with a deep sense of holiness, in accordance with Isaiah 20:2), bareheaded (i.e., with a mind that is devoid of the intellect's images and receptive to God's uncreated grace, in accordance with Isaiah 42:1 and Matthew 5:3) and openhearted in order to joyfully meet and be united with the non-declining Sun, namely, God.

---

6. Symeon the New Theologian, "Hymn 2," ed. Koder, *Sources Chrétiennes*, Vol. 156, 178.

7. Ibid., Preface to the Hymns: "The Mystical Prayer of Our Father Saint Symeon," ed. Koder, *Sources Chrétiennes*, Vol. 156, 150–52.

According to methexiology, which is founded on the works of Symeon the New Theologian and Gregory Palamas, the deifying vision of God's uncreated light is not a kind of divine reward or favor, since it is not an exclusive privilege of the "prizewinners" of the afterlife, but it is also a privilege of those who are spiritually cured in this life. The vision of God's uncreated light, to which Symeon the New Theologian and Gregory Palamas refer, is a consequence of *metanoia* (an ancient Greek word that means "changing one's mind," precisely, turning toward what is holy and eternal) and spiritual freedom in this life. In other words, by throwing off our soul's darkness (i.e., selfishness), and, thus, by being devoid of egoism, we automatically see God's grace, which flows unceasingly toward us. Those who advocate a rigid rationalist and egocentrically idealist attitude toward theology have no hope of gazing at the divine splendor in this life, because of the following reasons: (i) they identify free and intentional will—which is called *gnomikōn thēlema* by the Greek church fathers—with the concept of "natural will," in general, and, therefore, they are unable to conceive of a will or disposition that is not determined by egoism; (ii) they identify logic with the mind, and, therefore, they are unable to conceive of the intellect liberated from the "ego"; (iii) they identify God's uncreated light with God's uncreated essence, and, therefore, they render human participation in God's uncreated light impossible (since man cannot participate in God's essence, anyway), and they teach that, in the afterlife, a material form of fire will be burning the damned humans, while the saved ones will be rewarded with the vision of God and the *eudemonia* that stems from the concurrence between God's will and man's will. According to the scholastic theology of the afterlife, punishment and reward are determined by the judicial judgment of a judgmental and revengeful God, whose ethos reasonably incites humans to atheism, unless someone is neurotically fixated on the idea of God. In other words, the only genuine atheists are those who negate God's goodness and transform Him into an oppressive source of rules of correct conduct.

In his forty-sixth hymn, Symeon the New Theologian writes that we must know our divine father, and that the knowledge of our divine father can be achieved by experiencing our baptismal grace and not merely by studying and preserving religious doctrines and rituals. Religious formalism conveys the impression that the Incarnation of the divine Logos took place only formally, intellectually, but not substantially. Therefore, Symeon the New Theologian emphasizes that we should experience

God's uncreated light, and that our acts should reflect the Savior's mode of being.

Methexiology, in keeping with Hesychasm, emphasizes the essence–energies distinction and, by implication, the mind–intellect distinction. For this reason, it is very useful to delve into the controversy between Gregory Palamas and Barlaam. Barlaam argued that the Hesychasts' epistemology is similar to the heresy of Messalianism,[8] because, according to Barlaam, the Hesychasts aim at achieving a physical vision of God by experiencing what they regard as being God's essence. In keeping with the Augustinian and Thomistic theological traditions, which prevailed in the scholastic West, Barlaam maintains that the divine light to which the Hesychasts refer is a product of created grace. As I have already mentioned, the scholastic West, in general, maintains that the energies of God are either identified with God's essence, in which case they are inaccessible to man, or constitute created apparitions of grace, in which case they are accessible to man. By contrast, in his *Hagioritic Tome*, Gregory Palamas emphasizes that, unlike Messalianism, Hesychasm neither seeks a physical vision of the totally transcendent and unknowable essence of God nor identifies God's uncreated light with God's essence. In particular, in keeping with Plato's theory of spiritual vision and with the suprarational noetic experiences of the biblical prophets and of Christ's disciples, Palamas argues that the uncreated light mentioned by the Hesychasts is a manifestation of God's uncreated energies, which are distinct from God's essense, and that God's uncreated energies can be perceived by both the mind (i.e., the repository of God's energies in the human being) and the senses, but only after the senses have been purified and spiritualized by the return of the mind to the heart, wherein it is filled with God's uncreated grace.

After the aforementioned response by Gregory Palamas, Barlaam put forward another accusation against Hesychasm, claiming that, by advocating the essence–energies distinction, Gregory Palamas had posited the existence of two Gods. Palamas's response to the previous accusation was that both God's essence and His energies are uncreated, and that the distinction between them implies that man is capable of achieving deification by participating in God's energies, while God's essence remains

---

8. The term "Messalian" comes from the Syriac term *mesalyāna*, meaning "one who prays." Messalianism was a fourth-century Christian heresy, according to which, through prayer, man experiences the *essence* of God, and, therefore, he is freed from moral obligations and ecclesiastical discipline.

totally inaccessible, and, thus, God is above every essential or logical determination. Founded on the doctrine of the essence–energies distinction, Gregory Palamas's epistemology implies that humans can know the Good and the truth without the mediation of intellectual images. From this perspective, Palamas's epistemology is a Christocentric perfection of Plato's theory vision/knowledge, to which I referred in chapter 2. Moreover, like Plato, Gregory Palamas maintains that the experience of the Absolute (precisely, God's energies) presupposes a psychic cleansing.

From the perspective of methexiology, and in accordance with Gregory Palamas, the purpose of psychic cleansing is psychological transparency. A soul is transparent if it is cleansed from every element that may impede the descent of God's uncreated energies into the mind. If the mind is identified with the intellect, that is, if the mind is governed by reason (*ratio*), then the soul is not transparent, because, in that case, the mind is constrained to created sources of knowledge. Nicetas Stethatos, a distinguished eleventh-century Hesychast, in his work *On the Soul*, argues that the tree of knowledge of good and evil, which is mentioned in Genesis 2:9, symbolizes two spiritual paths: according to the path that corresponds to the knowledge of Good, man strives to cleanse his mind from every element that may impede the descent of God's uncreated energies into it, whereas, according to the path that corresponds to the knowledge of evil, man tries to discern good from evil by means of created reason, that is, without seeking his participation in God's uncreated energies. Hence, through rationalist theology, man repeats Adam's error, which caused Adam's exile from the uncreated Paradisiacal light.

Furthermore, Barlaam found fault with Hesychasm for teaching that "pure prayer" consists in praying by concentrating the mind (i.e., the repository of the Holy Spirit's uncreated grace) in the heart, that is, in the body. According to Barlaam and his followers, the mind should be freed from the body in prayer. The previous argument of Barlaam and his followers is derived from Augustinian mysticism, to which I referred in chapter 1. In his *Triads in Defense of the Sacred Hesychasts*, Gregory Palamas maintains that the previous argument of Barlaam and his followers contradicts the apostle Paul's doctrine that the body is the temple of the Holy Spirit within man.[9] According to Gregory Palamas, when the mind is cleansed from sin and selfish passions, it functions in concord with the

---

9. 1 Corinthians 6:19.

body, and man sees in himself the grace that Jesus Christ promised to the pure in heart.

In the first triad of his *Triads in Defense of the Sacred Hesychasts*, Gregory Palamas emphasizes that Hesychasm regards it "as evil for the mind to be concerned with the mindings of the flesh, and not wrong for the mind to be in the body, since the body is not evil." Moreover, in the first triad of his *Triads in Defense of the Sacred Hesychasts*, Gregory Palamas poses the following question: "We who carry as in vessels of clay, that is, in our bodies, the light of the Father, in the person of Jesus Christ, in which we know the glory of the Holy Spirit—how can it dishonor our mind to duel in the inner sanctuary of the body?" In the second triad of his *Triads in Defense of the Sacred Hesychasts*, Gregory Palamas answers the previous question as follows: "When spiritual joy comes to the body from the mind, it suffers no diminution by this communion with the body, but rather transfigures the body, spiritualizing it. For then, rejecting all evil desires of the flesh, it no longer weighs down the soul that rises up with it, the whole man becoming spirit."

The heart is the essence of the mind. The soul is united with the body into a unified psychosomatic nexus, and the mind is a power of the soul. But the mind is not an organic component of the soul, because it is derived from outside the soul, in the sense that it is the repository of God's uncreated grace within the human being. Hence, the mind should be filled only with God's uncreated grace, since it is the psychic faculty through which man can achieve direct knowledge of God and be deified. In the first triad of his *Triads in Defense of the Sacred Hesychasts*, Gregory Palamas argues that "the heart is the secret chamber of the mind and the prime physical organ of mental power." Therefore, the term "mind" should not be used interchangeably with the term "intellect." The intellect is a distinct power of the soul, and, particularly, it is the seat of reason, i.e., the psychic faculty of cognition. Whereas the knowledge that is based on the mind is derived from God's uncreated energies (i.e., directly from God), the knowledge that is based on the intellect is derived from a created source. "Paradise" as described in the book of Genesis is a symbol of that existential state in which man is united with the source of the significance of being, and, thus, in "Paradise," the human mind can see God directly. The "Fall of man" as described in Genesis symbolizes the loss of man's direct communion with God. Before the "Fall," the human mind was unceasingly oriented toward and concerned with God, whereas, after the "Fall," the mind of man became mingled with the intellect, and, therefore, it became dispersed upon the created world, and concerned with the created world.

In the first triad of his *Triads in Defense of the Sacred Hesychasts*, Gregory Palamas argues that, "after the Fall, our inner being naturally adapts itself to outward forms," and, in the second triad of the same book, he adds that the aim of the Hesychast is to prevent his mind from "straying hither and thither" and to restore the lost direct communion between his mind and God. Moreover, in the first triad of his *Triads in Defense of the Sacred Hesychasts*, Gregory Palamas quotes Basil the Great, arguing that "the mind, when not dispersed outwardly, returns to itself, and, through itself, ascends to God." With regard to the movements of the mind, Gregory Palamas follows Dionysius the Areopagite, and, thus, he discerns two movements of the mind: the mind is like the eye, in the sense that it sees and observes things other than itself, and, according to Dionysius the Areopagite, this movement of the mind is called the "direct movement" of the mind; but, according to Dionysius, the mind can return to itself, and this movement is called the "circular movement" of the mind. In the first triad of his *Triads in Defense of the Sacred Hesychasts*, Gregory Palamas maintains that the circular movement of the mind is the highest and most befitting mental activity, since, through its circular movement, the mind "even transcends itself and is united with God."

The thought of the Greek church fathers is founded on the fundamental distinction between the "uncreated" (absolute and timeless) and the "created" (relative and subject to temporality). The human soul is not essentially immortal, but it becomes immortal due to God's grace. Therefore, man is free to choose if the end of his life will be spiritual death—that is, existence in separation from God, who, according to John 14:6, "is the way and the truth and the life"—or, alternatively, deification and, hence, existential wholeness and eternal life in God.

5

Mystery, Grace, and Philosophical Theology: Through Unselfishness to Deification

"The time is fulfilled,"[1] "the times of ignorance"[2] passed. "The fullness of the time came,"[3] and the old world's "shadows flee away."[4] "The Logos became flesh, and lived among us."[5] "God sent out his Son, born to a woman, born under the law, that might redeem those who were under the law, that we might receive the adoption of children."[6] The Logos of God, "begotten of the Father before all worlds (aeons) . . . was incarnate by the Holy Spirit of the Virgin Mary, and was made man."[7] Jesus Christ was born *of* the Virgin Mary, not *through* the Virgin Mary, in the sense that he has a human body and soul, his human soul, like ours, has intellect and will, and, in general, Jesus Christ is like us in all things but sin. However, simultaneously, Jesus Christ has the infinite intellect and will of God. Jesus Christ is one divine person (hypostasis), namely, the Logos of God, having two natures, the human and the divine. Thus, Virgin

1. Mark 1:15.
2. Acts 17:30.
3. Galatians 4:4.
4. Song of Songs 2:17.
5. John 1:14.
6. Galatians 4:4–5.

7. The Creed of Christendom according to the First Council of Constantinople (381 AD).

Mary is called Theotokos, which is a Greek word that literally means "birth-giver of God."[8] "Without controversy, the mystery of godliness is great: God was revealed in the flesh."[9] The birth of Jesus Christ signals the entrance of the suprahistorical telos of history into historical becoming.

According to the New Testament, Jesus Christ started his earthly ministry when he became thirty years old. When adequately understood, the number thirty secretly proclaims Jesus Christ the Creator and Preserver of time, nature, and the world of ideas as follows:[10] seven symbolizes the Creator of time, because time is divided in weeks, and each week has seven days, and because, according to Moses's cosmogony, the creation of the world was completed in seven days; five symbolizes the Creator of nature, because there are five senses; eight symbolizes the Creator of the intelligible world, or the world of ideas, because the intelligible world transcends the sensible (temporal) world, and the latter is symbolized by number seven; ten symbolizes the Preserver of the world, because, according to the Holy Bible, God gave ten commandments for the moral perfection of mankind, and because the first letter of the name of the Incarnate Logos in Greek—namely, ΙΗΣΟΥΣ (JESUS)—is the tenth letter of the Greek alphabet. The sum of 5, 7, 8, and 10 is the symbolically important number 30. If we add 3, that is, the number of the Holy Trinity, to 30, then we get 33, which symbolizes the exaltation of Jesus Christ.

"In the fifteenth year of the reign of Tiberius Caesar,"[11] "the word of God came to John son of Zechariah in the desert, and he went into all the country around the Jordan, preaching a baptism of repentance for the forgiveness of sins."[12] "At that time Jesus came from Nazareth in Galilee"[13] "to the Jordan to John to be baptized."[14] "But John would have hindered him, saying, 'I need to be baptized by you, and you come to me?' But Jesus answering, said to him, 'Allow it now; for this is the fitting way for us to fulfill all righteousness.' Then he allowed him. As soon as

---

8. Gregory the Theologian, *Patrologia Graeca*, Vol. 36, 113, 633, 641.

9. 1 Timothy 3:16.

10. The following remarks about the spiritual meaning of various numbers associated with the person of Jesus Christ have originally been proposed by Maximus the Confessor; Maximus the Confessor, "First Century" (written for Thalassius), *Philokalia*, Vol. 2.

11. Luke 3:1.

12. Luke 3:3.

13. Mark 1:9.

14. Matthew 1:13.

Jesus was baptized, he went up out of the water; and behold, the heavens were opened to him, and he saw the Spirit of God descending as a dove and coming to him. Behold, a voice out of the heavens said, 'This is my beloved Son, with whom I am well pleased.'"[15]

As John Chrysostom has pointed out, Jesus Christ was baptized neither according to the Jewish baptism nor according to the Christian baptism, but according to John the Baptist's type of baptism.[16] These three types of baptism—namely, the Jewish, the Christian, and the Johannite baptism—are different from each other. The Jewish type of baptism was cleansing man from corporeal filths, but not from spiritual sins. Thus, according to the Mosaic Law, a sinful person shall "bathe himself in water," but he shall "be unclean until the evening."[17] According to John Chrysostom, cleansing instructions were incorporated into the Mosaic Law not because specific material objects (e.g., specific types of food, clothes, etc.) were literally unclean, but in order to instruct people who were still spiritually imperfect and, therefore, needed instructions for material cleansing to become more reverent toward God and pay more attention to their conscience.[18] The Christian type of baptism is not like the Jewish one, but it is much more important than that and full of God's uncreated grace. Therefore, the Christian type of baptism cleanses the soul from ancestral sin and gives the Holy Spirit to it. John the Baptist's type of baptism was spiritually superior to the Jewish one, because, in contradistinction to the Mosaic Law, which was preaching cleansing by instructing people to wash their clothes and bathe themselves in water, John the Baptist was preaching cleansing by instructing people to "produce fruit worthy of repentance."[19] However, according to John Chrysostom, John the Baptist's type of baptism is spiritually inferior to the Christian type of baptism, because it was neither giving the Holy Spirit to those who were being baptized by John the Baptist nor was it offering forgiveness of sins through God's uncreated grace.[20]

Jesus Christ said about John the Baptist: "among those who are borne of women there is no one greater than John, yet he who is least in

---

15. Matthew 3:14–17.
16. John Chrysostom, *Patrologia Graeca*, Vol. 49, 367.
17. Leviticus 17:15.
18. John Chrysostom, *Patrologia Graeca*, Vol. 49, 366.
19. Matthew 3:8.
20. John Chrysostom, *Patrologia Graeca*, Vol. 49, 369.

God's kingdom is greater than he."[21] The previous statement means that, of all people, no one fulfilled his God-given purpose better than John the Baptist, yet, in God's kingdom, all who come after John the Baptist have a greater spiritual heritage, because the human nature was restored to its Paradisiacal state, that is, it became capable of deification, as a result of the Incarnation of the divine Logos, namely, Jesus Christ. In other words, through his previous statement, Jesus Christ was contrasting life before Christ (mentioning that, throughout the pre-Christian era, the spiritually greatest person was John the Baptist) with life in the fullness of Christ's kingdom.

Why was Jesus Christ baptized by John the Baptist? According to Cyril of Alexandria, Jesus Christ received John the Baptist's type of baptism, whose nature was incapable of offering forgiveness of sins through God's uncreated grace, because, in this way, Jesus Christ taught us that he did not need to receive forgiveness of sins, since he assumed the human nature, with its infirmities, its liabilities, its temptations, but he was totally free from the law of sin, since he was the only-begotten Son and Logos of God.[22] Moreover, according to John Chrysostom, Jesus Christ received John the Baptist's type of baptism, whose nature was incapable of giving the Holy Spirit to those who were being baptized by John the Baptist, because, in this way, Jesus Christ taught us that he did not need to be given the Holy Spirit through baptism, since Jesus Christ is the Incarnate Logos of God, and his flesh was originally created by the Holy Spirit.[23]

However, the following question emerges: since Jesus Christ did not need to repent for anything, nor did he need to receive the Holy Spirit through baptism (since the totality of the Holy Spirit is in the only-begotten Son and Logos of God), why didn't he simply avoid John the Baptist's baptism? According to John Chrysostom, the answer to the previous question is that, by receiving John the Baptist's baptism, Jesus Christ was made known to the people by God, namely, through the Father's voice, saying that Jesus Christ is the Son of God, and through the Holy Spirit, who bore witness to Jesus Christ's divinity by descending like a dove and lighting upon Jesus Christ.[24] Thus, at the baptism of Jesus Christ, the Holy Trinity was revealed. Furthermore, John Chrysostom points

---

21. Luke 7:28.
22. Cyril of Alexandria, *Patrologia Graeca*, Vol. 72, 521.
23. John Chrysostom, *Patrologia Graeca*, Vol. 49, 367.
24. Ibid., Vol. 49, 367–68.

out that, by being baptized by John the Baptist, Jesus Christ fulfilled "all righteousness," and, thus, Jesus Christ revealed himself as the telos of the Mosaic Law.[25] After Jesus Christ's baptism, the Mosaic Law was terminated, since Jesus Christ preached the spiritual worship of God, instead of Moses's legalistic system of worship, he preached the deification of man, instead of Moses's legalistic system of morality, and he preached the kingdom of God, instead of an earthly kingdom. As John the Evangelist writes, "the law was given through Moses; grace and truth came through Jesus Christ."[26]

According to the Greek church fathers Theophilus of Antioch[27] and Irenaeus of Lyons,[28] before the Fall of man, the forebears of humanity were endowed with potential perfection, in the sense that they were endowed with the image of God from the start, and they were called to acquire the likeness of God by their own free will and efforts, assisted simultaneously by God's uncreated grace.[29] From the Greek church fathers' perspective, the narration of the book of Genesis is a story of man's struggle for spiritual progress and ontological perfection. In this context, the Fall of man can be interpreted as follows: in the state of Paradise, the first Adam, the Paradisiacal Adam, was existing unceasingly united with his archetype, that is, with his ontological telos, but, when he decided to assert his own reason's autonomy and self-sufficiency vis-à-vis the divine Logos, namely, vis-à-vis his effective and final cause, he interrupted his communion with God, and, therefore, he lost the divine Logos (i.e., he failed to keep the divine Logos in mind). Without the divine Logos, man was unable to actualize his ontological potential, that is, to achieve his deification. Thus, as Gregory the Theologian has pointed out, the first Adam, by losing the divine Logos, deprived humanity of access to

---

25. Ibid., Vol. 49, 369.

26. John 1:17.

27. Theophilus of Antioch was a second century Bishop of Antioch and Christian apologist. William Sanday, describes him as "one of the precursors of that group of writers who, from Irenaeus to Cyprian, not only break the obscurity which rests on the earliest history of the church, but alike in the East and in the West carry it to the front in literary eminence, and distance all their heathen contemporaries" (*Studia Biblica*, 90). He is venerated as a saint in both Eastern and Western Christianity.

28. Irenaeus of Lyons (d. 202) was Bishop of Lugdunum (now Lyons, France). He was a Greek from Smyrna in Asia Minor. He is venerated as a saint in both Eastern and Western Christianity.

29. Romanides, *The Ancestral Sin*.

Paradise.[30] However, the second Adam, namely, Jesus Christ, by fulfilling "all righteousness" and revealing the divine Logos, restored humanity's access to Paradise. Thus, by the term "Paradise," we should understand a state of perfect communion between man and God, and, since, after the Incarnation of the Logos in the person of Jesus Christ, the Father (divine Nous) sends the Holy Spirit to humanity in the name of the Jesus Christ,[31] man can experience Paradise in this life, too. Moreover, by the term "sin" we should understand the commitment of spiritual errors, that is, acts and attitudes that contradict the human telos, which is deification. There is a symbolic analogy between Noah's flood and Jesus Christ's baptism: through Noah's flood, the earth was cleansed,[32] and, through Jesus Christ, the human nature was cleansed.

After his baptism, Jesus Christ "was led by the Spirit into the wilderness."[33] "He was there in the wilderness forty days . . . with the wild animals,"[34] and "after fasting for forty days and forty nights, he was hungry."[35] After being tempted by Satan and defeating the tempter, "the devil left him, and behold, angels came and served him."[36] There is a symbolic analogy between the children of Israel who, after crossing the Red Sea, "walked forty years in the wilderness,"[37] and Jesus Christ, who was in the wilderness forty days. According to Epiphanius of Cyprus,[38] the "wilderness" is a symbol of our inner earth, what Cyril of Alexandria refers to as humanity's "fallen nature,"[39] and what Gregory of Nyssa refers to as a rough soul,[40] i.e., a filthy, dry, and tough soul. The "wild animals" that exist in the previous symbolic wilderness symbolize selfish passions and desires, and the worst of all these "wild animals" is the devil, who, according to the apostle Peter, "walks around like a roaring lion, seeking

---

30. Gregory the Theologian, *Patrologia Graeca*, Vol. 36, 353.
31. John 14:26.
32. Genesis 6–9.
33. Matthew 4:1.
34. Mark 1:13.
35. Matthew 4:2.
36. Matthew 4:11.
37. Joshua 5:6.

38. Epiphanius of Cyprus, *Patrologia Graeca*, Vol. 41, 1032. Epiphanius of Cyprus was a fourth-century Bishop of Salamis, Cyprus. He is venerated as a saint in both Eastern and Western Christianity.

39. Cyril of Alexandria, *Patrologia Graeca*, Vol. 77, 1188.
40. Gregory of Nyssa, *Patrologia Graeca*, Vol. 46, 593.

whom he may devour,"⁴¹ since the devil is an angel (spiritual being) who exercised his freedom of will in such an errant way that he became the paradigmatic representative of ontological failure, which is the essence of evil. However, due to the presence of Jesus Christ, the "wilderness" is transformed, or rather transmuted, into a cleansed soul in which the communion between man and God takes place. Thus, the prophet Isaiah rejoices, saying: "The wilderness and the dry land will be glad. The desert will rejoice and blossom like a lily."⁴² The previous transmutation is the essence of the mystery of the church of Christ.

Jesus Christ explicitly said to a Pharisee called Nicodemus that real theology and the salvation of humanity consist in human participation in the uncreated grace of God: "unless one is born anew, he cannot see God's kingdom . . . unless one is born of water and spirit, he cannot enter into God's kingdom. That which is born of the flesh is flesh. That which is born of the Spirit is spirit."⁴³ In the previous teaching of Jesus Christ, water symbolizes baptism. Basil the Great has pointed out that, if the Israelites had not crossed the Red Sea, they could not separate themselves from the Pharaoh, and that, similarly, through baptism, Christians separate themselves from "devil's tyranny."⁴⁴ According to Basil the Great, baptized Christians imitate the prophet Joshua (Jesus of Navi): they leave the "wilderness" (i.e., the sin) and cross the Jordan (i.e., the border between the kingdom of grace and the realm of devil's tyranny), just as Joshua "came up out of the middle of the Jordan";⁴⁵ they bear Christ's gospel, just as Joshua was bearing the ark of God's covenant;⁴⁶ they run toward the Christian polity, a polity flowing with uncreated grace, just as Joshua was moving toward the promised land, "a land flowing with milk and honey."⁴⁷

One day that Jesus Christ was passing through Samaria, "being tired from his journey," he sat down by Jacob's well, and he revealed the mystery of true worship to a Samaritan woman who came to draw water: "the hour comes, when neither in this mountain, nor in Jerusalem, will you

---

41. 1 Peter 5:8.
42. Isaiah 35:1.
43. John 3:3–7.
44. Basil the Great, *Patrologia Graeca*, Vol. 31, 428.
45. Joshua 4:18.
46. Joshua 4:9–11.
47. Joshua 5:6.

worship the Father . . . the hour comes, and now is, when the true worshipers will worship the Father in spirit and truth, for the Father seeks such to be his worshipers. God is spirit, and those who worship him must worship in spirit and truth."[48] In other words, the true temple for the true worship of God is the human soul, particularly, the mind (the repository of God's uncreated energy in man), and the perfect way of worshiping God consists in cleansing our mind from all created forms of knowledge (e.g., our own thoughts, sentiments, instincts, etc.) in order to be filled with God's uncreated grace. Jesus Christ contrasts worshiping God "in spirit and truth"—which is focused on taking care of our inner temple of God—with the Pharisees' religious legalism and formalism and with the Sadducees' ritualism and pietism. In this context, Jesus Christ said that "the Sabbath was made for man, and not man for the Sabbath,"[49] and he exposed the real ethos and the real motives of the scribes and the Pharisees, saying the following: "Woe to you, scribes and the Pharisees, hypocrites! For you clean the outside of the cup and of the platter, but within they are full of extortion and unrighteousness. . . . For you are like whitened tombs, which outwardly appear beautiful, but inwardly are full of dead men's bones, and of all uncleanness."[50] Moreover, whereas the Sadducees believed that the temple of Jerusalem could also be used as a place to transact business, "Jesus entered into the temple of God, and drove out all of those who sold and bought in the temple."[51]

Jesus Christ said to the Samaritan woman to whom he revealed the true worship: "You were right when you said, 'I have no husband,' for you have had five husbands; and he whom you now have is not your husband."[52] The Greek church father Euthymius Zigavenos, a prominent Byzantine theologian and author, has interpreted this biblical passage as follows: the Samaritan woman symbolizes the human nature, which, symbolically, has had "five husbands," that is, five laws, and, during the time of Jesus Christ, it had a sixth law; the first law that the human nature has had was the law of Paradise, the second was the law after the Fall of Adam (post-Paradisiacal law), the third was the law of the Flood of Noah (Noahic Covenant, found in Genesis 9:8–17), the fourth was the law of

48. John 6:3–24.
49. Mark 2:27.
50. Matthew 23:25–27.
51. Matthew 21:12.
52. John 4:17–18.

Abraham's circumcision (found in Genesis 17:23–27), the fifth was the law of Abraham's sacrifice of Isaac (found in Genesis 22:7–8; God did not want Isaac to die, but He wanted Abraham to sacrifice Isaac in his heart, so it would be clear that Abraham loved God more than he loved his son), and the sixth law was the Law of Moses (found in Exodus 20–31).[53] The Law of Moses was only the shadow of good things to come,[54] it could not bring about justification,[55] it could not bring about perfection,[56] it could not free man's conscience from a knowledge of sin,[57] and, therefore, when Christ was born, humanity was in need of a new law. "One of the scribes" asked Jesus Christ, "Which commandment is the greatest of all?"[58] Jesus Christ's answer was the following: "The greatest is, 'Hear, Israel, the Lord our God, the Lord is one: you shall love the Lord your God with all your heart, and with all your soul, and with all your mind, and with all your strength.' This is the first commandment. The second is like this, 'You shall love your neighbor as yourself.' There is no other commandment greater than these."[59] In addition, at the Last Supper with his disciples, before being crucified, Jesus Christ said: "A new commandment I give to you, that you love one another. Just as I have loved you, you also love one another. By this everyone will know that you are my disciples, if you have love for one another."[60] The new law, that is, the Law of Christ, is love.

In order to understand love as the Law of Christ, we must interpret love not as a sentiment, but as God's mode of being. A sentiment is an emotion endowed with an evaluative judgment. Love *qua* sentiment means that a person X loves a person Y because of the benefits (e.g., emotional gratification, material benefits, etc.) that come from that relationship, and, therefore, ultimately, the energy of X's love for Y returns to X. Sentimental, worldly love is self-seeking: when we love in this way, we seek to unite ourselves with some other mortal human being for immediate purposes, such as happiness, self-satisfaction, or worldly joys and pleasures. However, God loves because this is the way He exists, since He

---

53. Zigavenos, *Patrologia Graeca*, Vol. 129, 1193.
54. Colossians 2:17; Hebrews 10:1.
55. Acts 13:39.
56. Hebrews 7:19.
57. Hebrews 10:1–4.
58. Mark 12:28
59. Mark 12:29–31.
60. John 13:34–35.

is totally self-sufficient, and, thus, He does not need to receive any benefit from any relationship. In regard to God, communion is an ontological category, since God is a communion of three Persons, and God is in communion with creation, since the latter is an actualization of God's will. Thus, God's love stems from the ontological category of communion, and, in fact, it is the life of communion, that is, Paradise. Moreover, love as the Law of Christ, that is, love as God's mode of being, is equivalent to spiritual freedom, because it implies that one is free from any logical, natural, or historical necessity; such a person is even free from the logic of individual interest. This is the essence of the mystery of the Eucharist, which Jesus Christ instituted at the Last Supper.[61]

From the perspective of the Law of Christ, we can talk meaningfully about "philosophical theology" only if and to the extent that the term "philosophy"—which is a Greek word literally meaning "love of wisdom"—is understood as a way of life that manifests and expresses one's conscious choice to seek truth freely and "for the sake of *theoria*"; hence, from the previous perspective, philosophers do what they do for love. This is the essence of the classical Greek approach to philosophy. According to Herodotus's account (1.29.2), Solon, one of the so-called "seven sages" of ancient Greece (i.e., seven early-sixth-century BC philosophers, statesmen, and law-givers), having given the Athenians new laws, travelled around the world "for the sake of *theoria*."[62] In other words, philosophy is a self-sufficient conscious enquiry that is nurtured and enriched by the given activity itself, since *theoria* (i.e., gazing at the real truth) is the ultimate pleasure of the mind, and, therefore, an end-in-itself. In contradistinction to the previous Greek perception of philosophy, the Latin perception of philosophy treats philosophy in a rather instrumental way, that is, as a means to rhetorical and, ultimately, historical ends. Thus, whereas the Greek perception of philosophy is focused on man's participation in and, ultimately, union with the real truth, the Latin perception of philosophy is focused on the authority of reason and logical coherence. As I argued in the previous chapters, medieval Western philosophy is founded on the Latin approach to philosophy, and, therefore, it gave rise to scholasticism.

---

61. Matthew 26:26–28; Mark 14:22–24; Luke 22:19–20; 1 Corinthians 11:23–29.
62. Curd and Graham, eds, *The Oxford Handbook of Presocratic Philosophy*, 512.

Jesus Christ built his church on the "rock"[63] of mystery, that is, on a truth that was not revealed by "flesh and blood" (i.e., it did not originate from a created source of knowledge), but by God the Father himself,[64] and, therefore, the church of Christ transcends critical reasoning. By contrast, scholasticism has developed through critical reasoning, that is, through "the weak and miserable elemental principles"[65] of this world. As I argued in chapter 4, scholasticism perceives grace as something "supernatural," whereas Hesychasm perceives grace as something uncreated. In fact, from the perspective of Hesychasm, on which methexiology is founded, the term "supernatural," especially as it was used by medieval scholastics, is rather awkward and confusing: God's grace and God's energies are uncreated, and—apart from God, who is uncreated—every other being and thing is created.

According to Hesychasm, the only meaningful way of using the term "supernatural" is to define it as a synonym for the term "uncreated." In the second triad of his *Triads in Defense of the Sacred Hesychasts*, Gregory Palamas argues that, "among God's gifts some are natural; they are granted indiscriminately to all. . . . Others are supernatural and full of mystery. These latter gifts I hold to be higher than the former," and he continues as follows: "philosophy is one of the natural gifts of God, as are also the discoveries of human reason, the sciences." By perceiving grace as something uncreated, Hesychasm implies that real theology consists in man's participation in God's uncreated energies, that is, real theology consists in the deification of man. On the other hand, by perceiving grace as something "supernatural"—that is, as an extreme and superb, *yet created*, phenomenon—scholasticism constrains theology to created sources of knowledge, and, thus, ultimately, theology is subsumed to human reason.

Throughout the Middle Ages, the Roman Catholic church was providing Western societies with a rationalist way of thinking. The only difference between the medieval Roman Catholic church's rationalism and modern rationalism is that the first was controlled by the authority of the Pope, whereas the latter is independent of the Papacy. In fact, following a rationalist way of thinking, scholastics applied human reason even to the

---

63. Matthew 16:18.
64. Matthew 16:17.
65. Galatians 4:9.

"surpassing all understanding"[66] mystery of the Holy Trinity, primarily through the *Filioque*. The medieval Roman Catholic church's rationalist theology was systematized in the thirteenth century by Thomas Aquinas on the basis of a Western rationalist interpretation of classical Greek philosophy, as I pointed out in chapters 1–4. As explained in the previous chapters, the medieval West's rationalist interpretation of classical Greek philosophy consists in the thesis that Aristotle's universals were radically separate from the material world and in treating Platonic ideas as if they were logical substances. Thus, during the Council of Ferrara–Florence (1438–45), in which the Greek and the Latin churches tried to reach an agreement on their doctrinal differences, Papal theologians were not only invoking Aristotle's authority in their studies of the Holy Trinity, but also they were interpreting Aristotle's philosophy in a Western rationalist way that was spiritually alien to the Greeks.

Scholasticism espoused a rationalist theology and rejected the Hesychasts' doctrine of the essence–energies distinction, on which the Hesychasts' arguments about the deification of man are based. Thus, scholasticism investigates uncreated things as if they were created and, from the perspective of the Hesychasts, prefers "to trust in man" than "to take refuge in the LORD."[67] The previous attitude constitutes the humanistic core of scholasticism, and, for this reason, scholastics (rather involuntarily) paved the way to modern philosophy. Moreover, the previous peculiar humanistic attitude of scholasticism pervades Protestantism.

The pioneers of Protestantism, such as Martin Luther (1483–1546) and John Calvin (1509–64), had good intentions, and they sincerely attempted to liberate people from the authoritarian regime of the Papacy and to give them direct access to the Holy Scripture.[68] But they did not espouse the Hesychasts' doctrine of the deification of man, and they did not manage to find an equilibrium between spirituality and historicity; such an equilibrium can been safeguarded through the principle of the Holy Tradition, which was discarded by Luther and Calvin. Thus, the vigor of Protestantism was gradually weakened. The Lutherans' indifference toward the church's dogmatology gradually led them to cynicism and rationalist speculation. Thus, gradually, Lutheran piety became an overly subjectivist and extremely formalist religious system, and, ulti-

---

66. Philippians 4:8.
67. Psalm 117:8 (Greek/Septuagint numbering of the Psalms).
68. Sabine and Thorson, *A History of Political Theory*, chapter 19.

mately, it was degraded. Moreover, Luther's amphoteric attitude toward the relations between church and state gave rise to a type of Caesaropapism, which proved Luther an agent of German nationalism.

Calvin, like Luther, failed to fully grasp the notion of divine grace (as an uncreated source of knowledge), and he elaborated a cruel, rationalist Protestant movement, which, in its attempt to overcome the problems of Lutheranism, created new theological problems. Calvin's theology is centered on the grandeur, the sovereignty, and the juristic thought of a fair God-Punisher, thus giving rise to a coercive, formalist moral code and to religious fanaticism. In his *Institutio Christianae religionis* 1:XVII:1 and 1:XVIII:1, Calvin argues that criminals and Satan himself are instruments of divine providence and, more specifically, of divine wrath! Therefore, the Calvinists' morality is founded not on God's love (i.e., the Law of Christ), but on the fear of hell, and, in the context of Calvinism, the Christian value of mercy is subordinate to a strict penal code. In addition, from Calvin's perspective, grace is an arbitrary side effect of God's will, irrelevant to man's freedom of will, and, for this reason, in chapter 21 of Book III of his *Institutio*, Calvin deduced that "God has predestinated some to salvation, and others to destruction."

However, renouncing the flaws of Lutheranism and Calvinism, the Dutch Protestant theologian Jacobus Arminius (1560–1609) advocated the personal, free, and charismatic character of the relationship between man and God by stressing that "man has not saving grace of himself" and that, unaided by the Holy Spirit, no person is able to respond to God's will; additionally, according to Jacobus Arminius, the grace "of God is the beginning, continuance, and accomplishment of any good," yet man may resist the Holy Spirit.[69] Moreover, in the eighteenth century, the Anglican theologian John Wesley, following the theological legacy of Jacobus Arminius, wrote a series of sermons and treatises in which he emphasized prevenient grace, present personal salvation by faith, the witness of the Spirit, and sanctification. Jacobus Arminius's and John Wesley's theological systems express Protestants' quest for a hypostatic mode of existence, and, from this perspective, they can be considered as a "bridge" between Protestantism and Hesychasm, but, in contradistinction to Hesychasm, neither Jacobus Arminius's theology nor John Wesley's theology teaches the deification of man as man's participation in God's uncreated energies.

---

69. Bray, ed., *Documents of the English Reformation*, 453–54.

Because of the fact that the Roman Catholic and the Protestant West rejected the Hesychasts' teachings about the deification of man, Western Christianity gave primacy to the achievement of historical goals over the ontological perfection of man. This is the essence of the West's secularism and humanism, which render the Christ mystery inaccessible. It is worth noting that, in the sixteenth century AD, the Pope was more like a king, ruling over a large territory known as the Papal States; he was the largest land-owner in Italy. Thus, the Pope's authority was deeply entangled in nearly every aspect of worldly authority. During the Renaissance, at the zenith of the Papal regime's power, Popes collect taxes, use armies to confiscate their enemies' riches and amass fortunes by asserting their power like kings. Furthermore, due to its secularism and humanism, that is, due to its spiritual entrapment in the logic of historical necessity and in man-made logoi, the Roman Catholic and the Protestant West did not hesitate to justify religious crimes. For instance, according to the Fourth Lateran Council (1215), heretics should be "exterminated," and, according to Thomas Aquinas, heretics "deserve not only to be separated from the church by excommunication, but also to be severed from the world by death."[70] The previous violent mentality influenced Martin Luther, too, who, in his essay "Against the Robbing and Murdering Hordes of Peasants," argued as follows: "let everyone who can, smite, slay, and stab them, secretly or openly, remembering that nothing can be more venomous, hurtful, or devilish than a rebel."[71]

Thus, the West's rationalist theological systems have given rise to authoritarian regimes and religious crimes, which, in their turn, have given rise to the "fear-of-the-Holy-Inquisition" complex, which persecutes the modern Western soul. At the first mention of the terms "true faith" and "doctrinal theology," the modern Western soul, almost automatically, recoils from visions of heretics being burned at the stake, sinister monks torturing their victims to death in dark recesses of spooky monasteries, and Puritans' witch-hunts. All this really happened in the Roman Catholic and the Protestant West.[72]

---

70. Aquinas, *Summa Theologica* II:II, 11:3 corpus.

71. Included in Rupp and Drewery, eds, *Martin Luther*, 121–26.

72. Versluis, *The New Inquisitions*. In his book *The New Inquisitions*, Arthur Versluis has analyzed the following "archetypal dimensions of the inquisition": the first archetypal dimension of the inquisition is to have two hands that administer justice, instead of one (e.g., the one hand may be a judgmental religious institution, and the other hand may be a secular justice system); the second archetypal dimension of the

Even though, at the level of doctrinal theology, the Eastern Orthodox church officially endorses Hesychasm, the institutional authorities of the Eastern Orthodox church are not immune to rationalism, bureaucratization, ritualism, superstition, and authoritarianism. For instance, as I have already pointed out, before being ultimately canonized by the Eastern Orthodox church, Symeon the New Theologian and Gregory Palamas were persecuted by members of the administrative elite of the Eastern Orthodox church. Moreover, even though, during the Middle Ages, Constantinople, known also as the New Rome, was the major institutional guardian of the Eastern Orthodox church's doctrinal theology, the Byzantines began to pride themselves on the renown and glitter of their empire and capital city and to grow lax in theological affairs, as may be seen in the betrayals of the Eastern Orthodox church's faith that took place at the Second Council of Lyons (convened by Pope Gregory X in 1274 after Michael VIII Palaiologos, the Byzantine emperor, gave assurances that the Eastern Orthodox church was prepared to reunite with Rome in an irregular way, since Michael VIII Palaiologos was hoping that, by acknowledging the supremacy of the Pope, he would gain financial support for his wars of conquest) and at the Council of Ferrara–Florence (1438–45), where the German scholar Nicolaus Cusanus defended the *Filioque*, while several Byzantine delegates and the Byzantine Emperor John VIII Palaiologos himself were in favor of the unification of the Eastern Orthodox and the Roman Catholic churches for political and economic reasons; however, Mark Evgenikos, Archbishop of Ephesus, refused to sign the decrees of the Council of Ferrara–Florence, thus preventing the unification between the Eastern Orthodox church and the Papacy.[73]

As a result of the bureaucratization of church life, several church authorities in both Eastern and Western Christianity promote a distorted conception of obedience. In particular, in the context of secularized

---

Inquisition is criminalized thought, instead of action; the third archetypal dimension of the inquisition is the use of torture against persons who have 'wrong thoughts'; the fourth archetypal dimension of the inquisition is to instill fear into people to the point that the person's existential otherness is erased.

73. Mark Evgenikos is venerated as a saint in the Eastern Orthodox church. The Eastern Orthodox church praises Mark Evgenikos by chanting the following kontakion (Tone 3): "As one clad in invincible armor,/ thou didst cast down the pride of the Western rebellion;/ thou didst become an instrument of the Comforter/ and shine forth as Orthodoxy's defender./ Therefore, we cry to thee: Rejoice, O Mark, boast of the Orthodox."

churches, obedience underpins authoritarian and bureaucratic relations, whereas, in the context of genuine ecclesiastical relations, obedience means that one accepts to be spiritually guided by another person whom he acknowledges as a spiritual teacher and/or as the provost of the eucharistic gathering. Therefore, the fifteenth canon of the First-and-Second Council (861 AD)[74] allows each and every person to separate from and break communion with any bishop/overseer who publicly preaches a heresy, and, precisely, it states that "those who separate from communion with their president because of some heresy . . . not only are not subject to the penalty laid down by the canons, but are also worthy of the honor befitting the Orthodox," since, according to the same canon, "they have condemned not bishops, but false bishops and false teachers." In other words, according to the fifteenth canon of the First-and-Second Council, each and every member of the church has to be spiritually vigilant and is personally responsible for the maintenance of the true faith. For instance, in 658 AD, Maximus the Confessor, although he was only a simple monk, separated from and broke communion with every patriarch, metropolitan, archbishop, and bishop in the East and with Pope Vitalian of Rome because of their having been infected with the heresy of Monothelitism. In a letter to his disciple Anastasius, Maximus the Confessor wrote that, when he was asked what church did he belong to (since the churches of Constantinople, Rome, Antioch, Alexandria, and Jerusalem were united), he answered as follows: "The God of all pronounced that the Catholic [i.e., universal] church was the correct and saving confession of the faith in him when he called Peter blessed because of the terms in which he had made proper confession to him." Finally, the Sixth Ecumenical Council

---

74. This council is given this title by Theodore Balsamon (a twelfth-century canonist of the Eastern Orthodox church and Orthodox Patriarch of Antioch), John Zonaras (a twelfth-century Byzantine chronicler and theologian) and others. The First-and-Second Council was held in Constantinople and was assembled in the time of Emperor Michael, son of Theophilus, and of Bardas Caesar, his uncle on his mother's side, in the year 861 AD. It was attended by three hundred and eighteen church fathers. There was held a first convention of this council, and the Orthodox members won, and the heterodox (remnants of Iconoclasm) were defeated. But the heretics refused to have the records of this council preserved, and they made such a disturbance and fight that the first convention was dissolved without any definition and result being committed to writing. After some time had passed, a second convention of the same council was held, and again there was a discussion of the Orthodox participants with the heretics concerning the same subjects. This meeting's resolutions were written up. Thus, this council was called the First-and-Second, since it had held a first and a second convention.

(680–81 AD) vindicated Maximus the Confessor and his few disciples and condemned for heresy four Patriarchs of Constantinople, one Pope of Rome, one Patriarch of Alexandria, two Patriarchs of Antioch, and a multitude of other metropolitans, archbishops, and bishops, admitting that, during the Monothelite controversy, that simple monk and his followers were recapitulating the historical manifestation of the true Christian church, whereas all those notable bishops were wrong.

Moreover, several Roman Catholic and Eastern Orthodox clergymen have endorsed a misguided, superstitious approach to holy relics (and, especially during the Middle Ages, the Roman Catholic Church was engaged in a profane relic trade[75]), even though Jesus Christ has explicitly warned Christians against those priests who profiteer in holy relics and the bodies of saints in various ways.[76] One should hold the relics in respect, but not worship them. The genuine Orthodox Christian spirituality is focused on the deification of man, and it has nothing to do with superstitious attitudes. From the perspective of Orthodox Christianity, grace is neither a "privileged place" nor a "privileged object" controlled by the clergy, but it refers to a mode of existence that is characterized by psychic openness, existential heroism, and spiritual communion. However, several Christian clergymen, including members of the Eastern Orthodox clergy, cultivate superstitious mentalities, behind which they hide their spiritual inadequacy, and, through superstition, they manipulate people's neuroses.

In general, the language of Christ and his church is symbolic, but many people nominally identified as Christians are insensitive to symbolism and often prone to superstition. The word "symbol" is etymologically derived from the Greek verb *symbállo*, which means to place together and to join. In general, a symbol has the following qualities: (i) Not only does it refer to an external reality, but also it discloses within itself the nature of the external reality to which it refers. (ii) It participates in the spiritual reality of the symbolized object, function, or process. Therefore, a symbol is substantially different from an allegory; whereas the first participates in the spiritual reality of the symbolized object, function, or process, an allegory is something that passively and rather formalistically represents or stands for something else. (iii) Even though it participates in the spiritual reality of the symbolized object, function, or process, a

75. Herman, *Mistress of the Vatican*, 241.
76. Matthew 23:29; John 6:51.

symbol never represents the reality of the symbolized object, function, or process exhaustively, and, therefore, the spiritual reality of the symbolized object, function, or process always transcends the corresponding symbol; the reality of the symbolized object, function, or process always remains beyond any representation and image, and it can be disclosed only through an intuitive gaze, that is, through faith.

When faith is missing, then one can still be aware of the difference between a symbol and an allegory (effigy), but then one's experience of a symbol consists in either empathy or superstition. In order to understand the difference between empathy and symbolism, we may, for instance, think of an English social anthropologist who understands (empathizes with) a tribe in Sudan that he observes, but he does not experience that tribe's behavior and attitudes as his own personal behavior and attitudes. In order to understand the difference between superstition and symbolism, we must focus on the fact that the spiritual reality of the symbolized object, function, or process can be accessed only through faith, that is, spiritually and not representationally, whereas the superstitious approach to symbols is necessarily dependent on representation.

The fourteenth-century AD Byzantine theologian Nikolaos Cabasilas, who is venerated as a saint in the Eastern Orthodox church, wrote a treatise *On the Divine Liturgy*, in which he uses the term "symbol" as I previously defined it, in order to interpret the divine liturgy, in general, and Jesus Christ's command, "do this in remembrance of me,"[77] in particular. According to Cabasilas, the rite of the divine liturgy has been composed for two reasons: first, the holy liturgy does not merely narrate aspects of the divine economy (i.e., God's actions to bring about the world's salvation, and, generally, His interactions with the world), but it presents them in a dramatized way before our eyes; secondly, due to its symbolic character, the holy liturgy helps people's minds to remain firmly oriented toward events of the divine economy until the divine liturgy culminates in the Eucharist. Therefore, any superstitious approach to the Christian church's symbolic life and any attempt to treat symbols as if they were allegories preclude people from having an authentic experience of Christian life, which consists in union with Christ effected by Christian symbols.

Another problematic phenomenon in the historical life of the Christian church is the development of bureaucratic and authoritarian

---

77. Luke 22:19.

attitudes in both Eastern and Western churches. For instance, several Roman Catholic and Orthodox Christian clergymen advocate clerical celibacy and especially the bishops' celibacy in a way that attests to a grave lack of discretion of judgment, and they treat the lay members of the church in a bureaucratic and authoritarian way. However, the apostle Paul is clear on this issue: "someone who aspires to the office of a bishop desires a good work. A bishop then must be without reproach, the husband of one wife, . . . ruling well his own house, having his children in subjection with all reverence."[78] The apostle Peter, the first Bishop of Rome, himself, was married.[79] In the recorded church history, we find dozens of married bishops, at least until the seventh century AD; even married Patriarchs: Demetrius, a third-century Patriarch of Alexandria, Pharen, a fourth-century Armenian Patriarch, and John the Almoner, a seventh-century Patriarch of Alexandria. In regard to the genuine Christian church ethos, in general, Jesus Christ's rules are clear: "No longer do I call you servants, for the servant doesn't know what his lord does. But I have called you friends, for everything that I heard from my Father, I have made known to you";[80] and: "whoever wants to be first must be slave of all."[81] Jesus Christ's guidelines for the clergy emphasize unselfishness,[82] which has been perfectly exemplified by Jesus Christ himself; wherefore the apostle Paul has said: "He emptied himself."[83]

A very important issue that torments both Eastern and Western Christianity is the notion of the "catholicity," or universality, of the church. The Eastern Orthodox Patriarch of Constantinople is called "Ecumenical Patriarch," and the Pope of Rome claims primacy over the universal church. The first Patriarch of Constantinople to be called "Ecumenical Patriarch" was John the Faster, who was a most meek and gentle ecclesiastical person. The Byzantine Emperor Maurice gave John the Faster this title in 588 AD. In general, the Byzantines loved impressive titles. Thus, the bigger and more impressive one's title was, the happier that person was. For instance, in Byzantium, gradually, the title *Sebastōs* (Honorable)

78. 1 Timothy 3:1–4.
79. Matthew 8:14; Mark 1:30; Luke 4:38.
80. John 15:15.
81. Mark 10:44.
82. John 10:11.
83. Philippians 2:7.

became *Isosebastōs* (All Honorable), *Protosebastōs* (Supremely Honorable), and finally *Panhypersebastōs* (All Supremely Honorable).

In the sixth century AD, Constantinople was, indeed, the "ecumenical city," in the sense that it was the religious, political, cultural, economic, and legislative center of the *ecumēne*, that is, of the entire Roman Empire. The title "ecumenical" was not used by the Patriarchs of Constantinople alone. There was also, for instance, an "Ecumenical Librarian" in Constantinople. Therefore, since the term *ecumēne* referred to the Roman Empire, the term "ecumenical" carried the significance of "imperial." In this context, the "Ecumenical Librarian" was the chief librarian of the Imperial City, and he did not assume authority over other librarians of the empire. Similarly, the "Ecumenical Patriarch" was the Bishop of the Imperial City, and not the leader of world Orthodoxy. Furthermore, the term "Ecumenical Council" refers to a council of bishops from the whole *ecumēne*, that is, from the whole Roman Empire.

However, John the Faster's new title, "Ecumenical Patriarch," meaning Patriarch (Bishop) of the Imperial City, was translated into Latin as "Universal Patriarch." Thus, alarmed at the thought that one bishop was claiming to himself authority over all other bishops, the then Pope of Rome, Gregory the Great wrote to John the Faster, Patriarch of Constantinople, the following: "I pray you, therefore, reflect that by your bold presumption, the peace of the whole church is troubled, and that you are at enmity with that grace which was given to all in communion"; and he went on as follows: "What will you say to Christ, Who is the Head of the universal church . . . you who, by your title *universal*, would bring all His members into subjection to yourself?"[84] Finally, in the same letter, Pope Gregory asked Patriarch John the following question in regard to the assumption of the title "Universal Patriarch": "Whom, I pray you tell me, whom do you imitate by this perverse title if not [Lucifer] who, despising the legions of angels, his companions, endeavored to mount to the highest?"[85] In addition, far from reserving to himself the prerogative of "universal bishop," Pope Gregory explained that the See of Rome had refused a like title and honor.

Letter after letter, like an artillery barrage, Pope Gregory the Great's aforementioned epistle to the Orthodox bishops of his day accurately falls upon all those subsequent Popes of Rome who have been claiming

---

84. See Klingman, *Church History for Busy People*, 16.
85. Ibid., 17.

supremacy over all other bishops of the universal church of Christ. In his seminal book *The Papacy*, Abbé Guettée refers to the aforementioned dispute between Pope Gregory the Great and Patriarch John the Faster and to many other similar incidents that highlight and elucidate the ecclesiological departure of the modern Vatican from the ancient See of Rome. The dispute between Pope Gregory the Great and Patriarch John the Faster in regard to the title "Ecumenical Patriarch," which was assumed by the latter, was due to a mistranslation of the term "ecumenical," but it gave the opportunity to those two bishops, Pope Gregory and Patriarch John, to clarify and agree that the church of Christ has no "universal bishop," other than Jesus Christ himself. Thus, ultimately, the Eastern Orthodox church venerates both Pope Gregory the Great and Patriarch John the Faster as saints. On the other hand, in 1870, at the First Vatican Council, ultramontanism achieved victory over conciliarism, with the pronouncement of Papal infallibility and of Papal supremacy, that is, the Pope was officially proclaimed a "universal bishop."[86]

What is, ultimately, the mark of a true "catholic"? If we understand the ontological significance of "catholicity," then we realize that the nature of the answer to the previous question is definitely not administrative. Being a true "catholic" does not consist in being in communion with a supposedly "universal" episcopal See. The true and genuine "catholicity" that is, "universality," consists in being in ontologically grounded communion with God and, precisely, in participating in God's uncreated energies, through which and due to which man is deified, that is, he attains to the true and genuine "catholicity," or "universality," since a partaker of God's uncreated energies has an infinitely large psychic space, capable of receiving God, just as the Virgin Mary received God in her womb. In other words, the true and genuine "catholicity" or "universality" refers not to the size of a religious or a political ruler's jurisdiction, but to the size of man's soul. In fact, Jesus Christ has called each and every man, personally, to attain to universality through a psychic expansion that would transform one's soul into the true temple of God.

---

86. However, in the 1850s, members of the See of Utrecht, known as "Old Catholics," did not recognize any infallible Papal authority. In the 1870s, the Old Catholic communion of Germans, Austrians, and Swiss was formed at a public meeting held in Nuremberg under the leadership of the renowned church historian and priest Ignaz von Döllinger, following the First Vatican Council. According to the "Declaration of Utrecht" of 1889, the Old Catholic church accepts the first seven ecumenical councils and doctrine formulated before 1054, but it rejects the primacy of the Pope and the communion with the Vatican.

In order to overcome the Vatican's pretenses to universal ecclesiastical supremacy, the Church of England, the Protestant Episcopal Church in the United States of America, the Methodist Episcopal Church, the Presbyterian Church, the Lutheran Church, and other Protestant churches have declared their administrative autonomy, and each of those churches has its own administrative system. However, even though the aforementioned churches maintain their administrative autonomy from the Vatican, they are often closely aligned with particular state authorities, thus giving rise to several phenomena of Caesaropapism. For instance, in 1534, King Henry VIII of England separated from the Roman See and became supreme head of the Church of England. Other Protestant sovereigns, too, have exercised jurisdiction over their "state" churches. Several Lutheran and Calvinist groups have aligned with local and national political authorities from Northern Europe who were seeking to break from the Roman Catholic church's tutelage. Moreover, particularly from the sixteenth century onward, several local Eastern Orthodox churches started declaring their "autocephaly" (autonomy) from the Patriarchate of Constantinople, because several sovereigns were seeking to enhance their own and their nation's or empire's prestige and to project their cultural diplomacy by having an autocephalous (literally, "self-headed"), "ethnic" church. Thus, a series of autocephalous "ethnic" Eastern Orthodox churches have been instituted, such as the Patriarchates of Moscow, of Serbia, of Romania, of Bulgarian, and of Georgia, and the national churches of Cyprus, of Greece, of Poland, etc.

However, true and genuine Christians do not hold the errant belief held by many Jews in the time of the Incarnate Logos, that the Messiah was to establish an earthly kingdom. Jesus Christ told them clearly, "My kingdom is not of this world."[87] However, the leaders of the Jews did not endorse Jesus Christ's spiritual universalism, and, for the sake of an earthly kingdom, they went so far as to demand the crucifixion of the King of Glory. As the apostle John writes in his Gospel: "The chief priests therefore and the Pharisees gathered a council, and said, 'What are we doing? For this man does many signs. If we let him go on like this, everyone will believe in him, and the Romans will come and take away both our place and our nation.'"[88] Moreover, many who called themselves Christians paid no heed to Jesus Christ's spiritual universalism. Hence, we see

---

87. John 18:36.
88. John 11:47–48.

how the First Rome went so far as to declare the primacy of the Bishop of Rome over the universal church, and the Second Rome, Constantinople, in imitation of the First Rome, has in the modern era begun to teach that the Patriarchate of Constantinople is the source and the keystone of the canonicity of all local Eastern Orthodox churches, even though neither the Bible nor the Eastern Orthodox church's canonical tradition teaches such doctrines. Every authoritarian structure is inconsistent with the Eastern Orthodox church's ecclesiology, because, according to the Eastern Orthodox church's ecclesiology and triadology, the multiplicity of the church is constitutive of its oneness, and, thus, the "one" (provost) and the "many" always coexist as two aspects of the same being; in other words, "authority" (e.g., the bishop's authority) is always rooted in the church herself, that is, in the eucharistic gathering, and it cannot have any other source.

Additionally, under the influence of modern philosophy and nationalism, many who called themselves Christians fell into the mistaken belief of the superiority of their own particular nation and the phyletic notion of their nation's "messianic destiny" and "spiritual uniqueness," as though any Christian nation or people could have a particular spirituality superior to that of the universal Christian church. Each different local Christian community should love and respect its temporary homeland, not in a nationalist or chauvinistic way, but primarily because of the saints and the confessors of the Christian Faith who arose there and only insofar as the corresponding civilization is a pattern of things in the Heavens, in accordance with what we read in Hebrews 9:23.

The end of the twentieth century was strongly marked by a deep awareness of the crisis of the Enlightenment Project, which was founded on a confident belief that the human consciousness is an ontologically sufficient foundation of truth. In the twentieth century, Western Europe, that is, the cradle of the Enlightenment Project, caused two catastrophic world wars, and it gave rise to totalitarian regimes that transformed mass murder into a politically instituted national industry. Adolf Hitler's statement, "we do not want any other god than Germany itself,"[89] and Hanns Johst's statement, "when I hear culture . . . I unlock my Browning" (it is included in Johst's 1933 play *Schlageter*), often quoted by Nazi officials, such as Heinrich Himmler and Hermann Göring, disclose a genuine aspect of the modern Western civilization: Nazism. The essence of Na-

---

89. Quoted in Heiden, *A History of National Socialism*, 100.

zism consists in the decision of the modern man not only to declare his autonomy from God, but also to be liberated from his moral inhibitions and to express himself as a pure individual structure, even if this means that he should legitimize atrocities and construe atrocity as a virtue.

It is worth pointing that Hitler and the Nazi elite did not want to produce vulgar and uneducated torturers, but their goal was to produce properly educated and trained people whose point of reference would be the atrocious ideology of the Nazi "Superman" and the "Master Race." The Germans who proclaimed Adolf Hitler "Führer" (leader and guide) and served in the SS, in the Gestapo, and in Nazi concentration camps were bearers and spiritual representatives of a great Western culture—particularly, of the German culture, which can boast of its great achievements in philosophy, science, and art (e.g., the German writers Johann von Goethe and Johann von Schiller, the German philosophers and scientists Gottfried von Leibniz, Johann Fichte, and Georg Hegel, the German music composers Ludwig van Beethoven and Wilhelm Wagner, the German painters Caspar David Friedrich and Franz Marc, etc.). Moreover, when Hitler came to power, German universities were among the leading Western European academic institutions.

Hitler and Nazism are genuine spiritual descendants of the modern Western culture. For this reason, the following facts are not accidental, but they highlight Hitler as a genuine spiritual descendant of the modern Western culture: in the 1920s, the U.S. automobile manufacturer Henry Ford was financing Adolf Hitler's nationalist movement in Munich, and, in 1938—after Hitler had achieved power with the aid of U.S. and German business cartels—Henry Ford received the Grand Cross of the German Eagle, a Nazi decoration for distinguished foreigners;[90] during World War II, John D. Rockefeller Jr. owned a controlling interest in the Standard Oil corporation, but the next largest stockholder was the German chemical company I. G. Farben, through which the Standard Oil corporation sold huge quantities of gasoline and lubricants to Nazi Germany; members of the British nobility, such as Prince Charles Edward (Duke of Saxe-Coburg and Gotha and Duke of Albany), Lord Brocket, Lord Redesdale, the Duke of Westminster, etc., were supporters of Hitler and Nazism;[91] between 1936 and 1940, the then British Prime Minister Neville Chamberlain, acknowledging and treating Adolf Hitler's

---

90. Sward, *The Legend of Henry Ford*, 139.

91. James, *Aristocrats*.

Nazi Germany as a legitimate partner of the European balance-of-power system, made three trips to Germany in order to appease Hitler; many French socialist and radical leftist intellectuals, political activists, and trade-unionists supported or even joined the pro-Nazi French government of Philippe Pétain;[92] in 1998, Pope John Paul II "beatified" the notorious Nazi collaborator and convicted war criminal Aloysius Viktor Stepinac, who was a Croatian Roman Catholic cardinal and Archbishop of Zagreb from 1937 to 1960.[93]

Hitler, as a genuine spiritual descendant of the modern Western culture, exemplified, in a tragic way, the evilness of the modern Western culture. Apart from the millions of his victims, Hitler killed the "innocence" of Western man and the faith in the value and the power of the Western civilization, which is a bearer of created, humanistic lights. Similarly, in the twentieth century, Marxism, which, as a kind of inverted Hegelianism, is part of modern West's attempt to rationalize and universalize history, gave rise to the murderous and totalitarian regimes of Vladimir Lenin and Joseph Stalin.[94]

John Milbank, a renowned Professor in Religion, Politics, and Ethics at the University of Nottingham, in his book *Theology and Social Theory*, originally published in 1990, argues that theology "outnarrates" social science and social theory, and he announces theology's return to its old place as the "queen of the sciences," a title that it enjoyed at universities of medieval Europe. The source of his theological confidence is humanity's need for a holistic picture of reality, as opposed to the fragmentary way in which modern secular education approaches and tries to explain reality. In his aforementioned book, Milbank treats the emergence of postmodernism in the 1980s as a new moment of opportunity for theology. In the 1980s, the postmodernists (namely, scholars such as Michel Foucault, Jacques Derrida, and Jean-François Lyotard) declared the end of a certain modern confidence in science, progress, the European Enlightenment, and, generally, various secular utopias, what Milbank calls "secular reason." According to Milbank, the fact that postmodernism, following Nietzsche's intellectual legacy, wiped out any secure humanism and argued that everything is in flux signals a new moment of opportunity for theology.

92. Epstein, *Un Paradoxe Français*.
93. Cornwell, *Hitler's Pope*.
94. Domenach, *Une Morale sans Moralisme*.

In his book *The Gay Science*, Nietzsche argued that modernity brought about the event that he called the "death of God," which, in its turn, gave rise to a world without foundation or orientation.[95] According to Milbank, postmodernism is "a long footnote to Nietzsche," and the postmodernists try to think through the situation that Nietzsche found almost unthinkable, that is, a world without an existential horizon. Thus, Milbank maintains, postmodernism revealed that modernity, precisely, secularism, flows to nihilism. Postmodernism, in Milbank's view, makes us aware that the secular by itself is hollow, and, from this awareness, Milbank deduces that religion is not a matter of private concern, and that, if we assert that secularism is totally neutral toward religion, then moral and epistemological values become meaningless and inaccessible, and we are left only with the impersonal laws of matter and with the "thin values" of the economic and the political markets (as opposed to religion's "thick values," according to Milbank's terminology).[96]

Milbank has used the term "Radical Orthodoxy" in order to describe his radical attack on modern West's secularism. In the context of his Radical Orthodoxy, Milbank argues that modern science, on its own terms, does not say anything about ultimate truths (since it mainly describes observable regularities and re-enacts them in the mode of experiments), and that a completely secularized understanding of nature consists in an anarchic and meaningless world-conception, which often clashes with our common-sense understanding of things. In particular, Milbank points out that the modern scientific, secularized world-conception clashes with and undermines our common-sense understanding and experiences of feeling, loving, intending, being conscious, etc., and, that, therefore, to the extent that human beings actually feel, love, intend, and are conscious, they invoke metaphysical principles, such as God. In other words, Milbank emphatically argues that humanity escapes scientific explanation, and, for this reason, he anticipates that the twenty-first century will be a neo-religious and neo-metaphysical century.

Cognitive science, pioneered by Jerome S. Bruner, George A. Miller, and Ulric G. Neisser, studies the mind as a sort of computer, where the hardware is the brain, and the software consists in the human thoughts.[97] The previous metaphor is not surprising, since its first origins can be

95. See Laos, *The Metaphysics of World Order*, 87–94.
96. Milbank, *Theology and Social Theory*.
97. Neisser, *Cognitive Psychology*.

traced back to the seventeenth century, when clocks were metaphors for the mind. Basically, modern science has the propensity to draw analogies between the latest technology and the structure of the human mind. However, Milbank has correctly argued that cognitive science has not managed to fulfill its purpose, which was to provide an exhaustive explanation of humanity.

The philosophical origins of cognitive science can be traced back to Kant's theory of schemata, through which, Kant contends, intuitions (sense experiences) can be subsumed under categories ("pure concepts of the understanding").[98] Therefore, Kant gave primacy to the logical form over the real content of experience. Following Kant's legacy, cognitive science studies the human being as a subject who rationalizes the world by imposing logical forms (what Kant would call "pure concepts of the understanding") on sensible data. The basic problem with such a way of thinking about man's mental life is related to the following question: what is the ultimate criterion, or, in other words, the ultimate source of significance, on the basis of which the human mind rationalizes the world? As I argued in chapters 2 and 3, without God, the only source of significance is imagination, which is unstable and, hence, cognitively untrustworthy, especially because it has been scientifically proven that Kant's schemata are not *a priori* (since there are different geometries and models of space-time), and that logic is not a self-sufficient system of knowledge (due to Gödel's incompleteness and inconsistency theorems). Therefore, Milbank is right to criticize modern, secularized science, in general, and cognitive science, in particular, for being incapable of properly addressing issues related to meaning and ultimate truth.

On the other hand, Milbank's criticism of modernity and, particularly, of secularism is methodological, but not substantial, because he adheres to the Western tradition of "natural theology," and he discards the Hesychasts' doctrines of the essence–energies distinction and of man's deification. Milbank thinks of religion as a free exercise of reason within secular limits. In particular, Milbank supports religion, because, as he argues, it preserves the sense that there is a hidden underlying order in the world, or, in other words, that there is an unknown reason, whereas, Milbank continues, secular thought is always inclined either to infer reason, thus giving rise to a false perception that we know everything, or to adhere to an irrational model of reality, thus giving rise to the false

---

98. Kant, *Critique of Pure Reason*, A138, B177.

perception that we are subservient to chaotic forces. Milbank understands faith as an ongoing exploration of the hidden underlying order or reason of reality, and he defends religion on the grounds that it sustains this ongoing, free exploration. Therefore, Milbank's conception of religion underpins a "neo-religious" reformulation of Kant's theories about schemata and the unknowable noumenon; in the context of Milbank's theological thought, the unknowability of the thing-in-itself corresponds to the unknowability of God. Furthermore, Milbank's conception of religion underpins his rediscovery of subjectivism through the rediscovery of religion, since Milbank argues that humans are inside nature, they understand nature through their intuition about nature, and they need to recover the sense that the shapes of reality are the meanings of reality, which, according to Milbank, are structurally related to human feelings.[99]

Milbank adheres to the broad Western tradition of natural theology, and he tries to save the subject's freedom from a "crude" philosophical realism by arguing that there is a structural continuity between the reality of the world and the reality of consciousness, a structural continuity in the context of which, according to Milbank, the natural world goes on thinking itself, and humans go on shaping the natural world. In this way, he tries to merge the theology of Thomas Aquinas and the philosophy of Immanuel Kant into his system of "Radical Orthodoxy." Thus, Milbank seems to try to save the rationalist way of thinking that underpins natural theology from its destructive and self-destructive ultimate consequences, in which modernity has crashed, and which have been highlighted by the postmodern criticism of modernity.

However, as I pointed out in chapter 3, due to its limited access to the original sources of classical Greek philosophy, scholasticism misinterpreted Aristotle's notion of "form" as a substantial mode of being—that is, as a principle that is opposite to matter—and it postulated that the existence of being is due to its form, thus confusing shape with form. According to Aristotle, form is the energy, or the life of matter, but, according to the scholastics' variety of Aristotelianism, form has its own individual spiritual substance, and, therefore, for the scholastics, there is a sharp distinction between form and matter. Whereas, in the context of Aristotle's philosophy, form is equated with species, and, therefore, it is a universal attribute of being, scholasticism discards truth as species, and, therefore, it construes form merely as an individual attribute.

99. Ibid.

Thus, ultimately, in the context of modern subjectivism, form is merely a consequence of the intentionality of consciousness, and modern culture dignifies "innovation"—precisely, the production of new forms by the subject—as an end in itself. As I argued in chapter 3, what is significant to the Western subject is not the truth of the thing *per se*, but the subject's representations (*conceptus*, or *intellectio rei*), precisely, the form that the subject's imagination gives to the reality of the world and to the reality of consciousness (since, for the Western subject, the concepts "truth" and "reality" are distinct from each other). Moreover, as I pointed out in chapter 2, the scholastics' variety of Platonism is founded on their misinterpretation of Platonic ideas as logical substances, and, as I argued in chapter 3, the previous misinterpretation underpins the doctrinal innovation of the *Filioque* and the scholastics' natural theology, in the context of which God's wills are identified with logical substances.

The aforementioned, peculiarly Western interpretation (or rather misinterpretation) of Platonism and Aristotelianism determined the course of the entire medieval Western philosophy and philosophical theology, which have two fundamental characteristics: the attempt to find a sustainable compromise between human reason and human will, and the belief that human consciousness is an ontologically sufficient foundation of truth. Thus, in the context of medieval Western philosophy, in general, and in the context of the Roman Catholic church, in particular, philosophical realism/essentialism (e.g., Thomas Aquinas and Anselm of Canterbury), nominalism (e.g., Roscelin and William of Occam), conceptualism (e.g., John Duns Scotus), and mysticism (e.g., Bernard of Clairvaux) could coexist as legitimate expressions of the Western soul's belief in the ontological sufficiency of human consciousness as a foundation of truth. Therefore, scholasticism ignored the erotic character of Plato's and Aristotle's philosophies—whose ultimate purpose, as I argued in chapters 1, 3, and 4 was man's methexis (participation) in the Absolute—and it discarded the Hesychasts' doctrine that man has access to God's uncreated energies. In other words, as I argued in chapter 4, scholasticism confined theology and, generally, epistemology to created sources of knowledge, thus, rather involuntarily, paving the way to modernity.

A scholastic theologian (independently of whether he espouses Thomas Aquinas's essentialism, or William of Ockham's nominalism, or John Duns Scotus's conceptualism) asserts his epistemological autonomy from God by seeking truth through "natural reason," without seeking to participate and progress in God's uncreated energies, and, in fact, he does not even believe that man can really become a partaker of God's uncreated energies. This attitude is the humanistic and secular core of scholasticism, and, for this reason, I have argued that the scholastics, rather involuntarily, paved the way to modernity, which was inaugurated by René Descartes's declaration "cogito ergo sum" (I think therefore I am), which elevates the ego into an ontologically sufficient foundation of truth. Moreover, Protestantism is characterized by an even more radically humanistic and secular attitude than that of scholasticism, in the sense that, while the medieval scholastics asserted their epistemological autonomy from God's uncreated energies, in contradistinction to Protestantism, they did not assert their epistemological autonomy from the Papal community; the pioneers of Protestantism, however, asserted their epistemological autonomy from both God's uncreated energies (since, like the scholastics, they discarded the Hesychasts' doctrine that man has access to God's uncreated energies) and any visible church structure.

In general, in the context of scholasticism, it is believed that man cannot really, that is, *ontologically*, have a personal relationship with God; he can relate with God only through created sources of knowledge, that is, primarily through discursive reasoning (i.e., through the principle "I think"), through sentiments (i.e., through the principle "I feel"), or through intuitions (i.e., through the principle "I intuit"). Thus, the history of Western theology is pretty much characterized by an oscillation between rigid, oppressive rationalism, on the one hand, and sentimentalism and/or intuitionism, on the other. However, neither rationalism, nor sentimentalism, nor intuitionism can offer existential satisfaction to human beings, since, in all these cases, God himself, remains ontologically inaccessible and constrained by His uncreated essence, while humanity is limited to created truths about a so-called "Supreme Being," or "Absolute Reality." Because scholasticism limited humanity's spiritual horizon to created, speculative truths, and it "exiled" God to inaccessible intelligible realms, modernity, with all its problems and stalemates, which have been pointedly highlighted by Milbank and the postmodernists, was existing potentially within scholasticism until Cartesianism, operating as the midwife of modernity, allowed modernity to exist actually.

In order to overcome the problems and the stalemates of modernity, we must be aware of the reasons that brought about modernity and its secular thought. As I argued earlier in this chapter and in previous chapters, medieval Western theology is confined to created sources of knowledge, it argues that God's grace is a "supernatural," yet created, gift to humanity, it construes God's wills as if they were logical substances, and it engenders a "natural theology," in the context of which, even though God is believed to be uncreated and ontologically inaccessible, man can speculate about the natural attributes of God in a way that is similar to the way in which one can speculate about nature. Thus, medieval Western theology is mainly rationalist and secular. The most significant difference of the rationalism and the secularism of medieval Western theology from the rationalism and the secularism of modernity is that the first is theistic, construing God as the most abstract concept of the established rational system, and subservient to the Papacy, whereas modernity refuses to make any *a priori* rational commitment to the idea of God and is not subservient to religious authorities. Given that the rationalism and the secularism of medieval Western theology and mainly of the Papacy and the early Protestant movement nurtured a subject who thinks that theology is grounded in his consciousness and that he can know God through created knowledge—that is, mainly by theologizing in a way that is similar to theorizing about the natural world—it was only a matter of time before such a subject asserted his complete spiritual autonomy from an abstract, inaccessible ultimate principle (precisely, the scholastic God) and its repressive earthly religious representatives, with the well-known consequences.

In the context of modern Western theology, Oliver Davies, a renowned Professor of Theology at King's College London, departed from Milbank's Radical Orthodoxy by arguing that theology should emphasize the power of orthodoxy to change our lives.[100] Therefore, Davies has proposed a new theological system, which he has called "Transformation Theology." In particular, Davies argues that, whereas Milbank's Radical Orthodoxy is focused on the power of narrative and self-change, Transformation Theology emphasizes "the power of Christ himself, through the Spirit" who changes us, and that "change happens primarily in life and not primarily in thought."[101] However, Davies espouses the Western doctrine of created grace, and, therefore, he criticizes Milbank's perception that theology is rooted in narrative, not in order to replace it with the quest for an uncreated source of knowledge, but in order to replace it with another created source of knowledge, precisely with the percep-

---

100. Davies et al., *Transformation Theology*.

101. Davies, "Transformation Theology and Radical Orthodoxy." Online: https://www.academia.edu/1458552/Transformation_Theology_and_Radical_Orthodoxy

tion that theology is rooted in history. Thus, Davies argues that history is the place where "the natural world unfolds in [Christ]," and the "place of encounter."[102] Moreover, Davies argues that Transformation Theology is driven by "a more scientific and cultural 'return to the world,'" and he perceives Christian theology as "a distinctively cosmological thought-form."[103] Davies's Transformation Theology is, to some extent, a neo-religious reformulation of Hegel's philosophy of history, attempting, somehow, to Christianize Hegel's conception of the spirit of history, just as Milbank's Radical Orthodoxy is, to some extent, a neo-religious reformulation of Kant's metaphysics, attempting, somehow, to Christianize Kant's conception of the unknowable noumenon and Kant's theory of schemata.

As I argued in chapter 1, Hegel transcended the subject of German idealism in order to ascend to a quantitatively larger and, therefore, historically safer subject. In the context of Hegel's philosophy, the universal subject is history itself, and the universal subject's spirit is the reason of history. Thus, in the context of Hegel's philosophy, man is capable of knowing the historical truth (i.e., for Hegel, what Kant has called the "noumenon" is knowable, and, precisely, it consists in the historical truth), but man cannot be really united with history (i.e., man cannot *become* history), and, hence, he cannot be really united with the truth, since, for Hegel, the reason of history (i.e., of the Absolute) consists in the spirit's movement toward its self-awareness, and, for this reason, it is a historically determined truth. Davies's historical Christ can Christianize the reason of history through his Spirit, but he can neither liberate us from the logic of historical becoming nor ontologically unite us with him. In other words, in the context of Davies's Transformation Theology, man cannot *become* god, just as, in the context of Hegel's philosophy of history, man cannot *become* history. If we are not capable of participating in God's uncreated energies, and, thus, of ontologically transcending the logic of historical becoming, then any other change that may happen in our life as a result of an "encounter" with Christ (as it is perceived in the context of Davies's Transformation Theology) keeps us alienated from Christ within the context of an apparently Christocentric history, just as, in the context of Hegel's philosophy, our "encounter" with the historical truth keeps us alienated from history *qua* truth, even though we exist in

102. Ibid.

103. Davies, "Introducing Transformation Theology." Online: http://www.transformationtheology.com/what-is-tt.html

history. For this reason, the apostle Paul has warned us that history is not only the place of encounter with Christ, but also the place in which "the mystery of lawlessness already works,"[104] and Jesus Christ has explicitly warned us against putting our ultimate hopes in the change of historical conditions: "In the world you have trouble; but cheer up! I have overcome the world."[105] For the same reason, the apostle James writes the following: "You adulterous people, don't you know that friendship with the world is hatred toward God? Anyone who chooses to be a friend of the world becomes an enemy of God."[106]

Oliver Davies's philosophical and theological work is marked by a progression from metaphysics to phenomenology and hermeneutics, and from them to philosophies and theologies of the act. Therefore, his Transformation Theology is incapable of leading to the real union between man and God, since, for Davies, the relationship between man and God is necessarily mediated by the logic of history. Additionally, due to its hermeneutic-phenomenological stance toward the event of encounter between man and God, Davies's Transformation Theology is prone to extreme subjectivism, and it prompts a kind of love that—because it is construed as a sentiment and not as God's mode of being—subordinates doctrine to history (what Davies calls "the practices of love"[107]) and, ultimately, elevates history into the ultimate criterion of doctrinal truth.

Davies's hermeneutic-phenomenological stance toward the event of encounter between humans and God may be useful as an underpinning of some form of inter-religious diplomacy and of a syncretistic global moral code, but as a theological method is too risky. Adhering to the legal concept of religious freedom is one thing; indeed, Jesus Christ, himself, endorsed religious freedom and, generally, freedom of conscience.[108] But endorsing religious syncretism or a sentimental conception of love is a totally different thing. God can be truly loved only by upholding the true faith and His commandments. "God is love,"[109] and Jesus Christ is clear:

---

104. 2 Thessalonians 2:7.

105. John 16:33.

106. James 4:4.

107. Davies, "Transformation Theology in Its Historical Context." Online: https://www.academia.edu/1508691/Transformation_Theology_in_its_Historical_Context

108. Mark 8:34.

109. 1 John 4:16.

"Whoever has my commandments and obeys them, he is the one who loves me."[110]

Methexiology, as I expound it in this book, emphasizes a kind of knowledge that is not reducible to simple data gathering nor is it derived from created sources of knowledge, but, instead, it is experiential, unique to the person that experiences it, originated in God, and, at least in regard to rational and propositional language, incommunicable; hence, the apostle Paul referred to his experience of divine illumination by writing that he "heard unspeakable words, which it is not lawful for a man to utter."[111] But the previous divine knowledge is not entirely incommunicable. For this reason, in line with Jesus Christ's apostles and the tradition of Hesychasm, methexiology emphasizes symbolic ways of expressing and communicating things that, by definition, challenge and transcend propositional language. At this point, I should emphasize that, earlier in this chapter, I clarified the difference between the notion of "symbol" and the notion of "allegory." Therefore, by the term "church," we should understand a community of people who participate in the same symbolic universe, and, indeed, the event of people's participation in the same symbolic universe engenders the church's opposition to religious syncretism.

The book of Revelation clearly warns us against religious syncretism: "I testify to everyone who hears the words of the prophecy of this book, if anyone adds to them, God will add to him the plagues which are written in this book. If anyone takes away from the words of the book of this prophecy, God will take away his part from the tree of life, and out of the holy city, which are written in this book."[112] Many events of encounter between man and God have occurred throughout history in all religions; in some cases, prophesies have been confirmed, and such charismatic events have performed miracles and healings. But, from the Christian perspective, these prophesies and miracles do not testify to the truth of the doctrines taught in the corresponding experiences, because often they do not come from God.

The Bible, precisely the book of Deuteronomy, teaches us clearly that any prophesy or vision and, generally, any event of encounter between man and God must be evaluated on the basis of the doctrine it teaches: "If a prophet or a dreamer of dreams . . . gives you a sign or a

---

110. John 14:21.

111. 2 Corinthians 12:4.

112. Revelation 22:17–18.

wonder, and [it] . . . comes to pass, and he says, 'Let's go after other gods, . . . and let's serve them'; you shall not listen to . . . [his] words"[113]; the book of Deuteronomy explains that "the Lord your God is testing you, to know whether you love your God with all your heart and with all your soul,"[114] and it commands as follows: "You shall walk after the Lord your God. . . . And that prophet or that dreamer of a dream, shall die; for he has spoken to you to make you err from the Lord your God . . . so you shall remove the evil from among you."[115] Similarly, the apostle Paul tells us that we must be wary of anyone who claims to speak in the name of God: "even if we or an angel from Heaven should preach a gospel other than the one we have preached to you, let him be anathema! . . . If anybody is preaching to you a gospel other than what you accepted, let him be anathema."[116] Moreover, in his treatise "On Spiritual Knowledge" 36-37, Diadochos of Photiki (a Byzantine Hesychast included in the *Philokalia* and venerated as a saint by the Eastern Orthodox church) teaches us that many, indeed, have had the experience of visions and wonders that were not godly, and, thus, in their ignorance, they have been deceived.[117] Peter of Damascus (another Byzantine Hesychast included in the *Philokalia* and venerated as a saint by the Eastern Orthodox church), in his treatise "A Treasury of Divine Knowledge," amplifies the previous teaching further, by pointing out that, if we accept such delusions, our intellect, in its utter ignorance and self-conceit, depicts various shapes or colors, so that we think that we have experienced a manifestation of God or of an angel.[118]

In general, whenever we make sentimental "religious experiences" or various signs and wonders the criterion of our faith, we thereby become susceptible to every sort of delusion. If the standard of our faith reduces to sentimental "religious experiences" or various signs of spiritual encounter, and if we make history the ultimate judge of our doctrinal truths, then we are compelled to acknowledge the validity of any experience in which one's "religious" sensation is grounded; we can no longer distinguish God's truth from the devil's errors or from the intellect's delusions. But, according to the Hesychasts, who actually seek to experience

113. Deuteronomy 13:1-3.
114. Deuteronomy 13:3.
115. Deuteronomy 13:4-5.
116. Galatians 1:8-9.
117. Diadochos of Photiki, "On Spiritual Knowledge and Discrimination: 100 Texts," *Philokalia*, Vol. 1.
118. Peter of Damascus, "A Treasury of Divine Knowledge," *Philokalia*, Vol. 3.

the uncreated light of God's glory, all religious experiences must be tested for agreement with the orthodox faith before they can be accepted as genuinely godly.

History will really change for the good of humanity only when people change themselves, only when they undergo a spiritual conversion (in Greek, *metanoia*), which consists in a state of radical unselfishness. From the perspective of methexiology, radical unselfishness means that we acknowledge the human mind as the repository of God's uncreated energies, and, therefore, we are brave enough to empty our mind of all created elements of knowledge and detach it from the world of the senses in accordance with the arguments that I put forward in chapter 4. In other words, history will really become meaningful and will really change for the good of humanity only when we acknowledge that the end of history is neither a historical goal nor an abstractly transcendent goal, but an uncreated reality—the deification of man, that is, man's participation in the Good-in-itself (i.e., in God's uncreated energies). Hence, methexiology gives rise to a particular way of thinking about psychotherapy, which I will expound in chapter 6, and to particular way of thinking about axiology, ethics, and justice, which I will expound in chapter 7.

6

Psychotherapy: The Secret Potential of the Mind

As I have already argued, scholasticism—in the context of which Aristotle's universals were radically separated from the material world and Platonic ideas were construed as if they were logical substances—approached the soul as a naturally immortal substance radically separate from the material and mortal body. In the context of scholasticism, God is "exiled" to intelligible spheres, and, by implication, the human being is divided into two substances, that is, into the soul, which seeks God in the intelligible spheres through reason, and the body, which remains confined to the material world, "down here." Even though Descartes identified the soul with consciousness (i.e., with thought and will), thus laying the foundations of modern psychology, he maintained the previous dualistic arguments of scholasticism.

In the context of modernity, psychology was separated from philosophy, and it became an autonomous scientific discipline.[1] The history of psychology as a particular scientific discipline starts in 1879, when the German psychology researcher Wilhelm Wundt founded the first formal laboratory for psychological research at the University of Leipzig. Wundt identified the soul with consciousness, and he argued that scientific psychology should focus on analyzing consciousness, that is, a person's

1. The main sources that I have consulted regarding the development of the academic discipline of psychology are the following: Gross, *Psychology*; Hothersall, *History of Psychology*; Lundin, *Theories and Systems of Psychology*; Robinson, *An Intellectual History of Psychology*; Sternberg, *Pathways to Psychology*.

subjective experience of the world and mind. Wundt's method involved breaking consciousness down into elemental sensations and feelings, and, therefore, it was founded on structuralism. Wundt meticulously conducted the first psychological experiments, and he initiated the so-called "Volk psychology," which investigates issues related to language, art, social customs, myth, law, and morality. Moreover, Wundt highlighted the biological aspects of psychology, arguing that "all experimental methods of psychology appeal to physiology for support, since they can never ignore the physiological stimuli."[2]

In 1893, Eduard Titchener, an English student of Wilhelm Wundt's, founded his own formal laboratory for psychological research at Cornell University, after Oxford University had rejected the creation of a distinct department of psychology. Titchener placed psychological structuralism in a more scientifically rigorous setting than that of Wundt's theory. Titchener's psychological structuralism consists in analyzing consciousness into its constitutive elements (particularly, its experiences) in order to ascertain its structure. As a reaction to Titchener's psychological structuralism, which is focused on the questions "what" and "where," psychological functionalism is focused on the questions "how" and "why," it is concerned with the functions of the "mind," which Titchener identifies with consciousness, and it aims at applying psychology to everyday life. The development of psychological functionalism was originally encouraged by the biological research works of Charles Darwin and Francis Galton as well as by Herbert Spencer's social Darwinism, and it is intimately associated with the study of the nervous system.

Modern, or "scientific," psychology hinges on the principles of modern philosophy, and it is aimed at overcoming the problems that stem from the mind–body dualism, whose history is associated with the history of scholasticism and Cartesianism. Even though Wundt and Titchener studied the human soul *qua* consciousness in a positivist way, it soon became clear that the functions of consciousness and the nervous system cannot explain the entire spectrum of psychological phenomena, and, thus, "depth psychology" emerged. The term "depth psychology" was coined by the Swiss psychiatrist and eugenicist Eugen Bleuler (1857–1939) in order to refer to psychotherapeutic and research methods that seek the deep layers underlying behavioral and cognitive processes; in other words, depth psychology investigates not only consciousness, but

---

2. Wundt, *Logik*, Vol. 3, 219.

also the unconscious. Some of the most important representatives of depth psychology are Pierre Janet, William James, Sigmund Freud, Carl G. Jung, and Alfred Adler.

According to Freud's structural model of the soul, the psychic apparatus consists of the following three parts: (i) the "id," which comprises the unorganized and unconscious part of the personality structure, it contains the basic drives, and it acts according to the "pleasure principle"; (ii) the "ego," which comprises that organized part of the personality structure that includes defensive, perceptual, intellectual, and executive functions, and it acts according to the "reality principle"; and (iii) the "superego," which comprises that organized part of the personality structure, mainly but not entirely unconscious, which includes the individual's ego ideals, spiritual goals, and the psychic agency (called conscience) that judges and prohibits one's drives, fantasies, feelings, and actions. Freud maintains that the ego strives to find a balance between primitive drives and the reality of the world and, simultaneously, to satisfy the id and the superego.

From the perspective of depth psychology, scientific psychology strives to analyze the layers of the soul that are not conscious and are formed by wishes and desires that are repressed by social norms and by reason and common sense, which are regarded as adaptation mechanisms to external reality. Therefore, psychoanalysts maintain that the essence of psychological illness consists in painful explosions of censored and forbidden impulses or in more long-term symbolic manifestations of censored and forbidden impulses. According to Freud, there is "reason to assume that there is a primal repression, a first phase of repression, which consists in the physical (ideational) representative of the instinct being denied entrance into the conscious," and a "second stage of repression, repression proper, which affects mental derivatives of the repressed representative."[3] Moreover, Jacques Lacan has given particular emphasis to the role of the signifier in repression, arguing that "the primal repressed is a signifier," and he has examined how the symptom "is constituted on the basis of primal repression, of the fall, of the Unterdrückung, of the binary signifier . . . the necessary fall of the first signifier."[4]

Depth psychology, precisely, psychoanalysis, is mainly focused on particular psychological events, their functional unfolding, and the

---

3. Freud, *On Metapsychology*, 147, 184.
4. Lacan, *The Four Fundamental Concepts of Psychoanalysis*, 235.

dynamics of consciousness development, and, for this reason, it maintains that specific primal psychological processes, mainly events in early childhood (which are regarded as the psychological prime cause), are the most important psychological issues, whereas mental representations are regarded as issues of secondary importance and associated with secondary psychological processes. The prominent position that specific primal psychological processes occupy in psychoanalysis underpins psychoanalysts' attempt to interpret every cultural achievement of humanity, including religious, metaphysical, and scientific systems, independently of its context of validation; hence, psychoanalysts attempt to interpret every cultural achievement of humanity as a projection of a particular inner perception of the functions of the soul. In other words, the previous attitude of psychoanalysis implies that psychoanalysis refuses to create a world-conception.

For instance, when Freud, in his book *Moses and Monotheism*, argues that Christianity is simultaneously a regression[5] vis-à-vis polytheism and idolatry and a progression, in the sense that the murder of the father is confessed (confession being combined with a reward), he refers to the functions of the soul without assigning any normative value to the concepts of regression and progression. On the contrary, according to his own reasoning, Freud is compelled to connect the materialist-historical hypothesis of the murder of the dominant male with the notion of a primordial horde, and, therefore, he is compelled to create a myth, a supposedly "scientific" myth, in order to approach the unknown depths of the human soul. In particular, in his book *Moses and Monotheism*, Freud fashioned a myth about Moses that suits his psychoanalytical theory. In particular, according to Freud, Moses was an Egyptian who brought from his native country the monotheistic religion that he gave to the Jews, and he was murdered in the wilderness by Jews, but his memory was cherished by them, and his religious doctrine ultimately triumphed among them and then internationally through them. This myth combines the confession of the murder of the "father" (i.e., the dominant male) by the Jews with a reward for the Jews (i.e., the triumph of the new Jewish culture that was originally founded by the murdered "father"), and, because it suits Freud's theory, Freud regards the previous myth, which he himself has fashioned, as "scientific."

5. By the term "regression," Freud refers to a defense mechanism leading to the temporary or long-term reversion of the ego to an earlier stage of development rather than handling unacceptable impulses in a more psychological mature way.

From the aforementioned arguments about psychoanalysis, it follows that psychoanalysis is founded on the function of imagination, which I studied in chapter 2; more precisely, through his own imagination, the psychoanalyst creates new myths by means of which, and in the context of which, he tries to analyze censored and forbidden impulses and taboos, and the previous analytical activity leads to the revival of symbolically structured traumatic events and to the identification of those traumatic events' real dimensions, so that, ultimately, the patient achieves a balanced reconciliation with himself and with the world (external reality). Through psychoanalysis, one becomes consciously aware of his unconscious, that is, his consciousness assimilates repressed elements of his soul by establishing correspondences between symbolically structured elements that belong to the soul and elements that belong to the world (external reality). Therefore, as I have already explained, psychoanalysis takes place according to the criteria and the expediencies of the ego, whose reality may be of an imaginary nature, in the sense that the reality of the ego may merely consist in a socially legitimized and established fantasy. Moreover, as Jacques Derrida has pointedly noticed, Freud defines religion and metaphysics as displacements of the identification with the father in the resolution of the Oedipus complex, but the prominence of the father in Freud's own analysis is itself indebted to the prominence given to the father in Western metaphysics and theology.[6] In a similar spirit, Claude Lévi-Strauss has argued that, in essence, Freud's theory of the Oedipus complex is a reformulation of the Oedipus myth.[7]

As I have already pointed out, Freud's psychoanalytical theory invokes imaginative narratives in order to change the framework in which the patient experiences his or her psychological problems in conformity with Freud's analytical theory and in order to lend an aura of "scientific mythology" (whatever this obscure term means) to new myths that are, in the eyes of some, inappropriate or insipid abuses of sacred personages and, to others, entertaining and, to some degree, intellectually challenging plots penned by an artful and psychologically deep and complicated writer. However, if by the term "myth," we refer to the spiritual core of beings and things, and if we bear in mind that, as I argued in chapter 2, significance precedes imagination, then the purpose of a genuine myth is, through its symbolic language and plot, to disclose the ultimate

---

6. Derrida, *The Post Card*.
7. Lévi-Strauss, *Structural Anthropology*.

significance of being. This is, in fact, the value of the great mythological traditions. In contradistinction to the previous notion of myth, a "tale" is a poor substitute for myth, in the sense that, in the absence of a vital mythological tradition, tales are created in order to face the lack of communion between humans and the source of the significance of being (the "Absolute," or God) by resorting to imaginary sources of significance. Therefore, from the perspective of the previous definitions of "myth" and "tale," Freud's mythological creations are not exactly myths in the strict sense of the word, but rather tales.

In the context of his own variant of depth psychology, Carl G. Jung, one of Freud's most prominent students, attempted to make the mythological underpinnings of psychoanalysis more trustworthy by invoking the "collective unconscious." Jung was aware that myth—whose psychoanalytical significance lies not in the particular elements that it contains, but in the archetypes to which it refers and which it conveys—functions as an ontological underpinning of man and as a therapeutic message. However, Jung, like Freud, did not seek a path that leads to human participation in a transcendent truth, whose accessible universality could underpin the unity of the soul. Instead, by advocating the psychodynamic hypothesis, according to which parts of the unconscious (the id and the superego) are in constant conflict with the conscious, depth psychology cannot identify any transcendent truth, and it postulates that the human soul is naturally and necessarily characterized by contradictions, thereby restricting the goal of the psychoanalytical process to an attempt to invigorate the ego in order to be capable of facing the anxiety that stems from the supposedly constant and unavoidable conflict between the conscious and the unconscious. In other words, the purpose of psychoanalysis is to establish a psychological balance by developing a self-sufficient, ego-driven soul and by protecting social cohesion—in the form of a system of socially legitimate fantasies—against the destructive power of uncontrolled impulses.

In his seminal book entitled *The Red Book*, Jung openly and sincerely admits that he developed his theory of the collective unconscious based on his fantasies and dreams, particularly, on his personal imaginative experiences between 1913 and 1916. Despite being nominated as the central work in Jung's oeuvre, his *Red Book* was not published or made otherwise accessible for study until 2009, when the publishing company W. W. Norton published it in a facsimile edition edited by Sonu Shamdasani. This work is called *The Red Book* because its original form is a red leather-bound folio manuscript crafted by Jung. In 1957, Jung told Aniela Jaffé the following about his *Red Book*: "The years ... when I pursued the inner images, were the most important time of my life. ... My entire life consisted in elaborating what had burst forth from the unconscious and flooded me like an enigmatic stream and threatened to break me."[8]

As I pointed out in chapter 2, the function of imagination is characterized by creativity (particularly, manipulation of images) and by the subjectivity of man's conscious states; due to the latter, without the existence of a third factor—precisely, without the truth as a common vital meaning—imagination renders communication among conscious beings essentially impossible.

At this point, one could argue that human creativity originates in the development of an individual soul that refers to itself—that is, one could argue that, after the stage of infancy (during which the self-awareness of the baby—i.e., one's ability to differentiate the self from the non-self—is very limited), every activity and every attitude of the human being constantly refer to self-preservation and self-affirmation—and that the individual soul can survive in a competitive society through institutions, which, at a later stage, socialize the individual. If we advocate such an argument, then we must also advocate that the individual mode of assigning meaning to things produces and underpins social significations, that is, we are compelled to advocate that the solution to the problem of the individual soul's socialization exists potentially within the individual soul's imagination, and that the individual soul's imagination underpins the socialization of the individual soul through social imaginary significations. However, the individual soul would be capable of solving the problem of its socialization by itself if it expressed a form of social unconscious, which could function as the origin of an imaginative code of communication among individual souls, but, apart from the fact that the postulation of such a collective unconscious leads us deeply into the realm of metaphysics, we must mention that, by the fifth century BC, the Greek philosopher Xenophanes of Colophon[9]—the founder of Eleatic philosophy (according to which, despite appearances, real being is a changeless, motionless, and eternal "one")—had already pointed out the relativity of the images that originate from the collective unconscious and, according to Jung's terminology, can be called "archetypes."

8. Jung, *The Red Book*, vii.
9. References to Xenophanes's work can be found in Plato, *Sophist* 242c–d, and in Aristotle, *Metaphysics* 986b18–27.

According to Xenophanes, the collective unconscious, which underpins the intersubjectivity of images and, thus, the socialization of imagination, is characterized by particularity, and it is spatially determined, in the sense that it is a phenomenon of local, if not marginal, significance. Xenophanes, beginning with the thesis, "One god, greatest among gods and humans, like mortals neither in form nor in thought,"[10] declares that "the senses are deceptive and generally rejects reason along with them," as we read in Plutarch's *Miscellanies*, A32.

Jung treated the archetypes of the collective unconscious as if they were instinctive substances, in a way that is similar to the way in which medieval scholastics treated Plato's ideas as if they were logical substances, and, therefore, Jung, like medieval scholastics, precluded the spiritual freedom of the human soul. In other words, Jung sought to invigorate the imaginary foundations of depth psychology by presenting images that (supposedly) are essentially archaic, transpersonal, and even transcultural, and, therefore, he treated the archetypes of the collective unconscious as if they were instinctive substances, arguing that they are manifested as "*a priori*, inborn forms of intuition."[11] Jung argues that "instinct" and "archetype" are two sides of the same unconscious functional coin; in particular, he puts forward the following arguments: "Just as we have been compelled to postulate the concept of an instinct determining or regulating our conscious actions, so, in order to account for the uniformity and regularity of our perceptions, we must have recourse to the correlated concept of a factor determining the mode of apprehension," that is, what he calls "the archetype or primordial image," which he describes as "the instinct's perception of itself."[12]

Inherent in Freud's, Jung's, and the other depth psychologists' arguments about instincts are manifestations of ignorance about philosophical anthropology and cultural history. Human beings have always had instincts and brain (as a biological basis of mental events), and, throughout human history, to some extent, society represses human instincts in order to maintain its cohesion, while, simultaneously, it attempts to counterbalance social pressure through worship systems, rituals, celebrations, holidays, processes of professional and economic self-actualization, etc. Modern psychology has analyzed the previous phenomena, but it has not

---

10. Quoted by Clement of Alexandria; see Osborne, *Presocratic Philosophy*, 62.
11. Jung, "Instinct and the Unconscious," 133.
12. Ibid., 136–37.

sufficiently investigated the importance of the individual's participation in the community for the psychic cure of the individual.

From the perspectives of the ancient Greek and the Hesychast world-conceptions, the human being is a "person," that is, as I argued in chapter 1, an existential-otherness-in-communion. In particular, in the context of classical Greek civilization, the human being attained to personhood by experiencing existential otherness through the citizen identity and by experiencing communion through the "polis" (city-state), which was perceived as an image of the cosmic order and as the historical framework in which the citizen identity could be actualized and become meaningful. However, as I argued in chapter 3, the ancient Greek person faced an existential crisis when he realized the antinomy between the soul's freedom of will and the cosmic order. The previous existential crisis became even more difficult and painful when the ancient Greek person lost his polis, that is, the historical underpinning of his personhood, and he was compelled to live in the awesomely vast and multiethnic Roman Empire. Thus, the Greek person realized that he needed a new path to personhood, which was offered to him by Christianity.

The core message of Christianity has been accurately summarized by two early Greek church fathers, namely, Irenaeus of Lyons and Athanasius of Alexandria: Irenaeus of Lyons asserts that "if the Logos has been made man, it is so that men may be made gods,"[13] and, in the same spirit, Athanasius of Alexandria asserts that the divine Logos "was made man that we might be made God."[14] Moreover, as I have already explained, the Hesychast theological treatises have methodically expounded the Greek church fathers' doctrine of the deification of man through man's participation in God's uncreated energies. According to the previous Christian methexiological teachings, the human being attains to personhood through and in the context of his participation in God's uncreated energies; human participation in God's uncreated energies is founded on humanity's freedom of will, thus safeguarding human existential otherness, and it endows the human person with universality, in the sense that the human mind becomes a repository of the Absolute (precisely, of God's uncreated energies), while, simultaneously, the socialization of the individual soul is achieved through its communion with God, and,

---

13. Irenaeus, *Against Heresies* V.
14. Athanasius, *On the Incarnation*, 54.

therefore, the socialization of the individual soul does not imply submissiveness to any historical or natural necessities.

When human personhood is ontologically founded on human participation in God's uncreated energies, a human being can simultaneously be a person, a citizen of the world, and a citizen of God's uncreated "kingdom," since, as we read in John 18:36, Jesus Christ made clear that he and his disciples are spiritually free from historicity, by saying to Pilate: "My kingdom is not of this world." In the same spirit, the apostle Paul wrote to the Galatians: "You are all sons of God through faith in Christ Jesus, for all of you who were baptized into Christ have clothed yourselves with Christ. There is neither Jew nor Greek, slave nor free, male nor female, for you are all one in Christ Jesus."[15]

In contrast to classical Greek philosophy and political institutions and in contrast to Hesychasm, civil society, from the emergence of the first civil mentalities and institutions in the tenth-century Western Europe onward,[16] and modernity perceive the human being as a subject (a historical agent endowed with reason and will) and as a member of a partnership, called "society," whose primary purpose is the survival of its members, as opposed to the Greek philosophers' and the Hesychasts' notion of society as communion, which is founded on a vision of ontological wholeness. In the context of methexiology, which is founded on classical Greek philosophy and on Hesychasm, the human soul is an energy of communion, that is, it unites people together by understanding itself and the others as participants in the same universal truth (in the case of Platonism, that universal truth is the world of ideas, and in the case of Hesychasm, that universal truth is God's uncreated grace). By contrast, in the context of civil society and modernity, which are secular extensions of scholastic humanism, the human soul is identified with consciousness due to the rationalist underpinnings of civil society and modernity in general. Rationalism attempts to transform the soul from an energy of communion into an organ whose highest faculty is reason, rational thought. Therefore, in the history of the Western subject, rationalism caused an enormous repression of impulses, which, in

---

15. Galatians 3:26–28.

16. In the eleventh century AD, in his *History of Milan*, the historiographer Arnulfus of Milan writes that the union of the members of the civil class participated in the rebellion that broke out in Milan in 980 AD against the local archbishop, and he characterizes that union as a "conspiracy" (*coniuratio*), because its members were bound by mutual oaths.

its turn, caused a psychological reaction that was expressed through an attempt to justify and psychologically legitimize individual impulses. For instance, in the eighteenth century, Marquis de Sade's novel *Philosophy in the Bedroom* expressed this situation in a dramatic and eloquent manner.[17] Moreover, Bryan Chapell, an Evangelical minister, has published a survey among American Evangelicals according to which, in three major categories, specifically, use of illegal drugs, driving while intoxicated, and marital infidelity, behavior actually deteriorates after a commitment to American Evangelicals' legalistic Christianity (the incidence of drug use and illicit sex roughly doubles after conversion, and the incidence of drunken driving triples).[18]

As a consequence of rationalism, man developed a second, underground, soul that is constantly in conflict with the socially acknowledged and legitimate soul. In other words, in the language of depth psychology, due to rationalism, man is spiritually divided into the conscious and the unconscious. The concept of a man who is spiritually divided into a conscious soul and an unconscious one is irrelevant to the type of person that characterizes and underpins ancient Greek society, Byzantine society, and pre-modern societies, in general. In the context of pre-modern societies, in general, the essence of psychological illness consists not in the conflict between the conscious and the unconscious, but in the lack of communion, which may refer to one or more of the following types of communion: communion between humanity and the cosmos, communion between fellow-humans, and communion between humanity and God.

Modern Western culture is founded on a type of person whose soul is governed by either reason or by irrational passions—depending on one's personality type—and it precludes unselfishness. The soul of the modern subject seeks the ultimate pleasure through behaviors that are characterized by unrestrained hedonism and/or by the exercise of coercive power. But, in the previous way, instead of achieving psychic cure, the modern subject becomes even more psychologically ill. Psychoanalysis cannot offer real cure to the modern subject, because psychoanalysis postulates that the spiritual division of the human being between the conscious and the unconscious is a natural and inescapable attribute of the human soul, and, therefore, psychoanalysis merely helps man to manage his spiritual

17. De Sade, *Justine, Philosophy in the Bedroom and Other Writings*.
18. Chapell, *Christ-Centered Preaching*, 199.

fragmentation and to adapt to social constraints. Similarly, no rationalist religious system can offer real cure to the modern subject, because moralistic and legalistic recipes for good life cannot offer psychological unity to a psychologically fragmented subject whose soul is really obedient only to the law of individual desire.

According to methexiology, humanity is the image of God, and, therefore, humans are spiritually free. The spiritual freedom of man, which originates from his communion with God, implies that neither individual reason (with its logical imperatives) nor irrational desire (with its instinctive imperatives) is an organic part of the soul. According to methexiology, individual reason and irrational desire are only powers of the soul, and, therefore, the human soul is capable of making free decisions. By contrast, from Augustine of Hippo onward, as regards the structure and the functions of the human soul, the argument that has been prevailing among Western scholars and churches is that individual reason and irrational desire are organic parts, that is, essential attributes, of the human soul. In other words, in the context of Western culture, the human will is determined by reason and desire, and, therefore, the human being is spiritually fragmented into two psychic entities: the one is conscious and mainly governed by reason, and the other is unconscious and governed by desire. On the other hand, Hesychasm implies that human will is a free power of the mind, which is distinct from the intellect (the faculty of discursive reasoning), since the mind is humanity's repository of uncreated grace.

If we assume that will is an organ of consciousness, then the purpose of man's choices is his self-affirmation, and then freedom of will becomes a shadow of itself, because freedom of will is meaningful only if man's soul is capable of manifesting self-denial, that is, only if man's soul is capable of creatively transcending the ego. Freedom presupposes that man is capable of choosing between good and evil by using the power of his will. But, if the human will is an organ of consciousness, that is, if the will is naturally determined by reason and/or by irrational forces (instincts), then human freedom is an illusion. Therefore, as regards the structure of the human soul and psychotherapy, methexiology, espousing Hesychast psychology, is substantially different from scholastic and modern psychological theories, since the latter are predicated on the assumption that the human soul is naturally fragmented into a conscious and reason-driven entity and an unconscious and desire-driven entity and that the human will is an organ of consciousness.

The two major differences between Hesychast psychology and Western (medieval and modern) psychology are the following: (i) according to Hesychasm, human will is not an organ of consciousness, and, therefore, human will is free from both reason and irrational passions, whereas the Western (medieval and modern) "schools" of psychology maintain that the human will is an organ of consciousness; (ii) Hesychasm emphasizes the distinction between the mind and the intellect, whereas the Western (medieval and modern) "schools" of psychology discard the previous distinction. Gregory Palamas has emphasized the distinction between the mind and the intellect, because he argues that, while the intellect may (and, indeed, should) continue to apply human reason to the sensible world, the mind must be emptied of all rational and irrational elements in order to be filled with God's uncreated grace; then and only then can a human experience the freedom that characterizes God's mode of being. In other words, the first step toward the deification of man is mental emptiness (i.e., the mind must be cleansed from every element that originates from a created source of knowledge), and, hence, total unselfishness.

Reason, desire, and passion are innate powers of the soul, and, therefore, they are natural channels of knowledge. On the other hand, the mind is the faculty of suprarational wisdom. Reason is a structure within the framework of which there exist various functions of categories, which, when they are used properly, can connect isolated segments of sensation (i.e., empirical data) into a whole, and, therefore, they enable consciousness to formulate synthetic statements. In other words, reason processes sensible data, and, it organizes them into rational systems. If the mind were identified with the intellect, then the mind would be concerned with sensible data and would organize them into rational systems, instead of being unceasingly oriented toward the divine Logos. Thus, Gregory Palamas emphasizes the distinction between the mind, as the faculty of suprarational and uncreated knowledge, and the intellect, as the faculty of rational and created knowledge.

In the context of Hesychasm, the mind is the faculty of enlightened discernment, and it guides the soul as to which elements and stimuli it should pay attention or ward off. From the previous perspective, the mind is a divine psychic power. According to Hesychasm, nature is beyond good and evil, because good and evil are matters of personal choice and not of natural necessity. Hence, the choice between good and evil cannot depend on speculations about the essence of beings and things. The Hesychasts maintain that, for the mind, good consists in a state in which the mind is free from emotional disturbance and totally open to receive God's uncreated grace, whereas evil consists in a state in which the mind is passionately attached to sensation. Given that reason is concerned with sensible data, the intellect does not have free will, whereas the mind has free will, since it desires the suprarational Good, precisely, to participate in God. The mind can attain to the suprarational Good only if it is cleansed from the passions of the senses, and this can be achieved through metanoia, that is, through a mental change. According to Hesychasm, metanoia consists in the return of the mind to the heart and the liberation of the mind from bodily sensation. In the context of metanoia, the mind experiences a mental sensation that is free from the influence of the images of the external world.

If we discard the distinction between the mind and the intellect, then we are compelled to reduce the soul to the operation of the nervous system and to critical reason. Without the distinction between the mind and the intellect, the soul is not guided by the mind, which is the bearer of a suprarational truth, but it is guided by the intellect, that is, by reason, toward a truth that separates man from God and makes him ego-centric. Furthermore, without the distinction between the mind and the intellect, freedom of will is impossible, because freedom of will is meaningful only if one can make passionless choices. In other words, to have freedom of will means not merely that one can make choices, but also that one is not determined by his repressed desires, instincts, and/or logical necessities. If one is determined by his repressed desires, instincts, and/or logical necessities, then the fact that he makes choices does not mean that he has freedom of will. Without the distinction between the mind and the intellect, making passionless choices is impossible, and, by implication, freedom of will is impossible.

How does the mind relate to the passionate part of the soul? In order to answer this question from the perspective of methexiology, we must, first of all, mention that Hesychast psychology does not advocate the argument that we should deaden the passionate part of the soul. In the second triad of his *Triads in Defense of the Sacred Hesychasts*, Gregory Palamas mentions that Barlaam—based on Augustine's ascetic theory about a naturally immortal soul clothed in a mortal body—maintains that the passionate part of the soul must be deadened in order to stop influencing the body. In particular, according to Barlaam, the soul is a perfect gift from God, and, in prayer, it must be totally detached from sensation, since, Barlaam argues, the soul suffers from a spiritual darkness whenever it enjoys the powers of its passionate part and of the body. By contrast, Gregory Palamas points out that, if one adopts Barlaam's arguments, then prayer becomes a fantasy whose content is an idol of the soul.

According to Gregory Palamas, prayer is an act of heart purification, in which both the soul and the body participate. The purposes of ascetic practices, in particular, are to invigorate the soul in its fight against negative and destructive passions and to reinforce prayer. Thus purified and ruled, the body serves the soul, that is, it becomes a spiritual instrument, and, therefore, it is not an evil thing. In the context of Hesychasm, both the soul and the body, as a unified whole, participate in the journey to deification. If one's struggle for spiritual transformation and, ultimately, deification is limited to the soul and is not extended to the body, it is destined to fail and give rise to traumatic experiences. As regards the Hesychasts' asceticism, Georges Florovsky has argued that it is something that liberates human creativity, it is "a 'working out' of one's own self," and, "through ascetic trial, the very vision of the world is changed and renewed."[19] In other words, the Hesychasts' ascetic practices and their psychosomatic method of prayer, which I expounded in chapter 4, conduce to the preservation of their corporeal and mental faculties in their fullest energy, thereby enabling them to actualize their ontological potential.

Following the tradition of the Greek church fathers, methexiology emphasizes that no divine gift—not even the human soul—is actually perfect, since God's gifts to humanity are only potentially perfect, and the transition from potential perfection to actual perfection can take place only in total freedom, that is, it depends on a human's own will. Through the soul, God's grace is extended throughout the body, because the actualization of the potential qualities with which God endows humanity depends on the human body. Therefore, in contrast to Barlaam's teachings, Gregory Palamas argues that a passionless soul is not one that has deadened its passionate part, but one that has reoriented its passionate part away from evil toward God. Gregory Palamas points out that we love through the passionate part of the soul, and, therefore, if one deadens the passionate part of his soul, then he is unable to observe the Law of Christ, which is to love God and one's fellow-humans.

From the perspective of methexiology, the essence of psychological health consists in the soul's communion with God and with the other

19. Florovsky, *Christianity and Culture*, 127–28.

souls, and the essence of psychological illness consists in the loss of the soul's power of communion, where "communion" means participation in another being's or in another world's energies. In other words, according to methexiology, the essence of psychological illness consists in an injury to the sociality of the soul. Communion is a power of the human mind, but, if the mind loses the power of participating in God's uncreated energies, and if it is identified with the intellect, then man's life and behavior are determined by the ego and its selfish commands, which may be rational or sentimental. Sentiment does not have the power of communion, since it is, by definition, founded on subjective evaluative judgments. Reason does not have the power of communion either, because reason is based on a sharp distinction between the subject and the object, and, therefore, reason can lead to a unified perception of the object of knowledge, but it cannot unite the knower with the known. As a result, reason keeps man separated from God, perpetuating Adam's errant choice. Furthermore, a soul whose mind is not a partaker of God's uncreated energies is an unfree soul, since its desires are determined by the logic of the instinct. The soul's desires are determined by the way in which the soul assigns significances to beings and things and, particularly, by the way in which it evaluates beings and things. As I argued in chapter 2, God is the source of the significance of beings and things, and, therefore, if the human mind does not have access to God, precisely, if the human mind does not participate in God's uncreated energies, then the soul's desires are determined by the logic of the instinct. A soul is free if it can choose between good and evil independently of biological and egoistic commands. A human being is free only if and to the extent that he or she can conceive of the idea of Good as God's energy, that is, as a mode of life that is of universal value and can be really experienced by humans. On the other hand, only a spiritually unfree soul conceives of the idea of good in a selfish way, and a soul that is not spiritually free is ill.

Methexiology's aforementioned criticism of reason is founded on the Hesychast distinction between the mind and the intellect, and, therefore, its purpose is not to eliminate reason, but to liberate the mind from sense perceptions. As a consequence, neither methexiology's aforementioned criticism of reason nor the Hesychasts' method of prayer should be confused with Oriental theories of meditation. According to Oriental theories of meditation, the intellect should be detached from the sensible world, because they identify the mind with the intellect, and many of them contend that the sensible, material world is non-being. By contrast, the distinction between the mind and the intellect, on which my methexiological arguments and the Hesychasts' method of prayer are founded, implies that, in accordance with its natural function, the intellect should be concerned with the sensible world in order to endow the latter with a rational order that expresses the enlightened will of the mind, while the mind should be constantly oriented toward God and function as a pure repository of God's uncreated grace. In other words, it is the mind, and not the intellect, that should be detached from the sensible world.

The intellect provides knowledge that pertains to the sciences and technology of our secular world, such as grammar, rhetoric, logic, mathematics, astronomy, farming, road-building, sailing, plumbing, sky-scraper construction, information technology, space-engineering, medicine, nanotechnology, etc., and, therefore, it necessarily needs to interact with the world of the senses. If the intellect is detached from the sensible world, then it cannot function properly, and it falls into a state of sleep, which is totally irrelevant to the philosophy of methexis that I propose. On the other hand, the knowledge that is derived from the mind pertains to God's life-giving and uncreated wisdom, and, therefore, the mind should be detached from the sensible world.

When rationalism takes the lead, conformity and ego-satisfaction become absolute norms, psychology merely cleans the bars of the rationalist cage in which humans are imprisoned, and religious elites do not open up the person to the mystery, but rather they try to open up the mystery to the person according to their own discursive reasoning. However, there is a peculiar form of Orthodox Christian asceticism whose purpose is to revolt against the absolute domination of rationalism. This peculiar form of Orthodox Christian asceticism is called "foolishness for Christ," which highlights a particular form of madness as a manifestation of spiritual nobility. The Eastern Orthodox church venerates several "fools for Christ" as saints, such as: Domna the Martyr and Fool for Christ (she lived in the time of the pagan emperor Maximilian), Andrew the Fool for Christ (tenth century AD), Basil the Fool for Christ (he lived from the second half of the fifteenth century AD until the first half of the sixteenth century AD), Xenia of St. Petersburg the Fool for Christ (she lived from the first half of the eighteenth century AD until the beginning of the nineteenth century AD), John of Moscow the Fool for Christ (sixteenth century AD), etc.

As a special form of Christian asceticism, foolishness, madness, or *salōtis*[20]—which is a Greek term that is derived from the Syriac word *sakhla*, which means foolishness—appeared in the fourth century AD in Egypt concurrently with monasticism, and it is founded on the Bible, particularly on 1 Corinthians 1:20–25 and 4:10, where the apostle Paul writes the following: "Hasn't God made foolish the wisdom of this world? . . . the foolishness of God is wiser than men. . . . We are fools for Christ."

In the context of the form of asceticism that is called foolishness for Christ, foolishness is a façade put on by a charismatic bearer of the Holy Spirit. Divine eros burns in the heart of a fool for Christ. A fool for Christ is passionless in the sense that I mentioned above, that is, he has reoriented the passionate part of his soul toward God. Being a partaker of God's uncreated grace, a fool for Christ takes up a heavy cross: he or she lives in the world, among humans, pretending to be mad, insane, thus hiding his or her virtues, while striving to help others spiritually. Whereas "socially correct" people, treat a fool for Christ with contempt and derision, and they may even persecute him or her, a fool for Christ performs miraculous signs, and leads several people to metanoia and salvation. Fools for Christ sneer the world and its values, and they provoke "socially correct" persons and members of the social establishment, because fools for Christ have transcended the logic and the values of the world, and they lead people's souls to the ultimate source of the significance of being, that is, to a personal relationship with God, in the context of which one finds oneself experiencing what the apostle Paul meant by saying, "it is no longer I that I live, but Christ lives in me."[21]

A fool for Christ has emptied himself of egoism, and, thus, he has transcended all those circumstances that offer sentimental, intellectual, or material satisfaction to the ego, such as domestic warmth, worldly friendships, intellectual certainties, social dignity and acknowledgment, etc. He is a man who lives in the world according to the world's anti-doctrines, and he has ascended to such a high level of spiritual freedom and, hence, of psychic independence, that he does not strive to change institutions, but he unceasingly strives to change himself in order to become like Christ as much as possible. The ultimate goal of a fool for Christ is his metanoia and salvation, while the insolence that characterizes his behavior toward the world brings to the light of consciousness elements

---

20. Špidlík, "Fous pour le Christ en Orient," 753.
21. Galatians 2:20.

(e.g., motivations) that are not conscious, and, thus, helps people to know themselves better and to cure passions.

For instance, once, Andrew the Fool for Christ,[22] pretending insanity, was playing at a square. At some point, he entered into a nearby tavern, and he was sternly staring at a habitué, who reacted, saying to him: "What are you looking at, you fool? Get out!" Then Andrew responded to him as follows: "A miser demon, like a monkey, is sitting on your shoulder, you miserable wretch! Give me an obolus." The habitué said: "I have no money." Then Andrew continued as follows: "Indeed, you psychical cripple! You left your house carrying seven obolus—you paid one obolus in order to buy cabbages, one more in order to buy lupins, and you are having five more. Now demons are urging you to spend them in order to buy drinks." Then Andrew left the tavern, and the puzzled habitué admitted, in front of other habitués of the tavern, that what Andrew the Fool for Christ had just said was true.

According to the apostle Paul, one cannot become really wise, unless one renounces the wisdom of this world, that is, unless one is liberated from the law of the flesh, which inhibits the discovery of the personal logoi of beings.[23] In order to achieve the previous goal, the apostle Paul argues, one must imitate the life of Jesus Christ, who "emptied himself, taking the form of a bond-servant, and being made in the likeness of men,"[24] and he even suffered death and ignominy on the cross.[25] Moreover, the apostle Paul has pointed out that "God chose the foolish things of the world that he might put to shame those who are wise."[26] On several occasions, Jesus Christ himself was accused of being a demonic, immoral, and insane person.[27] However, his commandment about this issue is clear: "Blessed are you when people reproach you, persecute you, and say all kinds of evil against you falsely, for my sake."[28]

The role of a fool for Christ is tragic, because, according to his peculiar ascetic practice, a fool for Christ has to manifest sinful behavior, instead of piety, thus challenging established codes of moral and social

---

22. Andrew the Fool for Christ, *Patrologia Graeca*, Vol. 111, 621–888.
23. Romans 8:8.
24. Philippians 2:7.
25. Philippians 2:8.
26. 1 Corinthians 1:27.
27. Matthew 9:34; 11:19; 12:24; 27:63; Luke 7:34; John 8:48.
28. Matthew 5:11.

decency, and to manifest foolishness, instead of prudence. He is a person who perseveres through social marginalization and humiliation, because he is aware that the source of his value is not the social establishment, but God, and that being really valuable means actualizing God's will. Thus, a fool for Christ would not hesitate to put on even a façade of demonism in order to fight against demons in their own realm and turn their own weapons against them.

7

Axiology, Ethics, and Justice

By the term "morality," we refer to a conscious state in which the soul acts as a judge. In other words, conscience is a soul that judges. As I pointed out in chapter 6, in the context of modern psychology, the soul is identified with the consciousness of existence. Therefore, from the perspective of modern psychology, conscience is the consciousness of existence when it operates as a judge. If the soul is identified with the consciousness of existence, that is, if we exclude the mind as a repository of God's uncreated grace, then conscience is determined by its three natural powers, namely: the sentiment, the intellect, and the will.

In the context of modern philosophy, the most influential moral theories are those that have been put forward by Jeremy Bentham (1748–1832), John Stuart Mill (1806–73), Adam Smith (1723–90), and Immanuel Kant (1724–1804). However, as I will argue in what follows, none of these moral theories can stand as a general philosophy of morality.

Using ideas he inherited from John Locke, David Hume, Charles-Louis de Secondat Montesquieu, and Claude-Adrien Helvétius, Bentham attacked the received Lockeian doctrine, and he reformulated it by founding it on utilitarian principles. Bentham's political thought is mainly a quantitative theory of pleasure.[1] His moral theory, in particular, consists in a felicific calculus, according to which the value of a particular pleasure *per se* is determined by its intensity, duration, certainty, propinquity, fecundity, and purity. Moreover, by conceiving the ends of legislation to

---

1. Crimmins, "Bentham and Utilitarianism in the Early Nineteenth Century," 38–60; Hart, *Essays on Bentham*.

include security, subsistence, abundance, and equality, and by envisaging political structures to advance these ends, Bentham argued that the value of a pleasure is also determined by the number of the persons affected by it.

Bentham's felicific calculus implies that the quality of each pleasure is ultimately determined by its quantity, or, at least, by its intensity. Hence, the most important defect of Bentham's moral philosophy is that it cannot address qualitative issues as such. Another severe defect of Bentham's moral philosophy is associated with his argument that the value of a pleasure depends on the number of the persons affected by it. This argument is problematic because it contradicts the subjectivity of conscious states, and because one may define one's moral duties according to one's own individual interests. Accepting that one has moral duties does not *ipso facto* imply that one is a properly socialized person, since one's perception of one's moral duties may be mingled with selfishness. Thus, Bentham's moral philosophy may reduce to a mere philosophical justification of egoism. However, Bentham's moral philosophy may also underpin the suppression of individuality, because Bentham argues for the protection of social goods without having formulated a universal moral criterion that would unite individuals into a harmonious whole without suppressing individuality.

J. S. Mill attempted to improve Bentham's utilitarian moral philosophy by arguing that utility as a moral criterion is of a qualitative nature, and not of a quantitative one.[2] Under the influence of socialist and liberal ideals, Mill argues that the general interest of society must be respected and take priority over individual interest because of its intrinsic value, and not merely because it may coincide with people's individual interests. In Mill's own words, human happiness is intrinsically better than that of a particular individual, since it is of an altogether "higher" type. The central principle of Mill's utilitarian morality is the following: treat others as you would like them to treat you and practice charity. Thus, from Mill's perspective, a pleasure is worthy to be experienced by man only if it is intrinsically noble, and the value of man himself is the foundation of utilitarian morality. In Mill's own words, "it is better to be a human being dissatisfied than a pig satisfied."[3]

---

2. West, "Mill and Utilitarianism in the Mid-Nineteenth Century," 61–80.
3. Mill, "Utilitarianism," 9.

It goes without saying that Mill's utilitarian morality has significantly improved Bentham's utilitarianism. But Mill's moral philosophy has defects that are due to the intrinsically contradictory character of utilitarianism itself. In particular, following the logic of utilitarianism, Mill maintains that pleasure is the ultimate criterion of morality, and, simultaneously, he aims at deducing that a particular pleasure, that is, human happiness, is "higher" than all other pleasures. In other words, lacking a criterion of morality that transcends pleasure, Mill tries to create a universal hierarchy of pleasures, which is absurd. Furthermore, according to Mill, if no other factors interfere (e.g., coercion, restrictions, etc.), conscience is attracted, and it should be attracted, to the morally higher pleasures; hence, he makes a logically illegitimate inference from "is" to "ought."[4]

Inherent in the tension between "being," or what is, and "will," or what should be, is an expectation for a new beginning, for the sake of which and due to which a human may undertake enormous risks and jeopardize almost everything; in particular, someone may decide to sacrifice him- or herself, identifying being ("I am") with will ("I want"), or may choose evil, sacrificing his or her humanity to satisfy a selfish desire. Evil emerges and manifests itself when, during the tug of war between the ego and the ego's ideal self (or what psychoanalysts call the "superego"), someone sees himself as falling short of his ideal self. In that case, he internalizes his situation in a negative way, and he reacts vindictively by psychologically, that is, internally, annihilating humanity and the "other." Evil is not a product of social conditions. Evil is a tragic expression of one's impulse to complain and take vengeance for one's inner failure, in the sense that one has failed to respond effectively to the qualitative requests of one's own self. In other words, evil does not have an inherent basis, that is, its ultimate cause is neither lack of culture, nor nature, nor external oppression, but it springs from the will. Therefore, within the human will lies a link between humanity and evil. This link cannot be overcome through fair historical acts, that is, it cannot be overcome through the pretense that "the end justifies the means," because any act that is fair yet simultaneously causes pain, victims, and destruction cannot cancel evil.

Only a perverted person can legitimize evil (e.g., take measures that cause pain, death, destruction, etc.) by claiming that, in this way, he tries

4. George E. Moore has called the previous syllogism the "naturalistic fallacy"; Moore, *Principia Ethica*.

to overcome the contradiction between an ideal end and the actual state of affairs. One could try to justify evil by pointing out that a physician who prescribes a bitter medicine or inflicts pain through a lancet does something evil, too, and that, ultimately, a physician's "evil" practices cure patients. However, in the case of a capable physician, an apparently "evil" practice is transformed into something good because it is pervaded by the positive nature and spirit of medical science, whereas the evil that stems from a negativity bias causes evil for the sake of evil, since an avenger or a judgmental actor who is characterized by a negativity bias, far from successfully dealing with a negative situation, adds his psychological problems to an already negative situation.

Departing from classical utilitarianism, Adam Smith, the acknowledged father of classical political economy, has proposed a moral theory that is founded on the principle of "sympathy." From Smith's perspective, sympathy consists in the intuitive perception of the normative character of human behavior. In other words, according to Smith, "sympathy" combines empathy (i.e., the emotional interconnectedness that we feel with other humans) with the judgment and evaluation of individuals' behavior in particular situations.

Smith maintains that sympathy must be pure, unconditional, and universal. Additionally, he postulates that individuals make decisions based primarily on self-interest. Thus, he defines self-interest in a broad way; Smith's definition of self-interest includes sympathy. However, faced with Hobbes's and Rousseau's arguments that selfish desires may injure others, Smith has to answer the following question: how can the selfish desires of individuals be contained, while still enabling individuals to thrive by pursuing their self-interest? Smith answered to the previous question by developing a psychological metaphor called the "spectator."

According to Smith, we should think of the spectator as someone who observes our behavior and the behavior of others. When we are observing someone taking a decision or an action, part of us is judging that action: that is the "spectator." Smith argues that, "to approve of the passions of another, therefore, as suitable to their objects, is the same thing as to observe that we entirely sympathize with them; and not to approve of them as such, is the same thing as to observe that we do not entirely sympathize with them."[5] Smith relates sympathy to approval as follows: "To approve of another man's opinions is to adopt those opinions, and to

---

5. Smith, "Sympathy," 105.

adopt them is to approve of them[;] ... it is equally the case with regard to our approbation or disapprobation of the sentiments or passions of others."[6]

According to Smith, the aforementioned inner spectator judges according to his sense of what is proper behavior, and, simultaneously, he complies with the principle of sympathy. However, the following question emerges: how should we act when we do not know if others approve or disapprove of our actions? Smith answered to the previous question by arguing that we use the aforementioned inner spectator to evaluate our own actions, and, for this reason, we have self-contained mechanisms and dynamics for controlling selfish desires.

Smith attempted to create a coherent systematic science of man grounded in sympathy. However, sympathy is not a necessary conscious state, conscious states are characterized by subjectivity, and, since the sentimental and the volitional powers of conscience can influence sympathy, sympathy may not lead to the formulation of unconditional moral judgments. In order to confront the previous logical difficulties, Smith resorts to the psychological metaphor of the spectator, and he argues that an individual's own conscience can be used as a substitute for the conscience of an external sympathizing spectator whenever the first operates as an impartial spectator. However, the previous argument is a logical contradiction, because, in this way, Smith eliminates sympathy in the fields of deliberation and judgment, which are supposedly underpinned by sympathy. In other words, the way in which Adam Smith uses the term sympathy implies that he has not clarified if sympathy is a moral sentiment, as he has theoretically asserted, or if it is an expression of moral rationalism, as it is implied by the role that the impartial spectator plays in Smith's moral theory.

The contradictory character of Smith's moral theory corroborates the argument that I put forward in chapter 6, according to which a selfish soul can never be spiritually free. Smith postulates selfishness as an ontological attribute of the human being, and he tries to endow sympathy—which is a particular sentiment of the selfish individual—with universal authority. In order to endow sympathy with universal authority, thus protecting and dignifying the selfish ontological core of the individual, Smith's moral theory, by using the psychological metaphor of the spectator, makes the individual's inner life so shallow that sympathy is

6. Ibid., 106.

subjected to reason. In other words, ultimately, Smith's individuals can have sentiments only if their sentiments are not sentimental, that is, only if their sentiments, instead of expressing the person's existential otherness, conform to reason. Therefore, in the context of Smith's *Theory of Moral Sentiments*, individuals pursue their selfish interest, but, ultimately, they conform to the commands of the reason of the established system, in the sense that they pursue their selfish interest according to the established system's rationality, and, for this reason, they are ultimately, transformed into undifferentiated units of a self-regulating system that, in his *Wealth of Nations*, Smith described as the economic system of "natural liberty."[7]

Smith's economic system of "natural liberty" is a scientifically rigorous reformulation of physiocracy, which was the first systematic attempt to explain economic behavior in similar ways to natural (that is, inanimate) behavior. Physiocracy was pioneered by François Quesnay (1694–1774) and Anne-Robert-Jacques Turgot (1727–81). The physiocrats argue that there is a "natural order" that allows and enables human beings to live together. Samuelson and Nordahus have given a concise account of physiocracy as follows: "a remarkable description of the economy as a circular flow, still used in today's texts . . . was made by Quesnay, Louis XIV's court physician. He stressed that the different elements of the economy are as integrally tied together as are the blood vessels of the body."[8] The thought of the physiocrats, the mentality of industrialism, and Adam Smith's aforementioned moral theory converge in the publication by Adam Smith of *The Wealth of Nations* in 1776, which "marks the birthdate of modern economics."[9] The physiocrats and the modern economists, in general, follow a positivist epistemology, which has been summarized by John Elliott Cairnes as follows: "Political Economy is a science in the same sense in which Astronomy, Dynamics, Chemistry, Psychology are sciences. Its subject-matter is different; . . . but its methods, its aims, the character of its conclusions are the same as theirs."[10]

The physiocrats, the classical economists, and the neoclassical economists follow a positivist epistemology, which was summarized by Cairnes in the quotation above. In general, modern economics is dominated by the argument that there are economic laws and that the primary

---

7. Sabine and Thorson, *A History of Political Theory*, 624; Smith, *The Wealth of Nations*.

8. Samuelson and Nordhaus, *Economics*, 376.

9. Ibid., 376.

10. Cairnes, *The Character and Logical Method of Political Economy*, 35.

aim of economics is the discovery of those laws. Thus, the dominant theories of modern economics are fixated on essentialism (philosophical realism) and Newtonian mechanics. But, as Alexander Woodcock and Monte Davis have pointed out, even in the context of natural sciences, "Newton's triumph was not an explanation of anything," and "the twentieth century has taught us that the universe is a queerer place than we imagined, perhaps (in J. B. S. Haldane's words) queerer than we *can* imagine," that is, "much of reality is not so obliging."[11] In contrast to physiocracy and Newtonian mechanics, science is a consciousness orthosis, in the sense that the purpose of science is to create theories that help consciousness to approach reality (both the reality of consciousness and the reality of the world). Physical and historical reality is not merely an object whose particular manifestations are statically conceived by scientific consciousness; instead, physical and historical reality is a goal toward which scientific consciousness is dynamically oriented, and scientific consciousness seeks to identify physical and historical reality with scientific consciousness itself, that is, scientific consciousness seeks to eliminate any distance between scientific consciousness and any object of scientific research.

The economic system is a particular case of the general issue of the communication among conscious beings. If we leave the realm of unconscious communication, to which physiocracy is confined, and attempt to deal with problems of deliberate cooperation, we need a moral theory. Through his psychological metaphor of the spectator, Smith attempted to articulate a moral theory that gives rise to such a high level of conformity to the established system that, ultimately, degrades human beings to the level of inanimate, or purely instinctive behavior, so as to safeguard the rationality of the established system. In the context of Smith's moral and

11. Woodcock and Davis, *Catastrophe Theory*, 10, 14. According to Ilya Prigogine and Isabelle Stengers, "our universe has a pluralistic, complex character. Structures may disappear, but also they may appear. Some processes are, as far as we know, well described by deterministic equations, but other involve probabilistic processes" (Prigogine and Stengers, *Order out of Chaos*, 9). Furthermore, it should be emphasized that there is a fundamental asymmetry between physical (or astronomical) time and historical time, and, therefore, there is a fundamental asymmetry between natural science and social science. Whereas physical time is, more or less, uniform, historical time is subject to structural changes. Physical time obeys its own entropy, which means that it flows in a precise and unalterable (irreversible) direction toward a precise but unknown end, but historical time is not characterized by any entropy, because it is a free outcome of the action of human consciousness, and, therefore, it is subject only to the laws imposed on it by the intentionality of human consciousness.

economic theories, and, generally, in the context of the so-called "classical economics" (whose paradigmatic representatives are David Ricardo and Thomas R. Malthus), the "system" becomes a mechanism that obeys its own terms and logic, it gives rise to the autonomy of economics from real people's needs and will, and it is imagined as an impersonal and ruthless mechanism, while "systemic morality" is merely a training tool for making people judge, desire, and evaluate according to the rationality of the established system.

The so-called classical political economy (i.e., the economic theories of Adam Smith, D. Ricardo, and T. R. Malthus, as well as the economic theories that are based on the works of the previous pioneers of "classical economic thought") trains economists and, generally, economic actors to subordinate the concept of "value" to the concept of "price" and, by implication, to subordinate the creativity of the human being to the rationality of the established economic system. As Louis Lavelle has pointedly observed, a price is a fact, but a value is a judgment.[12] Value transcends action, and, simultaneously, it is integrated into action and guides action, since value is the structure of action, and action confirms the existence of value. Moreover, ultimately, values determine prices. The existence of values enables humans to develop their consciousness of existence, since, due to values and through values, a man is aware that he is not necessarily determined by "objective conditions," but he can change his existential conditions, instead of merely seeking ways of rational adaptation.

In the history of modern philosophy, the most prominent theory of moral rationalism was formed by Immanuel Kant. Kant's theory of morality is grounded in the principle of the "categorical imperative." A categorical imperative is a command, or a rule, that applies in all situations and at all times. This categorical imperative is that we should do what is rationally (logically) right for human beings.

Kant's moral theory has two basic assumptions, namely: (i) Only human beings are capable of rationality. Hence, Kant maintains, it is imperative to protect man's rationality and, precisely, his ability to be rational, since to take away our ability to be rational means to take away our humanity. In other words, for Kant, the distinctive attribute of humanity is rationality. (ii) As rational beings, only humans are autonomous, that is, they can make volitional choices, whereas all other creatures on

---

12. Lavelle, *Traité des Valeurs*.

the planet pretty much react instinctively. Moreover, according to Kant, man's autonomy should be protected.

In his *Groundwork of the Metaphysics of Morals*, Kant argues that the following two ethical imperatives should guide our actions: (i) We should do what is best for everyone equally. (ii) We should do what preserves the needs of each individual equally. Thus, the first formulation of Kant's categorical imperative is the following: "I ought never to act except in such a way that I can also will that my maxim should become a universal law."[13] In other words, Kant argues that, if it doesn't logically make sense that your action (that you are regarding as ethical) could be made dispositive,[14] then it is not the best ethical action. The second formulation of Kant's categorical imperative is the following: "Act in such a way that you always treat humanity, whether in your own person or in the person of any other, never simply as a means, but always at the same time as an end."[15] From the perspective of Kant's original assumptions, if someone uses other people as a means to achieve his own goals, for instance, if he deceives people, he trumps their rationality, instead of preserving their ability to be rational, and, therefore, he commits an assault on those people's humanity itself.

Kant's moral theory is focused on ethical duty, and it is intimately associated with the morality of modern civil society. Moreover, Kant's ethics, epistemology, and ontology have influenced the scholarly work of numerous Protestant theologians.

Even though Kant's moral theory helps the development of the rational power of conscience, it is seriously problematic. First of all, Kant's argument that the moral law is a categorical imperative leads to oversimplification. The following counter-example disproves Kant's universality claim: indeed, as Kant contends, we should not wish lying to become a universal law, but if you know that a person X is asking you information about a person Y in order to harm, or even kill, Y, then it might be neither psychologically easy nor rational to give X true information. Additionally, Michel Anteby, Professor of Organizational Behavior at Harvard University, has pointed out that so-called "moral grey zones" emerge in more or less every sector or enterprise when official rules are repeatedly broken with, at minimum, a supervisor's approval, and they

---

13. Paton, *The Moral Law*, 67.

14. By dispositive, I mean relating to or bringing about the settlement of an issue, a general settlement/rule.

15. Ibid., 91.

rely on personal trust at all levels.[16] According to Anteby, a characteristic example of such a "moral grey zone" is the following: "physicians often afford paramedics and EMTs considerable leeway to 'play doctor' or 'experiment' with certain drugs and dosages when they believe it is critical to a patient's survival."[17]

Kant has bought the logical power and coherence of his moral theory at an extremely high cost, since, in order to achieve such a high level of logical power and coherence, his moral theory eliminates the sentimental power of conscience, and it precludes sensitivity and discretion of judgment. Thus, given that conscience has three natural powers—namely, the sentiment, the intellect, and the will—Kant's moral rationalism inhibits the development of an integrated conscience, and it gives rise to a rather shallow personality.

The fallacy of Kant's moral theory originates from his ontological claim that the Good-in-itself is inaccessible to the human being. The Kantian subject is capable of knowing only the products of his or her own consciousness, and, therefore, ultimately, Kant's epistemology is grounded in imagination. In fact, this is Kant's conclusive argument in the first edition of his *Critique of Pure Reason*, published in 1781. In the first edition, Kant uses the term "transcendental imagination," by which he refers to the unknown common root uniting sense and understanding, but, frightened of the consequences of such a bold claim, he decided to omit the term "transcendental imagination" from the second edition of his *Critique of Pure Reason*, which was published in 1787.[18] Additionally, Kant argues that imaginative formation (*Einbildung*) is distinct from the power to give form to an intuition (*Bildungskraft*), because it makes images without the presence of a sensible object, either by invention (*fingendo*) or by abstraction (*abstrahendo*). As I argued in chapter 2, imagination is necessarily unstable. Faced with the consequences of his assumption about the unknowability of the Good-in-itself and with the inherent instability of imagination, Kant attempted to fortify the subject's ego and transform it into a substitute for the unknowable Good-in-itself through the categorical imperative, that is, by filling the human soul with moral duties, which, as I argued earlier, give rise to a person whose conscience is not integrated, and whose inner life is shallow.

---

16. Anteby, *Moral Grey Zones*, chapter 9.
17. Ibid., 143.
18. Makkreel, *Imagination and Interpretation in Kant*, 21.

In contrast to the aforementioned moral theories, methexiology implies that ethics consists neither in duty nor in the individual's selfish will, but in a radical sense of unselfishness that opens up our minds to the mysterious, yet knowable, Good-in-itself. According to Hesychasm, on which methexiological ethics is founded, the Good-in-itself, in the form of God's uncreated energies, is accessible to humans, if and to the extent that they rise above and sacrifice their individual certainties, that is, their selfish thoughts and desires. In other words, since humans can participate in the God's deifying uncreated energies—if and to the extent that they cleanse their minds from logic and sentiments, which keep humans confined to the realm of the ego—methexiological ethics consists in being godly. As I have already explained, the mind should be understood as the repository of God's uncreated energies, and, therefore as something distinct from both the intellect (the seat of reason) and the passionate part of the soul (the seat of emotion). Hence, humans can use their intellects and the passionate part of their souls wisely only if they are governed by the mind, which, in its turn, should be filled only with God's uncreated energies.

The essence of methexiological ethics can be understood by contemplating on the following story from the book *Gerontikon*,[19] which contains sayings of Eastern Orthodox monks: Abbé Serapion once went to the house of a prostitute, pretending he was a client. Before the prostitute started offering her services, he asked her to allow him to read his canon (prayer rule). Then Abbé Serapion started reading from the book of Psalms, and, after each particular psalm, he was praying to God to save that prostitute. Abbé Serapion's canon made the prostitute's conscience shudder, and, by the time Abbé Serapion finished his canon, the prostitute had undergone a spiritual conversion. Finally, the prostitute asked Abbé Serapion to guide her to a way of life that would be in accordance with God's will. Abbé Serapion led the prostitute to an abbey of nuns, where he left her with the abbess, but he ordered the abbess to give no prayer rule to the former prostitute and to let her do what she wanted. However, after two days, the former prostitute asked the abbess to give her a prayer rule, and, after a few more days, she asked the abbess to spend the rest of her life in prayer and by following the rules of that monastery. The abbess acted according to the requests of that former prostitute, thus following the guidelines that had been given to her by Abbé Serapion and what is

---

19. *Gerontikon*, 239–40.

written in 1 John 3:21–23: "if our hearts don't condemn us, we have boldness toward God; and whatever we ask, we receive from him, because we keep his commandments and do the things that are pleasing in his sight."

Abbé Serapion did not impose any correctional measures on the former prostitute, because he was primarily concerned not with her deeds, but with her soul, in accordance with Jesus Christ's teaching that, "from within, out of the hearts of men, proceed evil thoughts, sexual sins, theft, murder, adultery, greed, wickedness, deceit, lustful desires, envy, slander, arrogance, and folly."[20] Abbé Serapion discerned that the soul of that woman was longing for the Absolute and that the mismanagement of the quest for the Absolute had led her to the desecration of her being. Therefore, he led her to a way of life in which the Absolute, for which she had been longing for so long, could be disclosed, and he let her meet the Absolute of her own free will. Abbé Serapion did not even request that woman to confess her sins to him, because he was aware that the sacrament of confession is not a particular formal rite, but it is the mystery of metanoia, and that the essence of sin is the lack of metanoia. Therefore, the purpose of a spiritual guide and of ethics, in general, should be to save man's soul from remaining closed toward God and toward the fellow-humans.

From the perspective of methexiology, ethics should not treat man as if he were a being that should be deontologically corrected, or ethically "rebooted," according to a particular set of imperatives, but it should aim at opening up man's soul to the Good-in-itself, namely, to God, and to the fellow-humans. The essence of ethics is exactly the previous kind of psychic openness. Every other perception or criterion of ethics, whether it be atonement through self-inflicted pain and/or self-sacrifice, or rational self-control, or individual sentiments, proceeds from and is underpinned by a sense of self-vindication, and, for this reason, it keeps man's soul closed and, therefore, sinful, no matter how pious one's external behavior is. In fact, this is the meaning of Jesus Christ's Parable of the Pharisee and the Tax Collector.[21]

The aforementioned methexiological approach to ethics underpins and leads to a particular approach to justice: justice as restoration of the sociality of the human soul and, by implication, as social responsibility. The main purpose of positive law is to achieve, protect, and, in case of

---

20. Mark 7:21–22.
21. Luke 18:9–14.

social disorder, restore social peace. However, history has shown that positive law contradicts itself whenever some of its rules cannot convince people that they are in harmony with the essence of justice. For this reason, Pythagoras has pointed out that societies should be governed by benevolent laws.[22] When social consciousness disapproves of certain laws, it characterizes them as unjust, and, in this event, human consciousness becomes upset and is instigated to resistance. Therefore, humanity needs a stable and trustworthy measure and criterion of justice; this is the purpose of divine justice, because the foundation and the shelf of the just republic is the Good-in-itself. Both Plato[23] and Aristotle[24] maintain that the Good-in-itself is the foundation and the shelf of the just republic, because they conceive of the city-state as a society of free and equal persons whose purpose is the achievement of a perfect life, that is, a life in the image of God.

According to the Old Testament, the purpose of divine justice is the restoration of the communion between humanity and God, and, for this reason, the Old Testament's system of justice is characterized by mercy. Therefore, for instance, in Ezra 9:15, we read that people should be glad God doesn't give them what they deserve, in the sense that God's love and mercy had spared the Israelites when they did nothing to deserve it. In the same spirit, in his Proverbs 25:21–22, King Solomon writes the following: "If your enemy is hungry, give him food to eat; if he is thirsty, give him water to drink: for you will heap coals of fire on his head, and the LORD will reward you." Moreover, prompting man to act in a godly way, Lamentations 3:27–31 says: "It is good that a man should . . . give his cheek to him who strikes him, and let him be filled with disgrace. For the LORD will not cast off forever." However, according to the Bible, over the years, divine justice has been distorted into a license for revenge and into an instrument through which ruling elites impose their commands on people. In Matthew 5:39, Jesus delineates his approach to justice as follows: "If someone strikes you on the right cheek, turn to him the other also."

The aforementioned biblical passages make clear that injustice originates from an injury in the sociality of the human soul, that is, injustice is a consequence of a spiritual illness, and, therefore, the purpose of real

---

22. Iamblichus, *Life of Pythagoras*, 126.
23. Plato, *Republic*, 544a; *Statesman*, 302b5.
24. Aristotle, *Politics*, 1283b41–1284a3, 1288a33–b5.

justice is to restore the sociality of the human soul by properly training people to be in harmony with themselves, with their fellow-humans, and with God; any other kind of justice is a distortion of justice, because it serves worldly and selfish goals. Writing from a strictly philosophical perspective, Plato has also argued that injustice is an "illness" (*nōsema*),[25] and, therefore, he has characterized those political systems in which injustice prevails as "illnesses" (*nosēmata*).[26] Hence, a real system of justice neither legitimizes revenge through state institutions (e.g., prisons, firing squads, concentration camps, etc.) nor serves the selfish interests of social elites, but it treats criminals as spiritually ill persons who need spiritual cure, and it seeks to restore the sociality of the criminals' souls.

When the scribes and the Pharisees found a woman guilty of adultery, and, according to their laws, they were ready to stone her to death, Jesus Christ told them: "He who is without sin among you, let him throw the first stone at her."[27] Once, Peter asked Jesus: "Lord, how often shall my brother sin against me, and I forgive him? As many as seven times?"[28] Jesus's answer to him was the following: "I don't tell you seven times, but seventy-seven times."[29] Given that, in the context of the Bible, the number seven is the number of completeness and perfection (deriving much of each meaning by being associated with God's creative work), Jesus's answer, that, is "seventy-seven times," means that we should not even keep track of how many times we forgive someone. In other words, Christ's ethics of unselfishness underpins and gives rise to a system of justice grounded in forgiveness. This enlightened form of forgiveness corresponds and is inextricably linked to a program of spiritual training whose purpose is spiritual conversion (metanoia).

In keeping with its anti-legalistic attitude, methexiology implies that a just society is one in which laws of the state are kept to the bare minimum. According to a traditional saying of Athonite monks, "a good act is not really good, unless it has been done in a good way." Therefore, no good act is really good unless it is based on man's freedom of will. For instance, the welfare state appears to be something good, but, in reality, it is not good, primarily because of the following reasons: first, it is

---

25. Plato, *Gorgias*, 480b1.
26. Plato, *Republic*, 544c6–7.
27. John 8:7.
28. Matthew 18:21.
29. Matthew 18:22.

based on violence, in the sense that it presupposes and necessitates high levels of taxation and social security contributions; secondly, it increases the power of the state and restricts people's freedom of will; thirdly, the very existence of the welfare state indicates that people's conscience is not properly cultivated, since they are unable to voluntarily manifest their sense of social responsibility. Hence, unless people become capable of voluntarily manifesting their sense of social responsibility, the welfare state is manipulated by corrupt social elites that use it as an instrument for justifying the expansion of state power and social control mechanisms, which, ultimately, serve the selfish interests of the ruling elites (e.g., even though several people argue that taxation is justified on the grounds that it redistributes wealth, the truth is that the biggest portion of the taxes that are collected by the state benefit the economic elite through economic subsidies, business contracts between the state and private corporations, and state-financed educational, social-security, and public-order systems that reflect the mentality and serve the interests of the economic elite).

It is important to keep in mind the three temptations that Jesus Christ overcame in the desert, according to Luke 4:1–13. The first temptation was the following: "If you are the Son of God, command this stone to become bread." Symbolically, and in regard to politics, the previous temptation means that the devil tempted Jesus Christ to impose his authority on people by "purchasing" people's support, that is, by appealing to and manipulating people's basic instincts, primarily people's need for food and security. However, even when his human nature was starving, Jesus Christ steadfastly responded as follows: "It is written, 'Man shall not live by bread alone, but by every word of God.'" The second temptation was the following: "I will give you all this authority and their glory. . . . If you therefore will worship before me, it will all be yours." Symbolically, and in regard to politics, the previous temptation means that the devil tempted Jesus Christ to subordinate eternity and spiritual freedom to the logic of history and to adopt a pragmatic attitude toward historical becoming. However, Jesus Christ steadfastly responded as follows: "Get behind me Satan! For it is written, 'You shall worship the Lord your God, and you shall serve him only.'" The third temptation was the following: "If you are the Son of God, cast yourself down from here, for it is written, 'He will put his angels in charge of you, to guard you.'" Symbolically, and in regard to politics, the previous temptation means that the devil tempted Jesus to impose his authority on people through glamor. The intellectually weaker and more average types of people can be controlled and manipulated through "bread," that is, through tangible benefits, but strongly intellectual types are susceptible to intellectual illusions, and, therefore, the most effective way of manipulating the latter is through glamor. However, Jesus Christ steadfastly responded as follows: "It has been said, 'You shall not tempt the Lord your God.'"

From the perspective of methexiology, any discussion about justice is meaningful only if it involves the cure of injuries in the sociality of the human soul and the protection of people against the aforementioned temptations of Christ. As I have already argued, unless the injuries in the sociality of the human soul are cured, man cannot be spiritually free, since a selfish soul is imprisoned in the dark "cave" of natural necessities (e.g., instincts) and intellectual illusions. Unless the human soul is not liberated from the dark "cave" of natural necessities (e.g., instincts) and intellectual illusions, conscience cannot give rise to a just society. Justice is ultimately a matter of spiritual liberation, for which reason Jesus said: "If you remain in my word . . . you will know the truth, and the truth will make you free."[30]

The methexiological theory of justice, which I have just expounded, clearly clashes with secularism and, especially, with the most advanced form of secularism, which is the philosophy of action. The philosophy of action—either of the materialist type, such as Karl Marx's dialectical materialism, or of the spiritualist type, such as Alasdair MacIntyre's Roman Catholic Marxism and Oliver Davies's Theology of Transformation—is an extension of the medieval West's theology and of the modern West's humanistic thought. The essence of the philosophy of action is the negation of God's uncreated energies. Hence, "practice" contrasts not so much with "theory" as with "grace"; the conceptualizations of "practice" that I have in mind when I contrast "practice" with God's uncreated grace are mainly those that have been put forward by Karl Marx,[31] Alasdair MacIntyre,[32] and Pierre Bourdieu.[33]

The scholastics' argument that divine grace (i.e., God's energies) is created implies that the significance of beings and things is created, and, hence it reduces to practice. On the other hand, adhering to the

---

30. John 8:31–32.

31. Marx, "Theses on Feuerbach" (notes written by Karl Marx as a basic outline for the first chapter of his book *The German Ideology*).

32. MacIntyre, *After Virtue*.

33. Bourdieu, *Outline of a Theory of Practice*.

Hesychasts' doctrine of God's uncreated energies, methexiology emphasizes that God's grace is uncreated. The argument that God's grace is an uncreated gift of God to humanity implies that the significance of beings and things is never a practical issue, that is, it is never reducible to practice. In other words, from the perspective of methexiology, the purpose of existence is never derived from a historical or mechanical process.

The argument that the purpose of existence is not derived from any historical or mechanical process is corroborated by the fact that many people who had absolutely believed that the significance of beings and things was derived from practice, since they had identified a historical utopia (e.g., communism) with man's eschatological liberation, have been killed in social rebellions; their decision to sacrifice their lives for the sake of their beliefs indicates that they had never really adopted the argument that the significance of beings and things was a practical issue or a pragmatic truth. When one sacrifices one's life for "bread" or for an idea, he actually refuses to exchange the meaning of life for the practical experience of life. Hence, even in a negative way, a person who sacrifices his life for an ideal gives witness to the glory of God's uncreated energies. In other words, a person who sacrifices his life for his ideals—regardless of whether he is a supporter of a materialist ideology or not—proves that his spirit cannot be subjugated by any general law nor by any historical theory that aims at transforming human life into a practical process.

The philosophy of action *per se* produces two types of persons: bureaucrats and nihilists. On the other hand, the belief in God's uncreated grace underpins holiness, and, therefore, Hesychasm produces saints. In the context of any philosophy of action, justice is necessarily pursued through worldly means, and, therefore, it consists in a rational process according to which an institution collects fees/taxes (usually in a coercive way), and then, after keeping a portion of its proceeds for itself, it distributes goods to people. By contrast, a saint gives out everything. In particular, the difference between a communist and a saint is that the first needs to amass economic resources in order to distribute goods, whereas the latter wants everything to be given out in the context of a radical and metaphysically grounded kind of unselfishness.

The theories of justice that are derived from and underpinned by a philosophy of action can be categorized into the following three approaches:

Nihilistic theories of justice: From the perspective of nihilism, the theory of justice should be focused on individual rights and, especially, on individual ownership. A paradigmatic representative of what I call a nihilistic theory of justice is Robert Nozick.[34] Nozick's theory of justice is based on his self-ownership argument, which has been summarized by Will Kymlicka[35] as follows: (a) people own themselves; (b) the world is initially owned by nobody; (c) one can acquire absolute rights over a disproportionate share of the world, if one does not worsen the condition of others; (d) it is relatively easy to acquire absolute rights over a disproportionate share of the world; therefore, (e) given that private property has been appropriated, a free market in capital and labor is morally required. The previous perspective is nihilistic because, in Nozick's intellectual universe, humanity is disconnected from its significance, which is to say that humanity is disconnected from the source of the significance of being. Moreover, even though Nozick defines human autonomy as "self-ownership," he does not explain why self-ownership is equivalent to such strong property rights. Self-ownership is equivalent to such strong property rights only if we assume that one's ownership of oneself is equivalent to one's ownership of the commodities that one produces and/or purchases—but this assumption degrades the human being into a commodity. If a man degrades himself and other humans into commodities, then, not only does he lose his autonomy, but also he can logically establish neither his superiority vis-à-vis other commodified human beings nor the legitimacy of his ownership claims over commodities, since he himself is a commodity.

Bureaucratic theories of justice: A paradigmatic representative of what I call a bureaucratic theory of justice is Jon Elster, a prominent scholar of "analytical Marxism" (an individualist reworking of Marx based on game theory) and "methodological individualism."[36] Elster's theory of social choice and his approach to distributive justice are based on his assumption that preferences are endogenous to rational choice models. According to Elster, individual preferences are formed through the process of political decision-making itself, and, therefore, individual preferences are not *a priori* or exogenous. However, Elster himself, in his later writings, admitted that rational choice theory is not as powerful as he had initially contended. In his book *Explaining Social Behavior*, Elster argues as follows: "rational-choice theory has less explanatory power

---

34. Nozick, *Anarchy, State and Utopia*.
35. Kymlicka, *Contemporary Political Philosophy*, 172.
36. Elster, "The Market and the Forum: Three Varieties of Political Theory."

than I used to think. . . . *There is no general nonintentional mechanism that can simulate or mimic rationality.*"[37] As I have already argued, truth transcends logic, and the significance of life transcends life itself. Therefore, every regime that is based on a bureaucratic approach to justice, regardless of its rationality claims, is to some extent compelled to resort to absolutism in order to subordinate truth and the significance of life to the rationality of the established system and its practical processes; the regimes of Nazi Germany and Soviet Russia as well as the bureaucratic regime of the Eurozone during the first two decades of the twenty-first century are some of the most extreme examples of absolutism caused and underpinned by a bureaucratic theory of justice.

Mixed theories of justice: By the term "mixed theories of justice" I refer to any attempt to combine the egoistic voluntarism that underpins what I call a nihilistic theory of justice with the rationalism that underpins what I call a bureaucratic theory of justice. A paradigmatic representative of what I call a mixed theory of justice is John Rawls.[38] In his *Theory of Justice*, Rawls tries to find a balance between two goals: the goal of personal liberty (which is reflected in his first maxim[39] of justice and expresses the human attraction to life) and the goal of social equality (which is reflected in his second maxim of justice[40] and expresses human concerns about the sustainability of life). For this reason, Rawls resorts to Kant's moral rationalism, whose defects I explained earlier in this chapter. Hence, Rawls's theory of justice—his "Kantian constructivism"[41]— has inherited the defects of Kant's moral rationalism. In addition, Rawls's theory of justice has inherited many of the defects of utilitarianism due to Rawls's hypothesis about the "original position" of humanity. In particular, Rawls assumes that, in their "original position," people were not aware of any particular purposes in life, but they only knew that it would be useful to have various "primary goods," which, according to Rawls, are "the principles that rational and free persons concerned to further their

37. Elster, *Explaining Social Behavior*, 5, 25.

38. Rawls, *A Theory of Justice*.

39. Rawls's first maxim of justice is the following: "each person is to have an equal right to the most extensive basic liberty compatible with a similar liberty for others." Ibid., 60.

40. Rawls's second maxim of justice is the following: "social and economic inequalities are to be arranged so that they are both (a) reasonably expected to be to everyone's advantage, and (b) attached to positions and offices open to all." Ibid., 60.

41. Rawls, "Kantian Constructivism in Moral Theory."

own interests would accept in an initial position of equality as defining the fundamentals of the terms of their association."[42] Given that Rawls's hypothesis about the "original position" is actually based on a kind of utilitarianism, his theory of justice is susceptible to the criticism of utilitarianism that I put forward earlier in this chapter.

As I have already argued, the methexiological theory of justice starts from its refusal to put truth on the "Procrustean bed" of logic and from its refusal to put the significance of life on the "Procrustean bed" of history. Therefore, the methexiological theory of justice is substantially different from any secular theory of justice, since secular theories of justice are founded on practice, whereas the methexiological theory of justice is founded on the irreducibility of the significance of being to practice. Furthermore, methexiology implies that no one has a right to usurp a power which originates from God, and that no one is above his or her brother or sister, except by intellect, charity, and education. God has not authorized any human to replace and represent Him on earth, since God's uncreated energies are directly available to humans. The true purpose of spiritual authorities is to guide and help people to participate in God's uncreated energies and thus to be deified; any spiritual authority that pretends to be a substitute for God's uncreated energies or an ontologically necessary vicar of God should not be believed. Our ignorance and selfishness alone give these usurpers the power that they wield in order to establish systems of spiritual and/or political despotism. As a conclusion, methexiology is an invitation to join a Crusade whose purpose is the reconquering of those "holy lands" that are known as freedom, love, and truth.

The secular perception of individual autonomy, which underpins Nozick's theory of justice and classical political economy, envisages a time when each person will be doing what he or she wills. However, methexiology clashes with Nozick's and the classical political economists' perception of freedom of will, because, if the manner and the extent in which someone actualizes his or her freedom of will is determined by the commands of the instinct and/or of the established economic system, then, as I argued in chapter 6, human freedom of will becomes a shadow of itself. Moreover, methexiology clashes with both Elster's and Rawls's theories of justice, because Elster's and Rawls's theories of justice are founded on an "earthly" perception of justice, whereas methexiology is founded on a "celestial" perception of justice. By arguing that methexiology is founded

---

42. Rawls, *A Theory of Justice*, 11.

on a "celestial" perception of justice, I do not mean that we should seek justice in the sky. The argument that methexiology is founded on a "celestial" perception of justice means that, when one has to distribute the "economic pie," he must not cut the economic pie into pieces, unless he is really just, that is, unless conscience has primacy over the logic of historical or economic necessities. From the perspective of methexiology, justice never submits to any kind of necessity or law. Thus, the concept of justice that is derived from methexiology never dictates that you should coercively take another person's coat in order to give it to someone else, but it dictates that you should give your own coat to someone else, in case you have a second coat. Hence, from the perspective of methexiology, real justice is a consequence of humanity's spiritual freedom.

The aforementioned study of the methexiological approach to ethics and justice implies that methexiology has an important impact on policy analysis, too. Policy analysis underpins and informs political and economic decision-making, even if there is a lengthy lag between policy analysis and its gradual absorption into political and economic debates. Once established as common sense, a text of policy analysis becomes incredibly powerful, because it delineates not only what is the object of knowledge but also what it is sensible to talk about or suggest. If one thinks and acts outside the framework of the dominant text of policy analysis, he risks more than simply the judgment that his recommendations are wrong; his entire moral attitude may be ridiculed or seen as dangerous just because his theoretical assumptions are deemed unrealistic. Therefore, defining "common sense" and, in essence, what is "reality" and "realistic" is the ultimate act of political power. Policy analysis does not simply explain or predict, it tells us what possibilities exist for human action and intervention; it defines both our explanatory possibilities and our moral and practical horizons. Hence, ontology, epistemology, and ethics matter, and the stakes are far more considerable than at first sight seems to be the case.

Methexiology, as I have delineated it in the present book, underpins and implies the following ten, mutually equivalent, definitions of policy analysis:

1. A process for organizing information about the reality of the historical world as a repository of opportunities and about the reality of the historical actors' consciousness as a repository of intentions, in order to help decision-making on the basis of methexiology

(humanity's participation in a metaphysically grounded system of fundamental significations, or values).

2. The examination of questions related to the policy-making process, conducted with the intention to achieve an ontologically grounded overcoming of the antithesis between realism and idealism and, thus, to affect the policy-making process.
3. Analysis that generates information in such a way as to improve the basis for policy-makers to historically manifest their experience of a metaphysically grounded truth (*méthexis*).
4. Analysis that assists policy-makers in understanding complex problems of policy choice in a historical environment characterized by a dialectical relationship between necessity and freedom.
5. Analysis that assists policy-makers to develop, understand, select, and implement what should be done in an environment characterized by a dialectical relationship between necessity and freedom in order to change people's existential conditions according to their intentionality—and what consequences to evaluate.
6. The systematic examination and comparison of alternative future policies by applying methexiology.
7. The application of methexiology in order to solve problems an organization is called upon to do something about.
8. Analysis that assists policy-makers to ameliorate the problems and manage the policy issues they face by applying methexiology, utilizing scientific and technological advances, considering the larger contexts and uncertainties that inevitably attend such problems, and giving witness to the spiritual freedom of the human being.
9. Keeping policy-makers' consciousness constantly vigilant, warning them of the risks of leaving policy issues to the hands of any kind of "automatic pilot" and preventing them from confusing momentum with purpose.
10. Smashing the illusion that policy-makers can avoid recourse to personal judgment and responsibility as the final concern of policy and attempting to bring about an environment that constantly produces new and not yet imagined types of performance (instead of simply performing the familiar).

Bibliography

IN ADDITION TO THE following bibliography, I have used: Oxford's scholarly editions and Penguin Classics for the study of classical Greek and Latin philosophers; J. P. Migne's *Patrologia Graeca* for the study of the Greek church fathers; J. P. Migne's *Patrologia Latina* for the study of the Latin church fathers; P. Schaff's and H. Wace's *A Select Library of Nicene and Post-Nicene Fathers of the Christian Church*; the collection *Sources Chrétiennes* (a bilingual collection of patristic texts founded in Lyon in 1942 by the Jesuits Jean Daniélou, Claude Mondésert, and Henri de Lubac); the Nestle-Aland edition of the New Testament; the *Septuagint* and the *Biblia Hebraica Stuttgartensia* for the study of the Old Testament; the World English Bible (WEB) public domain; the *Philokalia* editions by Perivoli tis Panagias Publications (Thessaloniki, Greece) and by "Aster" Publishing (Athens, Greece) for the study of the Hesychasts (Neptic fathers); the *Little Russian Philokalia*, published by St. Herman Press (Saint Herman of Alaska Monastery, Platina, California); *To Gerontikon* (a Greek collection of sayings of Eastern Orthodox monks), edited by Monk Pavlos, published by the Orthodox Foundation "Apostle Barnabas" (Athens, Greece).

Anteby, Michel. *Moral Grey Zones*. Princeton, NJ: Princeton University Press, 2008.
Arquilla, J., and Ronfeldt, D. "The Promise of Noöpolitik." *First Monday*, Vol. 12, August 2007. Online: http://firstmonday.org/ojs/index.php/fm/article/view/1971/1846.
Avineri, Shlomo. *The Social and Political Thought of Karl Marx*. Cambridge: Cambridge University Press, 1968.
Bachelard, Gaston. *The Poetics of Space*. Translated by Maria Jolas. Boston: Beacon, 1994.
Balthasar, Hans Urs von. *Presence and Thought: An Essay on the Religious Philosophy of Gregory of Nyssa*. Translated by Mark Sebanc. San Francisco: Ignatius, 1995.
Bauer, Walter. *Orthodoxy and Heresy in Earliest Christianity*. Translated and edited by R. A. Kraft and G. Kroedel. Philadelphia: Fortress, 1971.
Bengtson, Hermann. *History of Greece: From the Beginnings to the Byzantine Era*. Ottawa: University of Ottawa Press, 1988.
Bergson, Henri-Louis. *The Creative Mind*. Translated by Mabelle L. Andison. New York: Citadel, 1992.

———. *Matter and Memory*. Translated by N. M. Paul and W. S. Palmer. New York: Zone, 1994.
Berry, Michael. "Quantum Physics on the Edge of Chaos." *New Scientist*, November 19, 1987, 44–47.
Bourdieu, Pierre. *Outline of a Theory of Practice*. Translated by Richard Nice. Cambridge: Cambridge University Press, 2013.
Brandom, Robert B. *Perspectives on Pragmatism: Classical, Recent, and Contemporary*. Cambridge: Harvard University Press, 2011.
Bray, Gerald, ed. *Documents of the English Reformation*. Cambridge: James Clark, 1994.
Brough, John B. "Husserl and the Deconstruction of Time." *The Review of Metaphysics* 46 (1993) 503–36.
Brzezinski, Zbigniew. "Interview." *Le Nouvel Observateur*, Paris, January 15–21, 1998. Online: http://www.voltairenet.org/article165889.html
Bull, Hedley. *The Anarchical Society: A Study of World Order in World Politics*. 2nd ed. London: Macmillan, 1995.
Byron, Robert. *The Byzantine Achievement*. Mount Jackson, VA: Axios, 2010.
Cairnes, John E. *The Character and Logical Method of Political Economy*. London: Macmillan, 1888.
Castoriadis, Cornelius. *The Imaginary Institution of Society*. Translated by Kathleen Blamey. Cambridge: MIT, 1987.
Catoe, Lynn E. *UFOs and Related Subjects: An Annotated Bibliography* (prepared under AFOSR Project Order 67-0002 and 68-0003). Washington, DC: U.S. Government Printing Office, 1969.
Chadwick, Henry. *Boethius: The Consolations of Music, Logic, Theology, and Philosophy*. Oxford: Clarendon, 1981.
Chapell, Bryan. *Christ-Centered Preaching*. Grand Rapids: Baker, 1994.
Chardin, Pierre Teilhard de. *The Future of Man*. New York: Image/Doubleday, 1969. Online: https://archive.org/stream/TheFutureOfMan/Future_of_Man#page/n13/mode/2up.
Chesterton, Gilbert K. *The Man Who Was Thursday: A Nightmare*. New York: Dodd, Mead & Co., 1908.
Churton, Tobias. *Aleister Crowley: The Biography: Spiritual Revolutionary, Romantic Explorer, Occult Master and Spy*. London: Watkins, 2011.
———. *Freemasonry: The Reality*. London: Allen, 2007.
Cohen, Paul J. *Set Theory and the Continuum Hypothesis*. Reading, MA: Benjamin, 1966.
Coleman, John, "What Really Happened in Iran." 1984. Online: http://coleman300.net/whatreallyhappenediniranupdate.aspx
Comte, Auguste. *Cours de Philosophie Positive, leçons 46–51*. Paris: Hermann, 2012.
Constantine, Alex. *Virtual Government: CIA Mind Control Operations in America*. Port Townsend, WA: Feral House, 1997.
Copenhaver, Brian P., ed. *Hermetica: The Greek Corpus Hermeticum and the Latin Asclepius in a New English Translation with Notes and Introduction*. Cambridge: Cambridge University Press, 1992.
Cornwell, John. *Hitler's Pope*. London: Viking, 1999.
Crimmins, James E. "Bentham and Utilitarianism in the Early Nineteenth Century." In *The Cambridge Companion to Utilitarianism*, edited by B. Eggleston and D. E. Miller, 38–60. Cambridge: Cambridge University Press, 2014.

Curd, Patricia, and Daniel W. Graham, eds. *The Oxford Handbook of Presocratic Philosophy*. Oxford: Oxford University Press, 2008.

Curtis, Mark. *Secret Affairs: Britain's Collusion with Radical Islam*. London: Serpent's Tail, 2010.

Das, Bhagavan. *The Science of the Sacred Word*, Vol. 1. Adyar: Theosophist Office; London: Theosophical Publishing Society, 1910.

Davies, Oliver. "Introducing Transformation Theology." No pages. Online: http://www.transformationtheology.com/what-is-tt.html

———. "Transformation Theology and Radical Orthodoxy." No pages. Online: https://www.academia.edu/1458552/Transformation_Theology_and_Radical_Orthodoxy

———. "Transformation Theology in Its Historical Context." No pages. Online: https://www.academia.edu/1508691/Transformation_Theology_in_its_Historical_Context

Davies, Oliver, et al. *Transformation Theology: Church in the World*. London: T. & T. Clark, 2007.

Deloire, C., and C. Dubois. *Circus Politicus*. Paris: Michel, 2012.

Delvin, Keith. *Sets, Functions, and Logic*. 3rd ed. Boca Raton, FL: CRC/Taylor & Francis Group, 2003.

De Sade, Marquis. *Justine, Philosophy in the Bedroom and Other Writings*. Translated by Richard Seaver and Austryn Wainhouse. New York: Grove, 1990.

Derrida, Jacques. *The Post Card: From Socrates to Freud and Beyond*. Translated by Alan Bass. Chicago: University of Chicago Press, 1979.

Dinmore, Guy. "Fascists and Jews United for Rome Mayor." *Financial Times*, May 4, 2008. Online: http://www.ft.com/cms/s/0/4d07386e-19fd-11dd-ba02-0000779fd2ac.html#axzz3vTG61R8l.

Domenach, Jean-Marie. *Une Morale sans Moralisme*. Paris: Flammarion, 1992.

Donaldson, Simon K. "The Geometry of 4-Manifolds." *Proceedings of the International Congress of Mathematics*, 43–54. Berkeley, CA: n.p., 1986.

Elster, Jon. *Explaining Social Behavior: More Nuts and Bolts for the Social Sciences*. Cambridge: Cambridge University Press, 2007.

———. "The Market and the Forum: Three Varieties of Political Theory." In *Foundations of Social Choice Theory*, edited by Jon Elster and Aanund Hylland, 103–32. Cambridge: Cambridge University Press, 1986.

Engdahl, William. *A Century of War: Anglo-American Oil Politics and the New World Order*. London: Pluto, 2004.

Epstein, Simon. *Un Paradoxe Français: Antiracistes dans la Collaboration, Antisémites dans la Résistance*. Paris: Éditions Albin Michel, 2008.

Evert-Kappesowa, Halina. "La Tiare ou le Turban." *Byzantinoslavica* XIV (1953) 245–57.

Florovsky, Georges V. *Collected Works. Volume 2: Christianity and Culture*. Belmont, MA: Nordland, 1974.

———. *Collected Works. Volume 5: Ways of Russian Theology: Part One*. Belmont, Mass.: Nordland, 1979.

Freud, Sigmund. *Moses and Monotheism*. Translated by Katherine Jones. 1939. Reprint. Eastford, CT: Martino Fine, 2010.

———. *On Metapsychology*, The Pelican Freud Library, Vol. 11. Harmondsworth, UK: Pelican, 1984.

Ganser, Daniele. *NATO's Secret Armies*. Oxford: Cass, 2005.
Gardham, Duncan. "Violent Videos of Oslo Killer's 'Mentor.'" *The Telegraph*, July 29, 2011. Online: http://www.telegraph.co.uk/news/worldnews/europe/norway/8671075/Violent-videos-of-Oslo-killers-mentor.html.
Garnier, Colonel. *Israel in Britain*. London: Banks & Son, 1890.
Gauld, Alan. *The Founders of Psychical Research*. New York: Schocken, 1968.
Gaza, Enea di. *Teofrasto*. Napoli: Salvatore Iodice, 1958.
Geostrategy-Direct Intelligence Brief. "U.S. Gave Green Light to Terrorists in Bosnia." April 24, 2002. Online: http://www.wnd.com/2002/04/13659/.
Ghosh, P. K., and Deguchi, K. *Mathematics of Shape Description*. Singapore: Wiley & Sons, 2008.
Gilens, M., and B. I. Page. "Testing Theories of American Politics: Elites, Interest Groups, and Average Citizens." *Perspectives on Politics* 12 (2014) 564–81.
Goricheva, Tatiana. *Talking About God Is Dangerous: The Diary of a Russian Dissident*. New York: Crossroad, 1987.
Graham, Daniel, W. *Explaining the Cosmos: The Ionian Tradition of Scientific Philosophy*. Princeton, NJ: Princeton University Press, 2006.
Greenfield, Allen H. *Secret Cipher of the UFOnauts*. Lilburn, GA: Illuminet, 1994.
Gross, Richard. *Psychology: The Science of Mind and Behaviour*. 6th ed. London: Hodder Education, 2010.
Guettée, Wladimir (Réné-François). *The Papacy: Its Historic Origin and Primitive Relations with the Eastern Churches*. Translated by Arthur Cleveland Coxe. 1867. Reprint. Whitefish, MT: Kessinger, 2013.
Harris, Roy. *Reading Saussure*. La Salle, IL: Open Court, 1987.
Hart, H. L. A. *Essays on Bentham: Jurisprudence and Political Theory*. New York: Oxford University Press, 1982.
Hawkes, C. F. C. *The Prehistoric Foundations of Europe to the Mycenaean Age*. London: Methuen & Co., 1940.
Heidegger, Martin. *Basic Writings: Key Selections from Being and Time and The Task of Thinking*. Edited by David Farrell Krell. New York: HarperCollins, 2008.
Heiden, Konrad. *A History of National Socialism*. New York: Knopf, 1935.
Henkin, Leon. "Completeness in the Theory of Types." *Journal of Symbolic Logic* 15 (1950) 81–91.
Herman, Eleanor. *Mistress of the Vatican*. New York: HarperCollins, 2008.
Heyer, Paul. *Nature, Human Nature, and Society: Marx, Darwin, Biology, and the Human Sciences*. Westport, CT: Greenwood, 1982.
Hilgenfeld, Adolf. *Die Ketzergeschichte des Urchristentums*. 1884. Reprint. Darmstadt: Wissenschaftliche Buchgesellschaft, 1963.
Hitchcock, Ethan Allen. *Remarks upon Alchemy and the Alchemists*. Boston: Crosby, Nichols and Co., 1857.
Hodapp, Christopher. *Solomon's Builders*. Berkeley, CA: Ulysses, 2007.
Holden, Michael. "The Knights Templar Europe: Far-Right Fact Or Fiction?" Reuters, July 26, 2011. Online: http://www.reuters.com/article/us-norway-knights-europe-idUSTRE76P4Y620110726.
Hollingdale, Stuart. *Makers of Mathematics*. London: Pelican, 1989.
Hothersall, David. *History of Psychology*. 4th ed. New York: McGraw-Hill, 2004.
Howells, Christina, ed. *The Cambridge Companion to Sartre*. Cambridge: Cambridge University Press, 1992.

Hunger, Herbert. *Die Hochsprachliche Profane Literatur der Byzantiner*, Vol. 2. München: Beck, 1978.
Iamblichus. *Life of Pythagoras*. Translated by Thomas Taylor. London: Valpy, 1818.
Jaeger, W. W. *Paideia: The Ideals of Greek Culture*. Oxford: Oxford University Press, 1965.
James, Lawrence. *Aristocrats: Power, Grace, and Decadence*. New York: St. Martin's, 2009.
Jaspers, Karl. *Reason and Existenz*. Translated by William Earle. New York: Noonday, 1955.
Jolley, Nicholas, ed. *The Cambridge Companion to Leibniz*. Cambridge: Cambridge University Press, 1995.
Jung, Carl G. "Instinct and the Unconscious." In *The Structure and Dynamics of the Psyche*, edited by Gerhard Adler, 129–38. *Collected Works*, Vol. 8. Princeton, NJ: Princeton University Press, 1969.
———. *The Red Book: Liber Novus*. Edited and translated by Sonu Shamdasani. New York: Norton, 2009.
———. *Flying Saucers: A Modern Myth of Things Seen in the Skies*. Princeton: Princeton University Press, 1978.
Kant, Immanuel. *Critique of Pure Reason*. Translated by Norman K. Smith. 1933. Reprint. Great Books of the Western World, Vol. 42. Chicago: Encyclopaedia Britannica, 1952.
Kinman, Dwight L. *The World's Last Dictator*. Woodburn, OR: Solid Rock, 1995.
Klingman, George A. *Church History for Busy People*. Cincinnati: Christian Leader Corporation, 1928.
Korzybski, Alfred. "A Non-Aristotelian System and its Necessity for Rigour in Mathematics and Physics." A paper presented before the American Mathematical Society at the New Orleans, Louisiana, meeting of the American Association for the Advancement of Science, December 28, 1931. In *Science and Sanity*, 747–61. Englewood, NJ: Institute of General Semantics, 1933.
Kymlicka, Will. *Contemporary Political Philosophy*. Oxford: Clarendon, 1990.
Lacan, Jacques. *The Four Fundamental Concepts of Psychoanalysis*. Translated by Alan Sheridan. New York: Norton, 1978.
Lafayette, Maximillien de. *The German UFOs, Extraterrestrials Messages and the Supernatural*. New York: Times Square, 2010.
Lambek, J., and Scott, P. J. *Introduction to Higher Order Categorical Logic*. Cambridge: Cambridge University Press, 1986.
Laos, Nicolas. *The Metaphysics of World Order: A Synthesis of Philosophy, Theology, and Politics*. Eugene, OR: Pickwick, 2015.
———. *Topics in Mathematical Analysis and Differential Geometry*, Series in Pure Mathematics, Vol. 24. Singapore et al.: World Scientific, 1998.
Lassen, Christian. *Indische Altertumskunde*. Leipzig: Kittler, 1858.
Lavelle, Louis. *Traité des Valeurs: Théorie Générale de la Valeur*. Paris: P.U.F., 1951.
Lazzaro, Sage. "It's Now Possible for One Person's Brain to Control Another Person's Movements." *Observer*, November 6, 2014. Online: http://observer.com/2014/11/its-now-possible-for-one-persons-brain-to-control-another-personss-movements/.
Leary, Timothy, et al. *Neuropolitique*. 2nd ed. Las Vegas: New Falcon, 1991.

Leparmentier, Arnaud. "Une Union Européenne Trop Orthodoxe." *Le Monde*, November 19, 2014. No pages. Online: http://www.lemonde.fr/europe/article/2014/11/19/une-union-europeenne-trop-orthodoxe_4526070_3214.html.
Lévi-Strauss, Claude. *Structural Anthropology*. Translated by Claire Jacobson and Brooke G. Schoepf. New York: Basic, 1963.
Levitt, Matthew. "Hezbollah Finances: Funding the Party of God." Washington, DC: The Washington Institute for Near East Policy, February 2005. Online: http://www.washingtoninstitute.org/policy-analysis/view/hezbollah-finances-funding-the-party-of-god.
Lipsius, Richard A. *Der Gnosticismus*. Leipzig: Brockhaus, 1860.
Lundin, Robert W. *Theories and Systems of Psychology*. 5th ed. Lexington, MA: Heath, 1996.
Luther, Martin. "Against the Robbing and Murdering Hordes of Peasants" In *Martin Luther*, edited by Ernest G. Rupp and Benjamin Drewery, 121–26. London: Arnold, 1970.
Lyne, William. *Pentagon Aliens*. New Mexico: Creatopia, 1999.
MacIntyre, Alasdair. *After Virtue: A Study in Moral Theory*. Notre Dame, IN: University of Notre Dame Press, 1981.
Makkreel, Rudolf A. *Imagination and Interpretation in Kant*. Chicago: University of Chicago Press, 1995.
Marcel, Gabriel. *The Philosophy of Existentialism*. Translated by Manya Harari. New York: Carol, 1995.
Marx, Karl. *Capital: A Critique of Political Economy*, Volume I, Part I. Edited by Friedrich Engels. Editor of the first American edition: Ernest Untermann. New York: Cosimo, 2007.
———. *The German Ideology*. Rev. ed. Edited, with an introduction, by C. J. Arthur. New York: International, 2004.
Maximus the Confessor. "Peri Theologias kai tes Ensārkou Oikonomias tou Hyiou tou Theou, Pros Thalāssion" ("Regarding Theology and the Incarnate Economy of the Son of God, to Thalassios"). In *Philokalia ton Hieron Neptikon, Vol.* 2 (Philokalia of the Sacred Neptic Fathers, Vol. 2), edited by Nicodemus of the Holy Mountain and Makarios of Corinth. Athens: Ekdotikos Oikos "Aster," 1975.
Merriman, Roger Bigelow. *Suleiman the Magnificent: 1520–1566*. Reprint. UK: Read Books, 2007.
Meyendorff, John. *Byzantine Theology: Historical Trends and Doctrinal Themes*. 1979. Reprint. New York: Fordham University Press, 1983.
———. *The Orthodox Church*. New York: St. Vladimir's Seminary Press, 1981.
Milbank, John. *Theology and Social Theory: Beyond Secular Reason*. 2nd ed. Hoboken, NJ: Wiley-Blackwell, 2005.
Mill, John S. "Utilitarianism." In *John Stuart Mill: Utilitarianism, Liberty and Representative Government*, edited by H. B. Acton. London: Dent and Sons, 1972.
Minkowski, Eugène. *Lived Time: Phenomenological and Psychopathological Studies*. Translated by Nancy Metzel. Evanston, IL: Northwestern University Press, 1970.
Millar, Angel. *The Crescent and the Compass: Islam, Freemasonry, Esotericism, and Revolution in the Modern Age*. Melbourne: Numen, 2015.
Misak, Cheryl J., ed. *Pragmatism*. Calgary: University of Calgary Press, 1999.
Mohler, Armin. *Die Konservative Revolution in Deutschland 1918–1932: Ein Handbuch*. Stuttgart: Vorwerk, 1950.

Moore, George E. *Principia Ethica*. New York: Prometheus, 1988.
Moran, Dermot. *Introduction to Phenomenology*. New York: Routledge, 2000.
Muller, R., and L. Zonneveld, eds. *The Desire to Be a Human: A Global Reconnaissance of Human Perspectives in an Age of Transformation Written in Honour of Pierre Teilhard de Chardin*. Wassenaar, Netherlands: Mirananda, 1983.
Nedelsky, Sergey. *Palamas in Exile: The Academic Recovery of Monastic Tradition*. MTh thesis. New York: St. Vladimir's Orthodox Theological Seminary, 2006.
Neisser, U. G. *Cognitive Psychology*, Englewood Cliffs, NJ: Prentice-Hall, 1967.
Nietzsche, Friedrich. *Beyond Good and Evil*. Translated by Judith Norman. Reprint. Cambridge: Cambridge University Press, 2002.
———. *The Gay Science*. Translated by Josefine Nauckhoff. Reprint. Cambridge: Cambridge University Press, 2001.
Nozick, Robert. *Anarchy, State and Utopia*. New York: Basic, 1974.
Nye, Joseph, Jr. *The Future of Power*. New York: Public Affairs, 2011.
Obolensky, Dimitri. *The Byzantine Commonwealth: Eastern Europe 500–1453*. New York: St. Vladimir's Seminary Press, 1971.
Orloff, Grégoire. *Mémoires sur le Royaume de Naples*. Paris: Duval, 1819.
Orton, Kyle W. "How Saddam Hussein Gave Us ISIS." *The New York Times*, December 23, 2015. Online: http://www.nytimes.com/2015/12/23/opinion/how-saddam-hussein-gave-us-isis.html?smid=fb-nytimes&smtyp=cur&_r=1.
Osborne, Catherine. *Presocratic Philosophy: A Very Short Introduction*. Oxford: Oxford University Press, 2004.
Papanicolaou, Nicholas F. *Islam vs. the United States*. 2nd ed. Fort Mill, SC: Oak Leaves, 2015. Online: http://www.movieguide.org/news-articles/bookguide-islam-vs-the-united-states.html.
Parfitt, Tudor. *The Lost Tribes of Israel: The History of a Myth*. London: Phoenix/Orion, 2003.
Paton, Herbert J. *The Moral Law: Kant's Groundwork of the Metaphysics of Morals*. London: Hutchinson University Library, 1948.
Peltonen, Markku, ed. *The Cambridge Companion to Bacon*. Cambridge: Cambridge University Press, 1996.
Peters, Francis E. *The Harvest of Hellenism: A History of the Near East from Alexander the Great to the Triumph of Christianity*. New York: Simon and Schuster, 1971.
Piaget, Jean. *The Child's Conception of Time*. Translated by A. J. Pomerans. New York: Basic, 1969.
Piper, David. *The Illustrated Library of Art*. New York: Portland House, 1986.
Pirenne, Jacques. *The Tides of History*, Vol. I. Translated by Lovett Edwards. New York: Dutton, 1962.
Poole, W. H. *Anglo-Israel*. Toronto: Bengough Bros., 1879.
Portal, Roger. *The Slavs*. London: Weidenfeld and Nicolson, 1965.
Prigogine, I., and I. Stengers. *Order out of Chaos: Man's New Dialogue with Nature*. New York: Bentam, 1984.
Psellus, Michael. *De Omnifaria Doctrina*. Critical text and introduction by I. G. Westering. Nijmegen, Netherlands: n.p., 1948.
Quigley, Carroll. *Tragedy and Hope: A History of the World in Our Time*. New York: Macmillan, 1966.
———. *The Anglo-American Establishment*. New York: Books in Focus, 1981.
Rawls, John. *A Theory of Justice*. Rev. ed. Cambridge, MA: Belknap, 1999.

———. "Kantian Constructivism in Moral Theory." *Journal of Philosophy* 77 (1980) 515–72.
Rickards, James. *The Death of Money: The Coming Collapse of the International Monetary System*. New York: Penguin, 2014.
Riemann, Bernhard. "On the Hypotheses which Lie at the Foundations of Geometry." Translated by Henry S. White. In *A Source Book in Mathematics*, edited by David E. Smith, 411–25. New York: Dover, 1959.
Robinson, Daniel N. *An Intellectual History of Psychology*. 3rd ed. Madison, WI: The University of Wisconsin Press, 1995.
Romanides, John S. *The Ancestral Sin*. Translated by George S. Gabriel. Ridgewood, NJ: Zephyr, 2002.
Ropp, Robert S. de. *Drugs and the Mind*. New York: St. Martin's, 1957.
Sabine, G. H., and T. L. Thorson. *A History of Political Theory*. 4th ed. Fort Worth, TX: Holt, Rinehart and Winston, 1973.
Samuelson, P. A., and W. D. Nordhaus. *Economics*. 14th ed. New York: McGraw-Hill, 1992.
Scholem, Gershom. *Major Trends in Jewish Mysticism*. New York: Schocken, 1974.
Scott, Peter Dale. *American War Machine*. Lanham, MD: Rowman & Littlefield, 2010.
———. "The Global Drug Meta-Group: Drugs, Managed Violence, and the Russian 9/11." *Lobster*, October 29, 2005. Online: http://www.lobster-magazine.co.uk/articles/global-drug.htm.
———. "Korea (1950), the Tonkin Gulf Incident, and 9/11: Deep Events in Recent American History." *The Asia-Pacific Journal: Japan Focus*, ID 2784. Online: http://www.japanfocus.org/-Peter_Dale-Scott/2784/article.html.
———. "Norway's Terror as Systemic Destabilization: Breivik, the Arms-for-Drugs Milieu, and Global Shadow Elites." *The Asia-Pacific Journal: Japan Focus*, ID 3590. Online: http://www.japanfocus.org/-Peter_Dale-Scott/3590/article.html.
Scruton, Roger. *A Short History of Modern Philosophy: From Descartes to Wittgenstein*. London: Routledge, 2002.
Sfeir, Antoine, "Les francs-maçons en terres d'Islam." *L'Express*, May 29, 2003. Online: http://www.lexpress.fr/actualite/societe/les-francs-macons-en-terres-d-islam_496022.html.
Shahak, Israel. "'Greater Israel': The Zionist Pan for the Middle East." *Global Research*, November 7, 2015. Online: http://www.globalresearch.ca/greater-israel-the-zionist-plan-for-the-middle-east/5324815.
Sluga, Hans D., and David G. Stern, eds. *The Cambridge Companion to Wittgenstein*. Cambridge: Cambridge University Press, 1996.
Smelser, Neil J., ed. *Karl Marx: On Society and Social Change*. Chicago: University of Chicago Press, 1973.
Smith, Adam. "Sympathy." In *Scottish Philosophy: Selected Writings 1690–1960*, edited by Gordon Graham, 99–114. Exeter, UK: Imprint Academic, 2004.
———. *The Wealth of Nations*. 1776. Edited with an introduction and notes by Andrew Skinner. London: Penguin Classics, 1999.
Špidlík, Tomáš. "Fous pour le Christ en Orient." In *Dictionnaire de Spiritualité*, edited by Joseph de Guibert et al., Vol. 5, 752–61. Paris: Compagnie de Jésus, 1964.
Soros, George, "The Capitalist Threat." *The Atlantic Monthly*, February 1997. Online: http://www.theatlantic.com/magazine/archive/1997/02/the-capitalist-threat/376773/.

Sternberg, Robert J. *Pathways to Psychology*. 2nd ed. Boston: Cengage Learning, 1999.
Storrs, Richard S. *Bernard of Clairvaux: The Times, the Man, and His Work*. New York: Scribner's Sons, 1901.
Sutton, Antony C. *America's Secret Establishment: An Introduction to the Order of Skull & Bones*. Waterville, OR: TrineDay, 2002.
Sward, Keith. *The Legend of Henry Ford*. New York: Reinehart, 1948.
Syméon le Nouveau Théologien. *Hymnes*. Edited by Johannes Koder. Paris: Cerf, 2003.
Tarn, W. W. "Alexander: The Conquest of the Far East." In *Cambridge Ancient History, Vol. VI*, edited by J. Bury et al., 387–95. Cambridge: Cambridge University Press, 1933.
Thual, François. *Géopolitique de la Franc-Maçonnerie*. Paris: Dunod, 1994.
Versluis, Arthur. *The New Inquisitions: Heretic-hunting and the Intellectual Origins of Modern Totalitarianism*. Oxford: Oxford University Press, 2006.
Waite, Arthur E. *The Real History of the Rosicrucians*. New York: Cosimo Classics, 2007.
West, Henry R. "Mill and Utilitarianism in the Mid-Nineteenth Century." In *The Cambridge Companion to Utilitarianism*, edited by B. Eggleston and D. E. Miller, 61–80. Cambridge: Cambridge University Press, 2014.
Whitehead, Alfred N. *Process and Reality*. New York: Free, 1979.
Winkler, Kenneth P. "Kant, the Empiricists, and the Enterprise of Deduction." In *The Cambridge Companion of Kant's Critique of Pure Reason*, edited by Paul Guyer, 41–72. Cambridge: Cambridge University Press, 2010.
Wolff, Christian. *Philosophia Prima, sive Ontologia*. Frankfurt: Officina Libraria Rengeriana, 1736.
Woodcock, A., and M. Davis. *Catastrophe Theory*. London: Penguin, 1991.
Wundt, Wilhelm. *Logik*, Vol. 3. Stuttgart: Enke, 1921.
Wurmbrand, Richard. *Marx and Satan*. Chicago: Crossway, 1986.
Zizioulas, John D. *Being as Communion*. New York: St. Vladimir's Seminary Press, 1997.

Glossary

Soul (Psyche): is the totality of the faculties and the attributes of the human being that transcend pure biology. Moreover, the term "soul" refers to the *personal* manner in which each human being manifests life.

Consciousness: is that state of being which enables us to develop the functions that are necessary in order to know our environment as well as the events that happen around us and within ourselves.

Conscience (moral consciousness): is the consciousness of existence, or, more broadly, a soul that judges. In other words, when the consciousness of existence operates as a judge, it is called conscience.

Human Individual: this term may refer to two things: first, it may refer to a physical sample of the human species; secondly, it may refer to a particular moral agent and to a particular actor who has intrinsic (*a priori*) value, and, hence, he or she is a morally autonomous and responsible human being.

Person: an existential otherness (individuality) in communion, that is, endowed with sociality.

Logos/Word: Throughout this book, when I refer to the second Person of the Holy Trinity, namely, Jesus Christ, I use the terms "Logos" and "Word" interchangeably, usually preferring the first in order to emphasize the philosophical and theological significance of the term "logos" (that is, the disclosure of truth), but often using the latter when I quote from the English translation of the Holy Scripture, since the term "Word" is more common in the English translations of the Holy Scripture than the term "Logos."

Civilization: is a structure that consists of technology and institutions. In other words, "civilization" refers to both the means by which a conscious community attempts to improve the terms of its adaptation to the world and the results of a conscious community's attempt to improve the terms of its adaptation to the world.

Culture: is the result of humanity's reflection on its life. In other words, "culture" is a reflective attitude toward institutions and technology as well as an attempt to transcend institutions and technology through myth, whose complex structure, however, is dialectically related to the structure of institutions and technology. The concepts of "civilization" and "culture" do not contradict each other. Even though civilization corresponds to "technical construction," and culture corresponds to "spiritual creation," culture is embodied in civilization and underpins civilization, which, in turn, underpins the integration of culture into history.

Individualism vs. Collectivism vs. Personalism: "Individualism" refers to a culture that emphasizes individuality, that is, the existential otherness, of conscious beings. In the context of individualism, one's identity is primarily subjective. "Collectivism" is a culture that emphasizes the sociality of conscious beings. In the context of collectivism, one's identity primarily stems from the group. "Personalism" refers to a culture that emphasizes personhood, that is, it treats humans as persons. In the context of personalism, the individuals (that is, the existential othernesses) are in communion with a common, transindividual principle, which underpins the socialization of the individual. My theory of transcendental mysticism is personalistic, that is, it gives rise to personalism.

Orientalism: refers to the family of civilizations that constitute the historical and geocultural entity that is called the "Orient." The major constituent parts of Orientalism are the Hindu civilization zone, the Chinese civilization zone, and the Islamic civilization zone. Orientalism has two complementary distinctive characteristics: in the context of Orientalism, society imposes relations of tight interdependence among its members, and, from this perspective, it contradicts individualism and gives rise to collectivism (holism), but, on the other hand, Oriental systems of mysticism allow and, indeed, encourage a mystic to pursue his independence from his social environment through the renunciation of the world. Thus, pursuing their individuation outside this world, Oriental mystics can be characterized as "otherworldly individuals," in order to be distinguished from Western "worldly individuals," who pursue their individuation within this world. However, due to their essentially individualistic character, many "schools" of Oriental mysticism, especially those associated with Buddhism and Sufism, are popular in the West.

For instance, in the context of Hinduism, collectivism (holism) is founded on the concepts of *dharma* (right, duty) and *danda* (force, punishment). According to Hindu political thought, human society reproduces the cosmic order (*rta*), and the essence of political government consists in using *danda* to maintain *dharma*; the major sources of *dharma* being the *Vedas*, the *Smritis*, and *Vyavahara* (custom). Nevertheless, Hindu mystics may follow an individualistic path, which is *samnyasa*, meaning renunciation or abandonment. Of the 108 Upanisads that are contained in the *Muktika*, twenty-three are focused on *samnyasa* as the path to *moksa*, meaning liberation. Moreover, Buddhism has invigorated the individualistic traits of Hindu civilization by rejecting the caste system, by founding monasteries, by articulating a non-theological religion, and by enjoying the support of inferior social classes (e.g., traders, craftsmen, merchants, and foreign settlers).

In the context of Islamic political thought, collectivism (holism) is founded on the concept of the Caliphate, which is an organic perception of society founded on the *Sharia* (religious law). Sunni Islam holds that political and religious authority should be vested in the person of an imam-caliph elected by the *Ummah* (community), while Shia Islam (whose main groupings are the Twelvers, the Ismailis, and the Zaidis) limits the legitimacy to Mohammed's son-in-law and cousin Ali, who was ruling over the Islamic Caliphate from 665–61 AD. However, both the Sunni and the Shia emphasize the maintenance of the *Sharia*. On the other hand, Muslim mystics may follow an individualistic path. In particular, the Sufi Orders (e.g., Alevi, Bektashi, Mevlevi, Ba'Alawi tariqa, Rifa'i, Chisti, Naqshbandi, Shadhili tariqa, etc.) follow an individualistic approach to Islam, emphasizing the transmission of the divine light from the teacher's heart to the heart of the student, independently of the worldly society and its values. In the eighth and the ninth centuries AD, great Sufi masters argued that they achieved the illumination of their individual souls by individual exertion, mortification, and austerity. Moreover, despite the Islamic tradition's general discomfort with parable, allegory, and metaphor, many Sufi masters make extensive use of parable, allegory, and metaphor.

In contrast to both Orientalism and Western individualism, the Greek East, being founded on Hesychasm, maintains that the world is neither a morally "neutral" object to be exploited by *homo economicus* nor something that must be renounced. Thus, Hesychast asceticism is substantially different from an Oriental mystic's path of renunciation. A Hesychast affirms the goodness of creation (in accordance with Genesis 1:31), prays for the entire world, participates in the communal life of the church, and, far from pursuing his individuation outside this world, he participates in the afflictions of the world through Christocentric love and prayer, and he aims at directly socializing with God, Whom he understands as the source of the significance of all beings and things. The Hesychasts understand the world as a structure of *logoi*, and, therefore, they do not fight against the body, but they aim at liberating the body from the law of sin (precisely, from impersonal, uncontrolled impulses and instincts and from selfishness) and at establishing there the mind as an overseer. Moreover, the Hesychasts emphasize the difference between the terms "mind" (in Greek, *nous*), which they conceive as the repository of God's uncreated energies (grace) within the human being, and "intellect" (rational faculty), and, therefore, in contrast to Oriental mystical systems of meditation, the Hesychasts' notion of stillness implies that it is the mind, and not the intellect, that must be detached from the world of the senses.

Science, models, and concepts: The description of objects is called modeling, and it can be achieved through various different means, the most important of which is language. A model is an abstraction, that is, it describes only some of the corresponding object's properties. However, every model is an object itself, and, thus, it can be further described (that is, modeled) by intellectually ascending to a higher level of abstraction. Thus, in the context of scientific modeling, by the term "object," we refer to the following things: (i) material objects and phenomena of the physical world, (ii) models that have been created by the scientific consciousness at different levels of abstraction, and (iii) syntheses (i.e., synthetic judgments) that are derived from models.

In the context of science, scientific consciousness creates objects from the scientific world w_0 by using a universal language E_0. In each different scientific field, scientists may use only particular segments of E_0, which, however, are subject to change (e.g., they can be enriched by other scientists in the context of "scientific progress"), and, therefore, they are open systems of models. Models are usually symbolized by terms of E_0 (the universal language of modeling), and phenomena are characterized through judgments.

Specific models of phenomena are called relations. The basic relations (i.e., models of phenomena) are the following: "segment" or "subset" (a ⊂ b), "if then" (a → b), "a, not a" (a, ¬a), "or" (a ∨ b), "and" (a ∧ b). In the context of science, the models (relations) of the previous five basic relations are formulated through the judgments, S_0, of formal logic, and they give rise to the axiomatic system, T^0 (R_0,S_0), of formal logic. The models that satisfy the axiomatic system of formal logic are called concepts. In other words, the axiomatic system of formal logic determines a type of model that is called concept. Science is concerned with the study of objects whose models are concepts. The objective of a "formal theory," in particular, is the creation of models of concepts.

Idea, idealism, and (philosophical) realism: In the context of Plato's philosophy, "ideas" are eternal cosmic energies, and, in a sense, they correspond to what the Hesychasts (Orthodox Christian mystics) call God's uncreated energies and wills. In other words, according to Plato and the Hesychasts, ideas exist independently of human consciousness, and, therefore, they are not concepts (concepts were discovered by Aristotle). Given that the reality of Plato's ideas is independent of human consciousness, Plato's theory of ideas is a variant of philosophical realism. On the other hand, in the context of modern philosophy, idealism is founded on the argument that ideas are concepts, and, therefore, reality is primarily a system of abstractions. The development of modern idealism took different forms in the eighteenth, the nineteenth, and the twentieth centuries. The most radical form of idealism is solipsism, according to which the only reality is one's own consciousness, and, therefore, knowledge of anything outside of one's own consciousness is unjustified. Moreover, idealism (in the modern sense of the term) coupled with collectivism underpins the most dangerous forms of fascism and autocratic totalitarianism.

In the history of philosophy and philosophical theology, the most important variants of (philosophical) realism are the following: (i) Platonic realism: ideas are eternal cosmic energies, which underpin the order of the world, and to which the human soul has partial access, according to the degree of one's intellectual and moral progress. (ii) Hesychast realism: ideas are divine wills, or God's uncreated energies, of which humanity can partake (thus, becoming god by grace) by transcending both logic and morality and by offering the mind, empty from every type of intellectual, sentimental, and volitional egoism, to the Absolute (i.e., the deity) in order to be mystically filled with God's uncreated energy, or grace. (iii) Scholastic realism: ideas are logical substances in the mind of God, which underpin *theologia naturalis*, that is, theological rationalism. Two important secular (atheistic) variants of scholastic realism are Hegel's philosophy of history and Marx's philosophy of history, which, in essence, is an inversion of Hegel's dialectic.

About the Author

Dr. Nicolas Laos was born in Athens, Greece, on July 2, 1974. His father, Kyriakos Laos, an officer of the Greek Gendarmery, and his mother, Eleftheria née Karaouli, a government employee at the Greek Ministry of Public Order, ensured a sound education for him and were the first persons who made him aware of the interplay between spirituality and politology. Dr. Laos is a philosopher, politologist, and political consultant. His primary areas of expertise are ontology, epistemology, ethics, philosophical theology, political philosophy, noopolitics, netwar, and cultural diplomacy; his secondary areas of expertise are geopolitics, geoeconomics, political economy, organizational behavior, hypergame theory, monotonic and non-monotonic logics, and history of intelligence.

Dr. Laos has a versatile academic and research background. He has studied Mathematics, Politics, and Humanities and has graduated from the University of La Verne (California) with Honors and awards from the same University's Department of Mathematics. At the University of La Verne, under the supervision of Professor Themistocles M. Rassias (Fellow of the Royal Astronomical Society, London, UK), he conducted advanced research in mathematical analysis, differential geometry, mathematical logic, and the history of science, and he authored the book *Topics in Mathematical Analysis and Differential Geometry*, which was published in 1998 by World Scientific Publ. Co. as Volume 24 in their prestigious research Series of Pure Mathematics. During his mathematical studies at the University of La Verne, he also completed the courses "Intellectual History of the U.S. Since 1865," "Development of American Democracy," "World Civilizations," "Principles of Sociology," "Classical Political Philosophy," "American Government & Politics," "Political Behavior," and "European Government & Politics" at the same University, and he conducted research in the applications of logic and mathematics in the study of international-political affairs. In this context, he has authored the book *Theory Construction and Empirical Relevance in International Relations*, which was published in 2000, in English, by the Greek academic publisher Ant. N. Sakkoulas Publications. He expanded the previous research work in his book *The Metaphysics of World Order: A Synthesis of Philosophy, Theology, and Politics*, which was published in 2015 by Pickwick Publications.

Dr. Laos has earned a Doctoral Degree in Christian Philosophy (*Summa cum laude*) from the Academia Theológica de San Andrés, Mexico (Ukrainian Orthodox Church in Mexico). He achieved an A grade in all the courses in his Doctoral Degree Program in Christian Philosophy.

He has taught theory of international politics and political philosophy at the University of Indianapolis (Athens Campus). He has also consulted in noopolitics, geopolitics, geoeconomics, and world security with the R-Techno private intelligence company (Moscow), with shipping, energy, and construction corporations, and with the Research Institute for European and American Studies (Athens, Greece).

He has authored several books and articles in philosophy (including philosophical theology), politics, and the foundations of mathematics that have been published in English and Greek. Between 2012 and 2015, he authored more than four hundred investigative articles on world affairs that were published in authoritative Greek newspapers and magazines as well as on informative websites and blogs. In 2014, he developed and launched a successful weekly investigative documentary program called "Geopolitiki kai Noopolitiki" (Geopolitics and Noopolitics) on the Greek web TV channel Vmedia.

At the 26th Investiture Ceremony of the Grand Priory of England, Wales, Isle of Man and Channel Islands of the Hospitaller Order of Saint Lazarus of Jerusalem, held on September 27, 2008 in the Priory Church of Saint Bartholomew the Great in the City of London, Dr. Nicolas Laos was awarded the title of Knight of Saint Lazarus of Jerusalem by the United Grand Priories of the Hospitaller Order of Saint Lazarus of Jerusalem, whose Patron is Lord Robert Balchin, Baron Lingfield, Kt, DL, a Conservative member of the UK House of Lords and Pro-Chancellor of Brunel University. In 2013, on Saint Theodosius of Kiev's feast day, Dr. Nicolas Laos was awarded the title of Chevalier-Grand Profès de l' Ordre des Pauvres Chevaliers du Christ et des Saints Cyrille et Méthodie by His Beatitude Dr. Daniel de Jesús Ruiz Flores, First Hierarch of the Ukrainian Orthodox Church in Mexico (Iglesia Ortodoxa Ucraniana en México). Moreover, on May 8, 2013, the Most Rev'd Dr. Norman S.

Dutton, Metropolitan Archbishop of the Anglican Episcopal Church International, bestowed upon Dr. Nicolas Laos the title of Ecclesiastical Duke of Bethphage.

Since 2015, with the collaboration of the Unione Massonica di Stretta Osservanza Iniziatica (Milan, Italy) and with the blessing of Orthodox church hierarchs, Dr. Laos is the Founder and President ("Grand Hierophant-General") of the "United Traditionalist Grand Sanctuaries of the Ancient and Primitive Rite Memphis-Misraim," an international scholarly fraternity that is founded on his theory of methexiology and noopolitical research work, and it also uses methexiology as a new paradigm for a spiritually rectified and restructured Freemasonry.

www.ingramcontent.com/pod-product-compliance
Lightning Source LLC
Chambersburg PA
CBHW071246230426
43668CB00011B/1612